Everette E. Dennis
University of Minnesota

THE MEDIA SOCIETY

Evidence About Mass Communication in America

wcb

WM. C. BROWN COMPANY PUBLISHERS
Dubuque, Iowa

Contents

Acknowledgments, **vi**

Introduction, **vii**

Part 1
The Impact, Influence and
Effect of the Media

Chapter 1. *Pathways for Understanding Media Impact*, **3**
Two Steps Forward, Two Steps Back. Shifting Viewpoints About Media Impact. Some Avenues for Investigation. Three Research Perspectives. Summary and Conclusion.

Chapter 2. *Public Policy and Media Effects*, **21**
Civil Disorders and the Press. Violence and the News Media. Obscenity and Pornography. Television and Social Behavior. Children and Advertising. Research and Public Policy. Summary and Conclusion.

Chapter 3. *The Political Impact of the Media*, **35**
Elections as a Research Target. Editorial Page Endorsements. The Robinson Studies. Chain Ownership and Endorsements. Is TV Power a Myth? Political Research Directions. Summary and Conclusion.

Chapter 4. *The Popular Culture Perspective*, **49**
Mass Society/Mass Culture Critics. Images and Heroes in Popular Culture. General McLuhanacy. The Popular Culture Movement. Summary and Conclusion.

Part 2
Looking Inside: The Media as
Social Institutions

Chapter 5. *The Press as a Social Institution*, **67**
The Media as Social Systems. The Press as a Living System. New Emphasis on Inner Workings. Publishers and their Power. Structural Control of the Press. Journalistic and Business Relationships. Summary and Conclusion.

Chapter 6. *The Journalistic Enterprise:
The Product*, **79**
The Nature of News. The Assault on
Objectivity. The New Journalism.
Investigative and Adversarial Journalism.
Summary and Conclusion.

Chapter 7. *Journalists at Work*, **93**
Journalists and their Work. Inside the
Newsroom. Who are the Journalists? The
Johnstone Studies. A Local Application.
Management Studies: Behind the Front
Page. Officials and Reporters. The
Press and the Courts. Summary and
Conclusion.

**Part 3
Media Criticism and Analysis**

Chapter 8. *Instruments for Media Criticism*, **111**
New Thrust for Media Criticism. A
Socially Responsible Press. Press Councils.
Journalism Reviews. Worker Participation
Committees. Ombudsmen. Schools of
Journalism. Summary and Conclusion.

Chapter 9. *The Media Critics*, **129**
Perspectives on Press Criticism. The
Wayward Pressman. Academic Interest in
Criticism. Quasi-Academic Critics. The
Editor as Critic. Trends in Criticism. Summary
and Conclusion.

Chapter 10. *The Press and the Public Interest*, **139**
The Issuer and the Consumer. Search for
Definition. Searching for a Standard.
Media Interest and Public Interest.
Summary and Conclusion.

Chapter 11. *Toward a Media Society*, **151**
The Reaction to Research.
Toward the Media Society.

Bibliography, **157**

Index, **159**

For My Parents

Acknowledgments

There are several persons whose assistance and encouragement helped bring this project to fruition. Professor Don R. Pember of the University of Washington, also a consulting editor to Brown, originally suggested that I write this book. Professors D. Charles Whitney of Ohio State University and Carol Oukrop of Kansas State University were valued critics of manuscript drafts. Several colleagues at the University of Minnesota were helpful in direct and indirect ways. Among them: Professor Emeritus J. Edward Gerald, Professors Roy E. Carter, Edwin Emery, Donald M. Gillmor, Arnold H. Ismach, Daniel Wackman and Phillip Tichenor. Conversations with three others engaged in communication study also helped shape my ideas for this book and I am indebted to them—Professors William L. Rivers of Stanford University, James Aronson of Hunter College and Arthur Asa Berger of San Francisco State University. Professors John Johnstone of the University of Illinois-Chicago Circle and Keith Sanders of the University of Missouri generously allowed me to use tables from their published research. My research assistants, Christopher Allen and James McCartney, helped me on several other projects which allowed time for this one. Finally, thanks go to Karen Daninger for meticulous preparation of the manuscript and to Natalie Gould, Brown's supportive and persistent editor. To these persons and others I am most grateful. Of course, responsibility for any shortcomings in this book is mine.

—Everette E. Dennis

Introduction

What was once confined to the press sections of the news magazines, what was once found mainly in professional and trade journals has gone public. The mass media in the context of contemporary society are clearly on the public agenda. If the news media in America were once reluctant to write about themselves and their own problems, this tendency was overcome by the mid and late 1970s.

Americans were bombarded with information about the impact and influence of the news media on individuals, groups and the society. Writers and critics asked questions about the media that ranged from the effect of television advertising on preschoolers to the role of the press in the maintenance and operation of government. And increasingly people wanted to know—and were given ample opportunity to find out—what was going on inside media organizations.

The contemporary mass media are no passive observers, no mere conduits for information sitting on the periphery of the society. They are instead a central force in the society as the offerings of popular culture so vividly demonstrate. In films and in television programs, media organizations and their employees are depicted with dramatic force. A hundred magazine articles want to know about media and politics, media and children, media and violence, and the list goes on.

There is good reason for this preoccupation with mass media for we have become a media society. Virtually every aspect of our national life is tied up with mass media. Can anyone imagine national politics without media involvement? Or business in America without advertising? The media and their messages engulf us, and we have a great need to know more about what they are doing to and for us.

There is a steady flow of information about the mass media. What is often lacking, though, in this ephemeral, case-by-case approach is a larger, more holistic view. Even in their best analysis, writers and commentators rarely go beyond the singular instance. They examine the trees while ignoring the forest. There are, of course, many books about the mass media that try to do something more. They attempt to document, mainly in descriptive terms, the shape, size, and nature of the media. And sometimes there is an effort to provide critical assessment. Occasionally these books draw on research findings about the media to support or amplify a point, but for the most part they do not use mass communication research as a starting point for an analytical commentary on the media.

That is the mission of this book. Here we attempt an analytical review of mass media in America based primarily upon and structured around systematic research. It is hoped that such an approach will give the knowledgeable reader greater insight into the mass media—how they are organized, how they work, and their impact on the society itself.

By communication research we mean systematic, scholarly inquiry about the process and effects of mass media in society. In an *external* sense we will examine the impact and influence of the media as a force in the society: what the media do (and do not do) to people and their social institutions. The mass media are themselves social institutions, researchers say, and as such their intercourse with the other institutions of society is worthy of study. Thus we find studies that consider the organization and structure of the media from an economic or a political perspective. But this is only one level of the media's interface with the society. The media as disseminators of information also beam messages to individuals, their families, and social groups. A wide range of studies of media impact ensue. These are some of the *external* concerns of communication researchers.

There are also *internal* matters that are studied. When researchers look inside the media they want to know how media organizations operate, how they generate their messages as well as something of the people involved and their work patterns. The researchers go beyond the *process* of manufacturing the media message, to the content of that message itself. Thus there are studies of media gatekeepers and gatekeeping, of conflict and cooperation between professional and business values. Researchers concerned mainly with content look at media coverage of specific issues or to such things as bias in news copy.

External and internal mass communication research is by no means mutually exclusive. A researcher may be interested in both arenas simultaneously. For example, one might study the impact of newspaper editorial endorsements on voters and their behaviors, obviously an *external* matter. The same researcher might also want to know something of the social system within the newspaper that produced the editorials, an *internal* matter.

Thus mass communications researchers pose questions about the mass media and they proceed to systematically find answers. The answers they get are, of course, only as good as their methods, including the tools they use to measure, codify, and explain. Mass communication research has a variety of research traditions. This book is openminded about research and researchers. While some accounts of communication research accept only the social scientific tradition of researchers who use such tools as survey research, experimental design, and content analysis, there is no compelling evidence that social scientists have a corner on the market of truth when it comes to systematic explanations of the mass media. Indeed, the documentary researchers, historians and legal scholars have a long and distinguished record of research and analysis. Similarly the literary scholars, those who use the methods of literary criticism in evaluating communication content and behavior, also offer evidence of a different kind.

It is important to understand not only what questions the researcher raises, but what philosophical system and research tools he uses to get answers. Research is, of course, evaluated in its context. We look at the researcher's objectives, how he has defined his terms and inventoried the various factors that might bear on the questions raised. We also need to know the full extent of the sources from which the researcher gathers his data, what is sometimes called the *universe of data*. We need to know how the data was collected and how it was analyzed and reported. Finally, are the conclusions of the research supported by the evidence? Research should always be seen in context. A survey and historical study may raise similar questions about the role of the press in presidential elections, for example, but their findings come from different traditions, use different evidence, and cannot be added one to the other. They must be examined carefully and conclusions should not go beyond the evidence marshalled.

The data gathered by communication researchers quite naturally lead them toward explanations, sometimes toward broad, general theories. And this points up a serious problem that is encountered when a broad definition of communication research is accepted, one that embraces many research traditions. The result is findings that come from different levels of analysis. Some researchers (historians) may ask: "What are the effects of media?" and cite singular instances to answer the question. Thus experiential case studies emerge. Other researchers (social scientists) may ask the same question and seek their answer in a broadly based national survey conducted during an election. It should be remembered that philosophers of science say that theories worked out at one level of analysis cannot be presumed to have any validity at a higher or lower level of analysis. Thus the intra-individual studies of how reporters work with public officials cannot automatically be added to broader-based studies of public perceptions of governmental reporting in the press to form a single conclusion. Some social scientific research about media effects, for example, sticks closely to the population group sampled, daring not to generalize to all of the American people, while a popular culture study using literary methods might generalize quite broadly from the content of television soap operas to societal acceptance of authoritarian values. We must be wary of these tendencies and be critical of research that goes beyond its specific findings.

While communication researchers use different tools and methods, they also come from different disciplines. The earliest communication researchers were mainly trained in political science, sociology, and psychology. In more recent times, the hybrid field of mass communication research borrowed methods and outlooks from other disciplines but found new perspectives of its own in researching mass communication phenomena. Others have joined the mass communication research effort from fields such as anthropology, geography, linguistics, management science, and more. However, most of the research reported in this book comes from mass communication researchers who usually find homes in university departments of journalism, mass communication, or media studies. Additionally, we look at the work of applied researchers who work for media organizations and groups.

In this introduction, indeed in this book, we will not dwell on the communication researcher but rather on his research. As one prepublication critic said, "the research is more important than the researcher and the meaning of the research is more important than either the research or the researcher." What follows, then, focuses on the meaning of communication research as it helps to explain and make sense of the relationships of the mass media to their society and the internal dynamics of the media.

This book is intended for students in university courses variously called, mass media and society, the press in a free society, introduction to mass communication and others. The book is directed mainly to the intermediate media and society course although many analytically oriented introductory courses might benefit from it as well. It is the author's intention to respond to the criticism of several generations of journalism/communication students who find their texts and materials too simplistic and unconnected to the main thrust of the rest of their academic work in other university departments.

Introductory courses in psychology, sociology, and other social sciences orchestrate an understanding of major principles by blending substantive findings of research with a discussion of the researcher's methods. Journalism instruction and textbooks should do the same thing and thus better integrate with the student's general education. That is another of the purposes of this book.

The book is divided into three parts. Part I probes the traditional puzzlement about the relative impact, influence, and effect of mass communication in society. Chapter 1 in that section explores some new pathways for understanding media impact and suggests a movement from the concept of a powerful media, to a notion of minimal effects, back to a somewhat different but still powerful mass media view. Chapter 2 looks at reasons why communication researchers pursue certain studies, certain research targets. Chapter 3 considers the political impact of the press mainly from the standpoint of social scientific-behavioral studies. Again, a new interpretation of media effects is evident. Chapter 4 moves away from social science toward the more literary inclinations of the popular culture scholars who also have much to say about media effects.

In Part II we endeavor to look inside the media to see their inner workings and dynamics. Here the main emphasis is on studies of news media organizations since little comparable work has been done with entertainment media. Chapter 5 reviews studies that regard the press as a social institution. Chapter 6 looks at the forces inside the press that determine the nature of its product or content. Chapter 7 takes us into the realm of media sociology with specific emphasis on the people of journalism, those who do the work.

Part III emphasizes media criticism and analysis, some of it internal, some external. Chapter 8 looks at instruments of media criticism, channels for the public, for special interests and for journalists to criticize the press. Chapter 9 focuses on some particular media critics and their work. Chapter 10 combines some of the elements of press philosophy and criticism raised in the two prior chapters and explores the concept of the public interest in a mass communication context. Chapter 11 offers a somewhat speculative summation and a commentary about the worth of communication research.

It is hoped that this book will enlarge the student's understanding of the mass media and at the same time provide a basis for appreciating the contribution of communication research to that endeavor.

Everette E. Dennis
Minneapolis, Minnesota

Part 1

Impact, Influence, and Effect of Mass Communication

"Three hostile newspapers are more to be feared than a thousand bayonets."
—Napoleon Bonaparte

Chapter
1

Pathways for Understanding Media Impact

Those who watched the ABC "Sunday Night Movie" on September 30, 1973 saw a gruesome film called *Fuzz*, which depicted sadistic teenagers who poured gasoline on waterfront tramps and set them afire. In Boston two days later a young woman ran out of gas while driving through a slum. As she returned to her car carrying a two-gallon gas can, she was surrounded by six young men who dragged her to a vacant lot. There they beat her and forced her to pour the gasoline on herself. Then, with a lighted match they turned her into a human torch. Though she tried to save herself by rolling on the ground, she died a few hours later.

Did the television movie "cause" the young woman's death? *Yes*, said Boston Mayor Kevin White, "I think there was a relationship." *Yes*, said the *New York Times*, "The dreadful coincidence cannot be ignored."

Three weeks later in Miami, four twelve- and thirteen-year olds, one who reportedly had seen *Fuzz*, doused three sleeping derelicts with lighter fluid and laughed as the men awoke crying out with pain. One of the men died.

Can violent content in the media cause violent behavior in the individual? Those who look for evidence to support this claim point to increased antisocial activity that follows massive news coverage of attempted assassinations, airline hijackings, and various other terrorist acts. An inmate at a penal institution tells how he and his prison colleagues "learn" about new crime techniques from watching television police dramas.

Add to these singular instances of individuals who say they are being influenced positively or negatively by media, a range of larger social concerns—the role of the media in shaping consumer and political behavior—and the full dimension of the problem of media influence becomes evident.

Few people doubt the ability of a particular television program to trigger antisocial behavior in a particular individual. Often these are the cases that attract considerable publicity, but by any accounting they are extremely rare. More vital questions about media influence have to do with the ability of the media to affect patterns of behavior over time. And that is where anecdotes about single instances don't help very much. Such dramatic examples as *Fuzz* seem to say that the media are powerful, but social scientists looking at the larger picture have some doubts. After studying, examining, and dissecting the "all-powerful" influence of the propagandist from World War I to the mass media merchants of the mid-twentieth century, researchers began to question whether media could so easily structure thinking, change attitudes, and move people to action. One contemporary researcher summed it up thusly, "Today, if I were to give an outline of the most important findings of 40 years of research into the effects of the mass media I would have to tell roughly the following: the effects of the mass media appear to be negligible."[1]

This is an assessment of a social scientist who is summarizing the work of other social scientists—communication researchers—who have studied the role and function of the mass media in a variety of social situations. They have tried to put media influence in context with other forces that might play some part in shaping thinking, attitudes, and behavior. In doing so they have considered such alternative explanations as personal influence of individuals in the family, church, or social group.

Historians however, are more likely to point to individual cases. For example, they remember the example of William Marcy Tweed, the once-powerful boss of Tammany Hall, who lived out his days in a New York City jail. Driven into exile by a vigilant and vigorous press that had exposed his political excesses, Tweed arrived in Spain only to be seized by a Spanish customs official who recognized him from a Thomas Nast cartoon in *Harper's Weekly*. No doubt Tweed, who once urged his henchmen to "stop them damn pictures," was convinced of the persuasive impact of the press. Surely, a historian might ask, that was a media effect, wasn't it? Of course. But it was also a single instance based on an individual level of analysis. It is not really possible to generalize very broadly from this limited evidence to explain media influence in a larger context.

Social psychologist W. J. McGuire demonstrates the broader view of social scientists over time, a view that contrasts considerably with the anecdotal evidence presented earlier in this chapter. McGuire writes:

> The measured impact of the mass media as regards persuasiveness seems quite slight. . . . A tremendous amount of applied research has been carried out to test the effectiveness of the mass media.[1] . . . The outcome has been quite embarrassing for proponents of the mass media, since there is little evidence of attitude change, much less change in gross behavior.[2]

Why the apparent dilemma between the historian and the social scientist? At a common sense level the impact, influence, and effect of the media seems obvious. Doesn't the growth of advertising, which parallels the growth of American business, prove that? Haven't newspaper and magazine exposes from the Muckrakers to Watergate brought social and political change? And what about the impact of television violence? The conflict between those who say the media have little direct effect on people and those who ascribe great power to them may seem puzzling at first, but two sociologists, Melvin L. DeFleur and Sandra Ball-Rokeach, offer this plausible explanation: "A trustworthy method—science—says the media have few effects. Another trustworthy method—careful study by insightful historians and other analysts of the broader picture—says that they have sweeping effects. Is this a flat contradiction, or have these two approaches operated on different levels of abstraction? We feel the latter is the case."[3] Different levels of analysis derive different "facts" because they come from different systems of structuring knowledge.

TWO STEPS FORWARD, TWO STEPS BACK

To understand how the two sociologists reached this conclusion, one must look at the forces in this century that have shaped our perceptions of the power of the press. In the days after World War I there was much enthusiasm about propaganda analysis. A right-wing political faction in Germany distressed by their nation's defeat claimed that allied propaganda had actually won the war. This led to the myth of the all-powerful propagandist who used the mass media as his vehicle in influencing and controlling attitudes, opinions, and behavior. As communication researcher Ithiel de Sola Pool has written, "This belief in a 'Schwindel' led to much writing about the supposed magical powers of propaganda."[4] Before long, popular writers, government officials, and researchers the world over were commenting on and celebrating the importance of propaganda and the power of the press. Harold D. Lasswell, a political scientist, in a now-classic study of propaganda would write, "Most of that which formerly could be done by violence and intimidation must now be done by argument and persuasion."[5]

What would later be regarded as the exaggerated importance of mass media in opinion formation was strongly supported by the pronouncements of world leaders. Scholars and laymen alike could not help but be impressed with the persuasive arguments of Nikolai Lenin on the role of the newspaper in revolutionary politics[6] or the carefully crafted plans of the German propaganda minister Joseph Goebbels.[7] Against the backdrop of the rise of Bolshevik and Nazi governments, there seemed to be good reason for concern.

Bringing the matter of media effects even closer to home was the terrified response of thousands of Americans to the radio dramatization of H. G. Wells' *War of the Worlds* on Halloween eve 1938. The broadcast, narrated by the brilliant actor Orson Welles, gave larger-than-life characterization to a supposed invasion from Mars. Although carefully qualified with announcements stating that the radio play was fiction, the broadcast struck terror into the hearts of many Americans. People tried to warn friends and some even fled from their homes, heading west to avoid the "invasion." Years later, communication researcher Wilbur Schramm would look back on the Orson Welles broadcast writing, "many people were emotionally aroused, and some of them abruptly changed their behavior in a way that could never have been predicted before the broadcast."[8]

But, the confidence of those who believed profoundly in the "power of the press" was shaken greatly by a study of voter behavior conducted in Erie County, New York during the election of 1940.[9] The study, carried out by respected social scientists who employed sophisticated research methods, reported that with regard to changes in voting during an election campaign, the media have relatively few direct effects. The Erie County study, which was the work of sociologist Paul Lazarsfeld and his associates at Columbia University, was replete with intriguing findings. They suggested that:

—rather than being an agent of conversion, the media were more likely to reinforce preconceived beliefs;

—and whatever influence media did have, it was likely to be filtered through opinion leaders, a concept that came to be known as the two-step flow.

Instead of being the unwitting dupe of the mass media, the individual voter was seen as a person with "selective perception" who would pick out of the swirling messages of the information marketplace those items that would support his own views. The individual would interpret and digest that information to suit his own convictions. This would later be explained convincingly in Leon Festinger's theory of cognitive dissonance, which posits that the individual avoids discomfort and uncertainty by selecting information likely to reinforce his convictions. Similarly, he would reject information that conflicts with previously held ideas.[10]

Study after study in the 1940s and 1950s limited and severely qualified the importance of media effects.[11] This led to a carefully stated notion of media influence that was based on thoughtful measurement and analysis. Sociologist Bernard Berelson probably said it best, *"some kinds of communication, on some kinds of issues, brought to the attention of some kinds of people under some kinds of conditions, have some kinds of effects."*[12]

Therein lies the rub. In the years that followed the classic Erie County study, social scientists from such traditional disciplines as political science, psychology, and sociology as well as the new, hybrid field of mass communication conducted carefully defined studies using such research methods as surveys, field experiments, and content analyses to measure media effects under certain conditions. Unlike their earlier colleagues in propaganda analysis who often spoke of the press as a monolithic entity instead of individual media with individual characteristics, the new researchers measured carefully and made few broad-based claims, borrowing the humble understatement of science.

Frequently, studies would show gains in *information* by people who used and relied upon the media but little change in their *opinions*. And without change in opinions, there was little likely change in *behavior*.

Still there was considerable discussion about the effects of the media and the power of the press. Popular books like Vance Packard's *The Hidden Persuaders* and others reinforced the idea of the all-powerful media. Yet reviews of social science studies, however fragmented, were steadfast. As British sociologist Denis McQuail explained:

For those who want a simple answer about the power of the mass media, it would have to be in the negative. Such an answer, although in many respects misleading, would fit most of the available evidence. The most careful experiments and surveys have failed to substantiate the wide claims on behalf of mass media or the fears of critics of mass communications.[13]

Media impact, researchers said, must always be looked at from a standpoint of selective exposure of the audience, selective interpretation of the contents of the message, as well as selective retention of it. Anytime a study was done there were questions of timing of the message, the nature of its content, the audience to be exposed, and dozens of other important factors to be considered. Add to this the complexity of explaining the differences between print and electronic media and it is clear that the task of sorting out the effects of media is awesome indeed. Researcher Joseph Klapper put it succinctly in his 1960 book *The Effects of Mass Communication* writing, "mass communication ordinarily does not serve as a necessary and sufficient cause of audience effects, but rather functions between and among and through a nexus of mediating factors and influences."[14] Operating on this assumption researchers have studied persuasive communication attempting to determine which effects can occur and what mediating factors are involved. What was learned from that investigation? McQuail thinks that the major contributions of the research on persuasive communication probing the effects of media can be summarized as follows:

(1) There is agreement that effects, where they occur, most frequently take the form of a reinforcement of existing attitudes and opinions.

(2) It is clear that effects vary according to

the prestige or evaluations attached to the communication source.

(3) The more complete the monopoly of mass communication, the more likely it is that opinion change in the desired direction will be achieved.

(4) The salience to the audience of the issues or subject matter will affect the likelihood of influence—'mass communication can be effective in producing a shift on unfamiliar, lightly felt, peripheral issues—those that do not much matter or are tied to audience predispositions.'

(5) The selection and interpretation of content by the audience is influenced by existing opinions and interests and by group norms.

(6) It has become clear that the structure of interpersonal relations in the audience mediates the flow of communication content and limits and determines whatever effects occur.[15]

For most thoughtful persons looking at the results of more than two decades of communication research on effects, there was an inescapable conclusion: that the media are not central to changing thoughts, opinions, and actions, but instead they are peripheral. Thus, thinking had come full circle from the belief that the media have massive effects on people to the conclusion that they have limited effects. The social scientists in their zeal to apply the orderly methods of scientific investigation to their studies may still have to take some responsibility for an all-too-broad and erroneous view. In a sense they did just what they accused the historians of doing—over generalizing from limited results. To explain: the social scientists conducted limited, carefully defined and refined studies. After each one, they could say that under these conditions, with these people,

and these messages, the following effect seems evident. Usually, the study showed that in the particular situation investigated, the media had less influence, less effect than conventional wisdom might think. But in time these were the stuff on which generalizations about mass media were made and negative notions of minimal effects grew up.

While each researcher or research team carefully qualified their findings, there was an unfortunate cumulative effect. Three small-scale, limited studies that were often not in any way comparable were added up to equal a generalized assumption. Three fragments would suddenly be foisted off on the public as a whole theory or explanation for media effects, or noneffects as the case was more often. One critic, decrying this sometimes subtle practice said that the emphasis on many short-term impact studies in reaching conclusions about the impact of media was like trying to prove that smoking one cigarette leads to cancer. Of course, social scientists were not oblivious to the need for long-term, longitudinal studies that would test out propositions about communication over time, making comparisons and controlling for bias and error. All too often there was an emphasis on research findings with little discussion of the methods and tools used to yield those findings. This is extremely important because methods of sampling, for example, were more refined with the passage of time, and it simply wasn't accurate to add old findings to new ones and assume that one plus one equals two.

Yet, the social scientists made an honest attempt to move away from the unsupported and unsupportable claims of the propaganda analysts as they looked for measurable and justifiable impact of media. Their work was by no means perfect, but they made a solid case for sound scientific rationales, careful pretesting, and objective, systematic post hoc evaluations. And this was a major step away from the simplistic notions of the past about the power of the press.

SHIFTING VIEWPOINTS ABOUT MEDIA IMPACT

The radical shift from the old power of the press position to the diminishing effects view was widely discussed by social scientists, but was largely unknown or unwelcome in many quarters. There was an "instinctive tendency not to believe the many nil results [of communication research] that: "The mass media have hardly any effect, or that there is no such thing as public opinion or opinion leaders, or that the presentation of brutality does not leave any imprint on the public."[16] Popular literature perpetuated the myth of media power almost as it had always been articulated. There were exceptions, of course, even some that came up with a new twist. T. S. Matthews writing in his book, *The Sugar Pill* in 1959, said:

> The press has a negative power to titillate, alarm, enrage, amuse, humiliate, annoy, even to drive a person out of his community or his job. But of the positive power to which it pretends, and of which the Press lords dream—to make war and break governments, or swing an election, to stop a war or start a revolution—there is no tangible evidence.[17]

But Matthews and many other media commentators were guilty of a logical fallacy—that of generalizing from an individual level of analysis to the society-at-large. Generally the communications industry has lagged far, far behind the social science view of media effects, preferring not to believe these modest assessments. Even in fields like public health where

considerable funds were expanded for information-education campaigns to do such things as reduce smoking and drug use, it was not until the late 1960s that the "word" about the limited impact of media filtered down. It was something of a revelation to health professionals in 1968 when researcher Harold Mendelsohn told them, "social science has revolutionized our thinking about the power of mass communication effectiveness."[18]

This obvious chasm between researchers and practitioners is something to keep in mind as we further examine media/society relationships in this book. The fact that the research knowledge is not readily known or welcomed by the professional community is a thorny problem that leads to much misunderstanding. Where the changing view of media effects was understood by practitioners and various nonscholarly commentators, there was a tendency to oversimplify and (without context or qualification) to assume that media have limited effects. If the propaganda theorists overestimated the impact of media, social scientists through the 1950s and 1960s probably underestimated the media's effect. "The fact is," wrote communication researcher Elisabeth Noelle-Neumann in calling for a return to a belief in the concept of a powerful mass media, "the decisive factors of mass media are not brought to bear in the traditional laboratory experiment designs."[19] Agreeing, researchers De Fleur and Ball-Rokeach said there are many effects that do not show up in laboratory experiments or in before and after studies of persons involved in information campaigns. They wrote:

> We are referring to the enlargement of people's belief systems that new media bring; to the formation of attitudes toward a constant flow of new topics; to subtle shifts of individual and collective sentiment that may not have been seen in the ac-

tions of individuals; and to a number of other kinds of society-wide changes. We believe these changes come about because mass media are present and operating, in the society.[20]

Researchers with new perspectives, moving out of the limited laboratory situation have begun to change their once narrow and cautious view of media effects. The idea of selective perception, for example, is being looked at from a different angle. Agreeing that selective perception describes the process by which readers or viewers pick-out those bits of information that reinforce their preconceived notions, Noelle-Neumann says it is important to go a step further and look at the way the media operate in producing messages. The limited, laboratory studies of media impact, says Noelle-Neumann, failed to take into account three decisive factors about mass media. The three factors, all of which work together to restrict selective perception, are:

Ubiquity of the media—the ability to be everywhere, to dominate the information environment. The media are so ubiquitous at times that it is difficult for a person to escape a message.

Cumulation of messages—One should look beyond the individual, fragmented messages to the cumulative effect over time. There is periodical repetition of the message that tends to reinforce its impact.

Consonance of journalists—There is amazing and unrealistic agreement and harmony among journalists and others involved in the message. There tends to be a sameness to newspapers and newscasts. This limits the options the public has for selective perception.[21]

These three factors working together reduce the individual's opportunity to form an independent opinion. Long-term studies by Noelle-Neumann and others demonstrate that "the more selective perception is being restricted . . .the more attitudes can be influenced or molded by the mass media . . .[and additionally] the effects of mass media increase in proportion to the degree in which selective perception is made difficult."[22]

By using a combination of content analysis of media messages and trend observation of public opinion polls over a long period of time, Noelle-Neumann was able to make an assessment that led to a call for a "return to the concept of a powerful media." But unlike the powerful media view of the 1920s, Noelle-Neumann's is carefully qualified and does not go beyond her data. There must be evidence of effects supported and confirmed over time.

This perspective is by no means the only reinterpretation of media effects that is generating comment in the social science community. Moving away from the narrow focus of the attitude change literature, Peter Clarke and F. Gerald Kline of the University of Michigan have asserted that "what people learn from communication activity is a more rewarding topic for media effects research than attitude formation or change."[23] Too often, say Clarke and Kline, studies of how people learn about public affairs have compared educational attainment with media use. When questions are raised about which has the greater effect, the evidence comes down resoundingly on the side of educational level. But this may be misleading, they say, because questions asked in surveys and polls "may have been cast in ways that bias results in favor of education as the all-powerful agent."[24] Why is this so? In part, it is because questions probing what people have learned emphasize facts about public events that usually interest educators. Those of public knowledge are tied to names of states-men, dates of events, and prevailing view-points. Additionally, researchers are often con-cerned with the amount of time readers and viewers spend with various mass media. Under these circumstances, there is little wonder that the media do not seem very important.

Kline and Clarke would correct this problem by measuring media effects in a more refined way. They would abandon *media use* as the major measurement of communication experi-ence and instead look at the way the individual person *discriminates* messages. They would focus on *informational learning* rather than *attitude change*. In doing so, three kinds of in-formation would most concern them:

Salience information—information that has personal relevance and a direct bearing on the individual. Persons answering survey research-ers' questions might be asked how they think a public affairs problem would affect their health, finances and property, or personal time.

Solution information—information about proposals that have been made to solve public problems pertinent to the individual. To what extent is the individual aware of these propos-als, good or bad, that have been advanced to deal with a public issue.

Actor information—information about people or organizations that are trying to influence public policy. The individual is asked to as-sess the influence he thinks a particular politi-cian, leader, or spokesman might have.

In these three ways, it is possible for re-searchers to more clearly see the impact of mass communication on the individual. One should remember, of course, that the communication content (that is, the messages) that Clarke and Kline were dealing with had to do with public affairs information. They would be among the first to admit that the impact of the media with regard to violence and pornography might be quite different.

Another startling finding for those who had a fixed view of minimal media effects was the as-sertion by communication researcher John P. Robinson that the media can affect political be-havior after all. Unlike Clarke and Kline who used individual data, Robinson studied aggre-gate data that led him to broader conclusions. In a somewhat understated way, Robinson wrote, "evidence now exists that under certain condi-tions, the media can have political impact."[25] Based on surveys conducted in the 1968 general election, Robinson concluded that "the largely pro-Nixon coverage carried by the newspapers in 1968 was associated with some shift in the vote in Nixon's favor."[26] Newspaper editorials endorsing presidential candidates loomed as in-fluential factors in the election, according to the Robinson study. Explaining, Robinson said, "...it was estimated that a newspaper's per-ceived support of one candidate rather than another was associated with about a 6 percent edge in the vote for the endorsed candidate over his opponent."[27] Based on national survey data, the study conducted under the auspices of the Survey Research Center of the University of Michigan by a respected researcher added fuel to the changing perception of media effects.

As the view of media impact, influence, and effect began to shift, it was evident that the change was a cautious one, offered only after analyzing empirical evidence. While earlier studies of communication effectiveness were mostly concerned about behavioral changes brought about by informational bombardment, newer studies have looked at mental or cogni-tive effects wherein informational learning is deemed important and significant. True, researchers still examine attitude change and behavioral change, but they do so with different questions and with more subtle methods. In a sense they are doing what Wilbur Schramm suggested when he wrote, "Communication researchers...have to face up to the need of studying quiet; continuing effects that, in perspective overshadow the more spectacular and more easily measurable ones. And there is no better place to make their importance clear than in their relation to the effects of mass communication. . . ."[28]

SOME AVENUES FOR INVESTIGATION

Much of the contemporary investigation of media impact and influence is following Schramm's guidance, looking toward the "quiet continuing effects" that previously were unmeasured. Recognizing that so many of the early, classic studies emphasized limited, laboratory situations and were concerned with precise relationships between messages and people, researchers now have broadened their perspectives to include the social millieu, the environment. As DeFleur and Ball-Rokeach have written, "the ultimate basis of media influence lies in the nature of the three-way relationship between the larger social system, the media's role in that system, and audience relationships to the media."[29]

In this context, some researchers have examined mass media as a part of the larger social system. And very quickly this points up the subtle effects of mass media in society generally. Three social scientists, George Donohue, Phillip Tichenor, and Clarice Olien have done extensive research to demonstrate that "mass

media represent subsystems which cut across other subsystems and transmit information among and between them."[30] What this means is that the mass media, because they carry information, have the ability to penetrate most other aspects of the society. Thus, the mass media can allocate and regulate knowledge, and "control of knowledge is central to development and maintenance of power,"[31] the researchers say. The consequences of the media's role in regulating information and knowledge is demonstrated in other research by the three scholars. Positing a "knowledge gap" hypothesis,[32] the researchers say that one major effect of the media may be transmitting information that gives special advantage to persons with higher socioeconomic status. This reinforces and widens the gap between information-rich and information-poor people, a distinction that is drawn mainly along class lines. While this research may seem less dramatic than some other studies discussed here, its importance in measuring the impact of the mass media is immediately evident. In part, the shift toward new avenues of investigation was brought about by a more realistic view of the mass media. Communication researchers Maxwell McCombs and Donald L. Shaw explain:

Most likely, some behavioral scientists overreacted after efforts to locate communication factors related to attitude change resulted in the discovery that attitudes simply resist direct challenge. Their focus, of course, was on *attitudinal change,* not *informational learning.* Yet in news coverage, modern mass media do not consciously attempt to shape day-to-day attitudes but rather to inform their diverse audiences about events. The job of a good newspaper is to convey some sense of the reality of events for the audience.[33]

In simpler terms, the functions of mass communication had long been identified as

(1) informing, (2) influencing, (3) entertaining, and (4) providing a marketplace for goods and services. This is a translation of and variation on the classic commentary of Harold D. Lasswell who discussed the structure and function of communication in society as: (1) surveillance of the environment (2) correlation of the parts of society responding to the environment, and (3) transmission of the social heritage from one generation to the next. To these communication researcher Charles Wright added a fourth—entertainment. Elaborating, Wright says:

> Surveillance refers to the collection and distribution of information concerning events in the environment, both outside and within any particular society. To some extent it corresponds to what is popularly conceived as the handling of news. Acts of correlation, here, include interpretation of information about the environment and prescription for conduct in reaction to these events. These activities are popularly identified as editorial or propaganda. Transmission to the social heritage focuses on the communicating of knowledge, values and social norms from one generation to another or from members of a group to newcomers. Commonly, it is identified as educational activity. Finally, entertainment refers to communicative acts primarily intended for amusement, irrespective of any instrumental effects they might have.[34]

It was a broad-based look at much more than the persuasive (or opinion) function of the media, that stimulated new lines of inquiry in communication research. Although there are several schools of thought, approaches to media inquiry, and trends in research, three are discussed here. The three are all active, vibrant arenas and are engaging some of the nation's most productive researchers. All of them have a bearing on mass media influence, although in some instances that may not be the only purpose of the research.

THREE RESEARCH PERSPECTIVES

The three approaches to the study of media impact and influence considered here are *agenda-setting, uses and gratifications* and *political socialization*. In their own way each of these new perspectives enlarges and enhances our understanding of how mass communication works, what impact its messages have and how people respond to them.

Agenda-setting—Agenda-setting research is concerned with the impact of the media on cognitive change in the individual. The concern here is with the structure of one's thinking and perceptions. Researchers are asking to what extent the media shape our social reality. As the leading investigators in this area—McCombs and Shaw—have written:

> Audiences not only learn about public issues and other matters through the media, they also learn how much importance to attach to an issue or topic from the emphasis placed on it by the mass media. For example, in reflecting what candidates are saying during a campaign, the mass media apparently determine the important issues. In other words, the media set the ''agenda'' of the campaign.[35]

This, the two men believe, may be the most important effect of modern mass communication. An early and explicit statement about the agenda-setting function of the press came from political scientist Bernard Cohen who argued that the press is much more than a purveyor of news and opinion. The media may not be particularly successful in telling people what to think, Cohen wrote, ''but it is stunningly successful in telling its readers what to think *about*.''[36] With a strong interest in how people learn from the mass media, McCombs and Shaw offered a hypothesis for agenda-setting ''that media emphasis on an event influences the audience also to see the event as important."[37]

Testing the agenda-setting hypothesis in a study during the 1968 Presidential election, McCombs and Shaw looked at the relationship between undecided voters and the media content available to them. Interestingly enough, there was a strong positive correlation between the issues the voters deemed important and those emphasized by the news media. Subsequent studies using news and advertising content offered important confirmation although the two key researchers wondered whether the media really *set* the agenda or simply *reflect* the agenda of their news sources.

Several researchers pursuing the agenda-setting hypothesis have not only demonstrated through studies that there is a strong positive relationship between issues emphasized in the media and those regarded by the public as important, but have also shown that there is a similar relationship between one's exposure to a particular news medium and agreement with its agenda of public issues. The earliest agenda-setting research was quite limited in its objectives focusing mainly on the link between media content and the extent to which the public found the same information to be important during election years. This emphasis on studying informational learning rather than subsequent behavioral effects led to some criticism of agenda-setting. After all, the relationship between content and issues "takes on greater significance . . .if it can be shown that the rankings on issues have consequences in affecting voting or other behaviors,"[38] one study indicates.

One agenda-setting study that did consider *behavior* examined the relationship between press attention to negative aspects of air travel (for example, crashes and skyjackings) and the public's willingness to fly. The result: the public saw the chances of danger as personally relevant to them and it seemed clear that this led them to do less flying or to buy more insurance if they did fly.[39]

Agenda-setting research is not without its critics. Studies have not really been universally supportive of the agenda-setting hypothesis, say communication researchers Jack M. McLeod, Lee B. Becker, and James E. Byrnes. They believe there are inconsistencies in the findings of the various reported studies. For example, some studies say that agenda-setting is strengthened when there is little interpersonal discussion of the issues and heavy reliance on the media. Others disagree saying that high interpersonal discussion facilitates agenda-setting. McLeod and his colleagues say that most agenda-setting studies have used static designs and have been based on relationships that were measured at a single moment in time. They seem to be saying that it might not be wise to generalize too widely from such studies. There might be other explanations for the agenda-setting hypothesis, they assert. These could include the extent to which people have political interest and involvement among others.[40]

Whether agenda-setting is the most important effect of mass communication or simply a fragmented clue to a more persuasive explanation is not clear, but what is certain is—agenda-setting is a fertile ground for media effects research and the results of this research are raising intriguing new questions.

Uses and Gratifications—Somewhat confused by the apparent discrepancy between scholarly consensus on the minimal effects of mass communication in the face of massive media use by the public, researchers began searching for answers. Urging a change in perspective, psychologist Elihu Katz said that there should be less attention on what the media do to people and more attention on what people do with the media. What "use" do people make of the media in the social and psychological context of their lives? This grows naturally out of the concept of media functions discussed earlier in this chapter. Closely related to the work of Katz was the research of W. Phillips Davison who probed the role the media played in "enabling people to bring about more satisfying relations between themselves and the world around them."[41]

This approach, which became known as uses and gratifications, has two main advantages according to Denis McQuail. "It helps both in understanding the significance and meaning of media use and it suggests a range of new intervening variables to be taken into account in the search for effects."[42] Katz and two colleagues explain:

> The uses and gratifications approach has proposed concepts and presented evidence that are likely to explain the media behavior of individuals more powerfully than the more remote sociological, demographic and personality variables. Compared with classical effects studies, the uses and gratifications approach takes the media consumer rather than the media message as its starting point, and explores his communication behavior in terms of his direct experience with the media. It views the members of the audience as actively utilizing media contents, rather than being passively acted upon by the media. Thus it does not assume a direct relationship between messages and effects, but postulates instead that members of the audience put messages to use, and that such usages act as intervening variables in the process of effect.[43]

Thus, the role of the audience and the motivation of the audience comes into full view as a priority on the communication researcher's agenda.

While some researchers have assumed that audiences are passive, uses and gratifications researchers look upon the audience as active and goal-oriented. The individual audience member is looked upon as someone who selects media messages that not only have a particular, utilitarian use, but also provide satisfaction. All this gets more complex as one realizes that the media compete with many other social forces that can also provide useful, gratifying information. Such "traditional media" as bars and taverns, for example, can consume audience time and provide information of a sort that is useful and gratifying. Much of the uses and gratifications research flies in the face of the more humanistic popular culture critics of the media and offers an empirical test for some of the questions they raise. (See Chapter 4.)

Uses and gratifications research has begun to isolate ways in which individuals experience and use the mass media. Studies have examined different media in different social situations in an attempt to measure effects. Researchers look at such variables as media content, the nature and circumstances of the individual's exposure to the medium and the social context, whether alone or with others. Still, the research is mainly concerned with scoping out the dimensions of audience-message relations. Often, the work proceeds in a somewhat backwards fashion looking first at gratifications, then at information. As Katz and colleagues have summed it up:

> Much uses and gratifications research has still barely advanced beyond a sort of charting and profiling activity: findings are still typically presented to show that certain bodies of content serve certain functions or that one medium is deemed better at satisfying certain needs than another. The further step, which has hardly been ventured, is one of explanation.[44]

While some areas of communication research seem to have mainly theoretical implications, uses and gratifications research might have important practical, policy effects in daily mass media operations. As researcher Harold Mendelsohn has written, if properly used "audience gratifications research becomes a powerful instrument for changing those media policies that do not facilitate the satisfaction of actual media-related needs, wants and expectations."[45] The enthusiasm of communication researchers for this approach was emphasized in 1974 when the important Sage Annual Reviews of Communication Research devoted a full volume to uses and gratifications research. As with other areas, this research emphasis is somewhat fragmented offering findings related to particular media instruments in particular situations. A general theory based on broad mass media applications still seems somewhat distant.

Political Socialization—Political socialization as mass communication research grows out of the older and better-established field of socialization research. Socialization is a process by which the individual acclimates himself to society by learning its norms, values, and expected behavior patterns. Political socialization simply applies this concept to the way that a person learns political behavior. Political scientist Kenneth B. Langston defines political socialization as "the process, mediated through various agencies of society, by which an individual learns politically relevant attitudinal dispositions and behavior patterns."[46] One of those agencies of socialization is, of course, the mass media.

Because learning takes place most significantly in childhood, political socialization studies have most often focused on children. Scholars are asking to what extent mass communication is a factor in a way that children learn their political behavior. Importantly, mass communication as an agency of socialization is examined in context with other variables, including the family and peer groups. In approaching study in this area, a leading researcher, Fred Greenstein says there is the possibility of answering questions about who learns, what is learned, which agents of political socialization have what effect, what the circumstances of political socialization have to do with the process and finally, what the effects of political learning are.[47] Dean Jaros in a book *Socialization to Politics* writes:

> There are two broad categories of modern influences on the political socialization process: mass-mediated communication and direct personal contacts through peer groups. . . .It should be noted that it seems quite likely that whether a youngster pays any attention to the mass media is in part dependent upon his peer group relationships.[48]

Studies have probed the social origins of political socialization as well as the processes by which it is learned and maintained over time. They have looked carefully at the role of television as a teacher and at children's perceptions of government that have been projected through the mass media.

Political socialization, like uses and gratifications, is an area rife with implications for communication policy. It has brought together political scientists, sociologists, psychologists, and communication researchers. Perhaps in time findings from political socialization studies will answer a question posed by psychiatrist Robert Coles: "How does a nation maintain a certain notion of itself over a given span of time—so that policies pursued by one government with or without the consent of a particular citizenry become policies believed in, accepted quite eagerly and casually by succeed-ing generations of men and women?''[49] This is a natural arena for communication researchers since political content is a major stimulus in the learning of political cognitions, opinions and behavior.

Sidney Kraus, another leading political socialization researcher, believes that the mass media and especially television play decisive roles in political socialization. ''There are a va-riety of reasons for this,'' he says, ''not the least of which is the significant change in the way in which children grow up today. Other reasons are the growth and dominance of televi-sion in our daily lives and the increased technology in transmitting information.''[50] Kraus has chided his fellow researchers for pay-ing too little attention to media's role in politi-cal socialization. The mass media, he says, must be regarded as an important variable in the child's perception of the political process, if for no other reason than the considerable amount of time spent with television while growing up. Kraus and other researchers are pushing studies of political socialization into harmony with other communication research findings (like those reported earlier in this chapter) that are slowly but surely redrawing our notions about media effects.

SUMMARY AND CONCLUSION

''The mass media,'' Herbert Hyman has writ-ten, ''are a larger and better echo chamber than all the valleys of the Alps.''[51] In this chapter we have discussed the efforts of communication researchers to probe that echo chamber. In doing so, they are trying to bridge the gap be-tween the conventional wisdom of the layman and the simplistic interpretation of early social

science research on the effects of the media. One thing seems certain: the press is neither the all-powerful giant imagined by the propaganda researchers nor the peripheral influence seen by political researchers in the 1940s.

There is, as this chapter has indicated, a con-siderable distance between *conventional wis-dom* about the effects of mass communication and *research* on that subject. Part of this is due to different perspectives and different levels of analysis. For example, the case of ''Fuzz'' was a singular instance which in spite of its gro-tesque nature could not be generalized very widely. By contrast, the social science studies of political campaigns and the role of media in-fluence therein have broader inferences. This chapter explains how the individual cases of media effects from an historical perspective re-late to those derived from other methods of in-vestigation. Changing perceptions of media in-fluence and impact from the propaganda period to the current period when the ''informational learning'' effect of media is in vogue is re-viewed. Several leading commentators whose work is changing our view of media influence are discussed. Finally, we explore three new arenas for investigation of media influence: agenda-setting, uses and gratifications, and political socialization.

Contemporary researchers are raising new questions about the effect of the press on think-ing, opinion-formation and behavior by moving far beyond the simple cause/effect ideas that viewed communication process in an isolated fashion, stripped away from the rich interaction with many social influences. Perhaps scholars had to go through the up and down cycle of the 1940s and 1950s to arrive at the present formu-lations that look at people in the midst of an information-laden society where the bombardment of messages cannot be avoided. Contemporary research seems to be closer to social reality acknowledging that people *use* the media and asking how and for what purpose and under what circumstances. Still researchers are quite modest in their claims, perhaps remembering the dangers of overstatement and enlarging too much on intuition, however compelling it may seem.

Notes

[1] Elisabeth Noelle-Neumann, "Return to the Concept of Powerful Mass Media," in *Studies of Broadcasting, An International Annual of Broadcasting Science,* ed. H. Eguchi and K. Sata (Tokyo: Nippon Hoso Kyokai, Mar. 1973) p. 68.

[2] W. J. McGuire, "The Nature of Attitudes and Attitude Change," in *The Handbook of Social Psychology,* ed. Gardner Lindzey and Elliot Aronson, 2d ed., vol. 3, (Reading, Mass.: Addison-Wesley Publishing Comp., 1969), p. 229.

[3] Melvin L. DeFleur and Sandra Ball-Rokeach, *Theories of Mass Communication,* 3rd ed. (New York: David McKay Co., 1975), pp. 258-9.

[4] George Gerbner, "Mass Media and Human Communication Theory," in *Sociology of Mass Communications,* ed. Denis McQuail, (Middlesex, Eng.: Penguin Books), p. 43.

[5] Harold D. Lasswell, "The Theory of Political Propaganda," *American Political Science Review,* 1927, vol. 21, p. 627.

[6] V. I. Lenin, *What Is To Be Done?* (New York: International Publishers, 1929).

[7] For an excellent discussion of the German propaganda effort *see,* Leonard W. Dobb, "Goebbels' Principles of Propaganda," in *Public Opinion and Propaganda,* Daniel Katz, et al. (New York: Holt, Rinehart & Winston, 1964), pp. 508-522.

[8] Wilbur Schramm, *Men, Messages and Media, A Look at Human Communication* (New York: Harper & Row, 1973), p. 193.

[9] Paul F. Lazarsfeld, Bernard Berelson and H. Gaudet, *The People's Choice: How the Voter Makes Up His Mind in a Presidential Campaign* (New York: Duell, Sloan & Pearce, 1944).

[10] *See* Leon Festinger, *A Theory of Cognitive Dissonance* (New York: Harper & Row, 1957).

[11] *See* an excellent discussion of many of these studies in Denis McQuail, *Towards a Sociology of Mass Communications* (London: Collier-Macmillan, 1969), pp. 44-51.

[12] Bernard Berelson, "Communication and Public Opinion," in *Communications in Modern Society,* ed. Wilbur Schramm (Urbana: University of Illinois Press, 1948), p. 172.

[13] McQuail, *Towards a Sociology of Mass Communications,* p. 45.

[14] Joseph T. Klapper, *The Effects of Mass Communication* (New York: The Free Press, 1960), p. 8.

[15] McQuail, *Towards a Sociology of Mass Communications,* pp. 47-48.

[16] Noelle-Neumann, "Concept of Powerful Mass Media," p. 70.

[17] T. S. Matthews, *The Sugar Pill* (New York: Simon & Schuster, 1959), p. 166.

[18] Harold Mendelsohn, "Which Shall It Be: Mass Education or Mass Persuasion for Health?," *American Journal of Public Health,* vol. 58, no. 1, (Jan. 1968): 136.

[19] Noelle-Neumann, "Concept of Powerful Mass Media," p. 67.

[20] DeFleur and Ball-Rokeach, *Theories of Mass Communication,* p. 260.

[21] Noelle-Neumann, "Concept of Powerful Mass Media, passim.

[22] Ibid., p. 109.

[23] Peter Clarke and F. Gerald Kline, "Media Effects Reconsidered, Some New Strategies for Communication Research," *Communication Research,* vol. 1, no. 2, (April 1974): 225.

[24] Ibid., p. 228.

[25] John P. Robinson, "Perceived Media Bias and the 1968 Vote: Can the Media Affect Behavior After All?," *Journalism Quarterly,* vol. 49, no. 2 (Summer 1972): 239.

[26] Ibid., p. 241.

[27] Ibid., p. 245.

[28] Schramm, *Men, Messages and Media,* p. 233.

[29] DeFleur and Ball-Rokeach, *Theories of Mass Communication,* p. 261.

[30] G. A. Donohue, P. J. Tichenor and C. N. Olien, "Mass Media Functions, Knowledge and Social Control," *Journalism Quarterly,* Winter 1973, pp. 652-53.

[31] Ibid.

[32]*See* P. J. Tichenor, G. A. Donohue and C. N. Olien, "Mass Media Flow and Differential Growth in Knowledge," *Public Opinion Quarterly,* 34:159-70. The "knowledge gap" hypothesis is stated as follows: "As the infusion of mass media information into a social system increases, segments of the population with higher socio-economic status tend to acquire this information at a faster rate than the lower status segments so that the gap in knowledge between these segments tends to increase rather than decrease."

[33]Maxwell McCombs and Donald L. Shaw, "A Report on Agenda-Setting Research," Association for Education in Journalism, Theory and Methodology Division, San Diego, California, Aug. 18-21, 1974, pp. 10-11.

[34]Charles R. Wright, *Mass Communication: A Sociological Perspective,* 2d ed. (New York: Random House, 1975), p. 9.

[35]Donohue, Tichenor, and Olien, "Mass Media Functions . . .", p. 1.

[36]Bernard C. Cohen, *The Press and Foreign Policy* (Princeton, N.J.: Princeton University Press, 1963), p. 13.

[37]McCombs and Shaw, "A Report on Agenda-Setting Research," p. 16.

[38]Jack M. McLeod, Lee B. Becker, and James E. Byrnes, "Another Look at the Agenda-Setting Function of the Press," *Communication Research,* vol. 1, no. 2, (April 1974): 135.

[39]Unpublished study by Alexander Bloj, reported in McCombs and Shaw, "A Report on Agenda-Setting Research," p. 48.

[40]McLeod, Becker, and Byrnes, ". . .Agenda-Setting Function of the Press," p. 135.

[41]*See* W. Phillips Davison, "On the Effects of Communication," *Public Opinion Quarterly,* vol. 24, 1959, 343-60; *see also* Elihu Katz, "Mass Communication Research and the Study of Culture," *Studies in Public Communication,* 2: 1-6.

[42]McQuail, *Towards a Sociology of Mass Communication,* pp. 71-72.

[43]Elihu Katz, Jay G. Blumler and Michael Gurevitch, "Uses of Mass Communication by the Individual," in *Mass Communication Research, Major Issues and Future Directions,* ed. W. Phillips Davison and Frederick T. C. Yu, (New York: Praeger, 1974), p. 12.

[44]Ibid., p. 22.

[45]Harold Mendelsohn, "Some Policy Implications of the Uses and Gratifications Paradigm," in *The Uses of Mass Communications, Current Perspectives on Gratifications Research,* ed. Jay G. Blumler and Elihu Katz (Beverly Hills, Ca.: Sage Annual Reviews of Communication Research, vol. III, 1974), p. 317.

[46]Kenneth P. Langston, *Political Socialization* (New York: Oxford University Press, 1969), p. 5.

[47]Fred I. Greenstein, *Children and Politics,* rev. ed. (New Haven: Yale University Press, 1969).

[48]Dean Jaros, *Socialization to Politics* (New York: Praeger Publishers, 1973), p. 124-25.

[49]Robert Coles, "What Children Know About Politics," *New York Review of Books,* (Feb. 20, 1975), p. 22.

[50]Sidney Kraus, "Mass Communication and Political Socialization," *Quarterly Journal of Speech,* Dec. 1973, p. 391.

[51]Herbert H. Hyman, "Mass Communication and Socialization," in *Mass Communication Research,* Davison and Yu, p. 36.

"Any crisis, however mild, arouses popular excitement and leads to the formation of a public, consisting of those who are in some way concerned with an event that had disturbed the routine of organized life."
—*Tamotsu Shibutani, in*
Improvised News *(1965)*

Chapter 2

Public Policy and Media Effects

The practical implications of the effect of media on human behavior raise nagging questions about everyday dilemmas. And cause-effect relationships are often suggested. Take for example this scene in a magazine article by the brilliant prose stylist Gay Talese: "She was completely nude, lying on her stomach in the desert sand, her legs spread wide, her long hair flowing in the wind, her head tilted back with her eyes closed. She seemed lost in private thoughts, remote from the world, reclining on this windswept dune in California near the Mexican border, adorned by nothing but her natural beauty. She wore no jewelry, no flowers in her hair, there were no footprints in the sand, nothing dated the day or spoiled the perfection of this photograph except the moist fingers of the seventeen year-old schoolboy who held it and looked at it with adolescent longing and lust."[1]

The scene was Chicago, 1957 and the boy, Harold Rubin. Talese cuts away and brings Rubin into focus again nearly 20 years later, thusly: "Harold did not merely want a model studio, he wanted a sexual supermarket that would offer a wide assortment of commodities and services for sale."[2] The innocent teenager is transformed into a publicity-seeking pornographer who has frequent skirmishes with the police. Known as "Weird Harold," Rubin operates a business that Talese says is "an extension of his boyhood bedroom."[3] And despite many and varied sexual ventures, Rubin never finds a fulfillment for the desire aroused in him by the seductive photograph in the 1957 magazine.

Although there are many facets to Rubin's personality, Talese clearly implies that his preoccupation with erotic material in his teenage years was a factor in his later life. As Talese demonstrates so vividly, questions about whether and under what conditions the mass media can affect behavior continue to be bothersome. Parents wonder whether television violence will do harm to their children's personalities; politicians wonder whether the press can incite riots, judges wonder whether pornography is linked to antisocial behavior. When seen in the context of public problems and contemporary social dilemmas, media effects become quite pertinent to life itself. And, it is no wonder that those who fashion public policy have asked questions, called for evidence and sought answers in this disputed and troublesome debate.

Conflicting views of media impact (as spelled-out in the previous chapter) led those concerned about effects in the public and private sector to fund research that would provide answers and suggest directions for public policy. As one somewhat cynical psychiatrist put it, "ideas flow where the money is," and to some extent the direction of communication research has been influenced by the pattern of government and foundation funding.

If there have been two dominant concerns that have stimulated the flow of research monies in the years after World War II they were (1) the innovation of television and its widespread use, and (2) the social and political upheaval of the 1960s. While there was a good deal of research with communication implications conducted during the war years for purposes ranging from promotion of war bonds to indoctrination of soldiers, public funds flowing to communication research through the late 1940s and 1950s were minimal. Some exceptions were in areas like programmed instruction wherein communication researchers got their projects funded by riding on the coattails of public and private funding of education research. And for years a variety of communication research was funded by agricultural projects concerned with the diffusion of information.

The rapid introduction of television into American homes profoundly changed the way people used their leisure time, and children began to log many, many hours of television viewing. Television's potential for good in enlarging a person's world view as well as its potential for harm in transmitting negative impulses worried layman and scholar alike. The need for effective study was clear and leader, citizen, and researcher shared interest and enthusiasm for a sustained probe.

It was in a relatively calm period, the 1950s, that the inquiry into television impact and influence got underway. That research and other studies of media influence would be accelerated considerably by the turbulent events of the 1960s when Presidential commissions, Congressional committees, and other official sources asked hard questions about the role of the media in what was then termed "contemporary disarray." Assassinations, urban riots, student unrest, and generalized concern about violence and obscenity seemed to demand ex-

planation and communication researchers were called upon to help in the search for answers.

CIVIL DISORDERS AND THE PRESS

In the wake of riots in several American cities, President Lyndon B. Johnson appointed a National Advisory Commission on Civil Disorders in July 1967. Directing his commissioners to answer three basic questions: "What happened?, Why did it happen?, and What can be done to prevent it from happening again?," the President also asked, *"what effect do the mass media have on the riots?"* [4] Even though presidents since George Washington had keenly observed the media, none of them had asked a question in these terms before.

The Commission decided an examination of press performance would yield at least a partial answer, while admitting, that any "sure answer is beyond the range of presently available scientific techniques." [5] Looking first at the performance of the press and broadcasting during the riots, researchers hired by the Commission also considered overall media treatment of Black ghettos, community relations, racial attitudes, and poverty. In their probe, they:

—conducted in fifteen cities a quantitative content analysis of the content of television programs and newspaper reporting during the period of the disorders and in the days immediately thereafter.

—interviewed (using survey methods) ghetto residents about their attitudes of riot coverage;

—questioned government officials, law enforcement agents, media personnel, and ordinary citizens about their attitudes and reactions to reporting the riots;

—discussed riot coverage with representatives of the news media;

—held media conferences in several cities to gain further understanding of how the media responded to what happened in the riots and in urban disorder generally.

Much of the research was on the *content* of the media and how it was perceived by the audience. In addition, consideration was given to how the media work and the process by which they processed certain messages to the public. One doubts that such an approach can really provide a satisfactory assessment of effects, but certainly it would lead to greater understanding of the news media and their operations. Not incidentally, the Commission found that:

> Despite instances of sensationalism, inaccuracy and distortion, newspapers, radio and television tried on the whole to give a balanced, factual account of the 1967 disorders.

> Elements of the news media failed to portray accurately the scale and character of the violence. . . .The overall effect was, we believe, an exaggeration of both mood and event.

> Important segments of the media failed to report on the causes and consequences of civil disorders and on the underlying problems of race relations. . . .[6]

Whether and to what extent the media has an impact on race relations, "its role in shaping attitudes, and the effects of the choices it makes on people's behavior, is in a rudimentary stage,"[7] the Commission lamented in begging the question. The report of the Commission contained several unanswered questions and the suggestion that much further research was needed.

VIOLENCE AND THE NEWS MEDIA

A few months after the National Advisory Commission on Civil Disorders (known commonly as the Kerner Commission for its chairman then-Illinois Governor Otto Kerner) published its report, another outbreak of violence occurred. It happened in Chicago during the Democratic National Convention of August 1968 when there were bloody battles between police and youth, between police and press, between the counterculture and the establishment. This conflict against the backdrop of the assassinations of Dr. Martin Luther King and Robert Kennedy in the spring seemed to demand government action. Again, President Johnson (for the third time* in his presidency) appointed a blue-ribbon study commission—The National Commission on the Causes and Prevention of Violence. Urged by the President to "go as far as man's knowledge takes," the Commission appointed a staff that included communication researchers and also arranged for a number of studies.

The Commission's Task Force on Mass Media and Violence produced a bulky report titled, *Violence and the Mass Media,* which represented one of the largest and most complete government-sponsored studies of media ever assembled. The three-part report (including I. An Historical Perspective, II. The News Media and III. Television Entertainment and Violence) drew on historical, legal, and behavioral studies in its analysis of the media and their impact. The analysis considered media purposes and functions as well as newsroom practices and concluded: "Today, the press is less dependent upon violent content—upon titillation in general—than it may ever have been. The hard fact is that violence is not primarily what the news media have to offer today. For those who suppose that it is, that may be because it is what they have come to expect—or

---

*Including the Warren Commission, which investigated the assassination of President Kennedy and the two groups mentioned here.

choose to see and read.''[8] While decrying the paucity of solid scholarship about the press, the Commission staff in its use of resources and consultants made an important statement, suggesting in fact that study of the media requires historical and legal research as well as social organizational study to understand the dynamics of media operations. Beyond this, they said, the relationship of message to audience must be probed to determine real effects. The Violence report was a synthesis of existing studies in addition to new ones commissioned for the task at hand.

When the researchers looked at television entertainment and violence, the emphasis was much more heavily on behavioral studies. Chapter headings for this section of the report give a clue to its direction:

—Posing the problem of effects;
—Mass media as producers of effects: an overview of research trends;
—The effects of media violence on social learning;
—Value modifications by mass media;
—Mass media as activators of latent tendencies;
—The television world of violence;
—The actual world of violence;
—The two worlds of violence: television and reality;[9]

Concerned that mass media portrayals of violence attract huge audiences, the staff noted that much of the research on media and violence asks whether exposure to symbolic violence in the media actually triggers violent acts. But this, they said, is only a part of the picture, and perhaps one of the least important segments since the evidence is not compelling. What about the media portrayal of violence that might build a climate of attitudes, norms, and values as conditions that might lead to actual violence? This question pushed the staff toward three additional questions:

(1) Does mass media content cultivate acceptance of the idea that this is a violent world where there is nothing one can do but accept violence as a norm?
(2) Does mass communication tend to teach its audience that they live in a kind of world against which they must take up arms?
(3) Even if the mass media focus on violence does not instigate violent behavior, is there an opportunity lost because the media do not promote alternatives to violence by the audience?[10]

Content analytic studies probing the nature of television content and especially content containing violence as well as experiments and surveys that attempted to sort out people's attitudes and behavior patterns toward violent content brought several conclusions. The conclusions rejected the notion that mass media portrayals of violence have no effect on individuals, groups, and society. In instances where effects can be traced, the report continues, most persons would view them as costly and harmful to the individual and society. Putting media violence in context, the staff report said violence as it is depicted on television extends ''the behavioral and attitudinal boundaries of acceptable violence beyond legal and social norms currently espoused by a majority of Americans.''[11] Rejecting the television industry's claim that there is no conclusive evidence violence on television causes viewers to behave violently, the report states: ''Even a nodding acquaintance with the research literature on the causes of violent behavior teaches that violent behavior is usually the result of interacting social forces of which television program content may be one.''[12] The report says that depending on the emotional state of the individual, exposure to television violence can have important short-term and long-term effects. It links violent content with social learning and socialization and suggests that the person who has experienced prolonged violent media content sees the world as more violent than it really is. Such a view, while not actually stimulating violence in the individual, might support greater toleration for violence in the community. These and other findings were presented to citizens in surveys of their attitudes toward violent content. The majority of adult Americans surveyed were in substantial agreement with the conclusions of the Mass Media and Violence Task Force. These judgments, which agreed with the scientific evidence, were not themselves scientific evidence, but as the commission task force put it, "they do demonstrate the widespread concern that adults express about the effects of television violence."[13] The findings reported in the conclusions of the commission staff did not provide straightline directions about how they should be integrated into public or broadcast network policy. Yet some guidelines were offered and perhaps more importantly suggestions for further research were quite explicit. Speaking out against short-term, piecemeal studies of a single medium, the report called for more *long-term cumulative studies*. After all, the researchers reasoned, the impact of violence on a person's values or socialization to a group might be measured only in painstaking studies over several years. *Experimental studies* to test out notions of socialization would also be useful, the report said. This would allow researchers to test the effects of television violence on a population under different combinations of conditions and circumstances. Both pro and antisocial learning patterns might be studied and reinforced. *Epidemiological studies* looking at variations in rates of occurrence of violent activity and response were also recommended. This would allow for analysis of such variables as crime rates and media exposure rates, for example.

The violence commission studies, while not answering all of the questions that members of the public might have had about media influence and impact, did draw on the energies of leading researchers and effectively brought research knowledge to bear on a matter of concern to the public. Public interest in television and its effects would again occupy the attention of the government a few years later. (See section of this chapter dealing with the Surgeon General's report.)

OBSCENITY AND PORNOGRAPHY

Concurrent with the social and political upheavals of the 1960s was what some commentators chose to call "the sexual revolution." Along with it came traffic in obscenity and pornography that the Congress of the United States declared to be "a matter of national concern." That national concern translated itself into Public Law 90-100, which created a Commission on Obscenity and Pornography to be appointed by the President. One of four directives that Congress gave the Commission was "to study the effect of obscenity and pornography on the public, and particularly minors, and its relationship to crime and other antisocial behavior."[14]

The Commission appointed an "effects panel" to summarize existing research and to organize studies addressed to the obscenity and pornography dilemma. The panel was headed by sociologist Otto Larsen and included among its members psychologist Joseph Klapper of CBS whose work on media effects we have already cited. Though limited considerably by time (the commission was to be in existence only two years), the panel members moved ahead with an ambitious research plan. First, they oriented themselves to the study of effects and explored popular conceptions of pornography. In the process they designed effects studies that followed a multiple method approach. Surveys employing various types of sampling procedures, quasi-experimental studies of selected populations, studies of rates and incidence of pornography at community levels as well as controlled experimental studies were all part of the researchers' armamentarian.

Secondly, the researchers thought it would be useful to evaluate the previously mentioned effects studies against the backdrop of public opinion about sexual materials. They looked at the general public and such selected publics as psychiatrists and psychologists.

Thirdly, attention was given to behavioral responses to erotica. The researchers wanted to know whether exposure to erotic stimuli sexually excites and arouses the viewer and whether such exposure affects the subsequent sexual behavior of the user.

Fourthly, attitudinal, emotional, and judgmental responses to erotic materials were studied. Of particular concern here was the possible effect of erotic material on moral character and one's sexual orientation and identification.

Finally, erotica were related to antisocial and criminal behavior. Even though this was an area where research had once been restricted, the effects panel felt at the time of the study that there was sufficient scientific information to discuss the issue intelligently.

After conducting their studies, the researchers would conclude that "empirical evidence designed to clarify the question [of the case against pornography] has found no reliable evidence to date that exposure to explicit sexual materials plays a significant role in the causation of delinquent or criminal sexual behavior among youth or adults."[15]

In reviewing studies of public opinion and professional opinion toward pornography, a wide range of attitudes were reported. Those who had personal experience with erotic material were less likely to believe in harmful effects. Yet accumulated research on psychosexual stimulation demonstrated that exposure to erotic materials produced sexual arousal in substantial proportions in both males and females. Other studies indicated that persons who have experienced erotica were more likely to have more liberal or tolerant sexual attitudes. Perhaps the most striking research finding: "analyses of the United States crime rates *do not* support the thesis of a casual connection between the availability of erotica and sex crimes among either juveniles or adults."[16]

The findings of the communications researchers who leaned away from the notion that obscenity and pornography had a harmful effect on social behavior were the center of much controversy. The report of the Commission itself in spite of the best persuasive efforts of its chairman, a law school dean named William P. Lockhart, was rebuked both by a Republican president (by this time Richard Nixon) and a Democratic Congress. Perhaps this response demonstrated that research on questions related to controversial public policies may have a difficult time winning acceptance, of course, the questions addressed by the researchers were complex, and the evidence they gleaned was qualified, leading to a somewhat ambiguous interpretation. The research findings flew in the face of deeply-held popular beliefs, based largely on personal, anecdotal experiences. The best efforts of researchers using available social science tools and theories could turn up no hard

evidence that obscene content in media has undesirable effects. Indeed, there was even some
evidence that suggested desirable effects. This
was a substantial research effort, conducted by
competent scholars and it should have had considerable potential in influencing media and
governmental policy. But it failed miserably,
not because the research was poorly conceived,
but because the findings became the captive of
political controversy in an election year. In addition, it is unlikely that public policy on
obscenity and pornography will ever be determined primarily by research evidence. In this
instance, research findings ran into ethical concerns and moral constraints. As a result, the researcher's voice, neutral and dispassionate,
could not be heard above the roar of the crowd.

TELEVISION AND SOCIAL BEHAVIOR

Fearful that the Violence Commission (mentioned previously here) would not adequately
address the issue of televised violence, Senator
John Pastore took steps in the spring of 1969
that brought about a comprehensive and far-
reaching government sponsorship of communication research. In a letter to the Secretary of
Health, Education and Welfare, the Rhode Island Senator urged that the Surgeon General be
directed to appoint a committee "to devise
techniques and conduct a study . . .which will
establish scientifically insofar as possible what
harmful effects, if any, these programs have on
children."[17]

Three years later, after the issuance of a significant five-volume report, *Television and Social Behavior*, the Senator would declare:

> When the Surgeon General appeared to tender the
> Report of his Committee on televised violence and
> its impact on children, I said our journey was just

beginning. In my judgment, what has taken place
in the past few days is nothing less than a scientific
and cultural breakthrough. For we now know
there is a causal relationship between televised
violence and antisocial behavior which is sufficient to warrant immediate remedial action. It is
this certainty which has eluded men of good will
for so long.[18]

The report was the work of the Surgeon General's Scientific Advisory Committee on Television and Social Behavior which was appointed
by the Secretary of HEW in June 1969. Never
before did a group of communication researchers have more support for their efforts. A
budget of $1.8 million provided funding for
twenty-three independent research projects and
more than forty technical papers. The advisory
committee itself had a distinguished membership that included such leading social scientists
as Irving L. Janis, Joseph T. Klapper, Ithiel de
Sola Pool and others; additionally it was able to
draw upon other active researchers who carried
out studies on a contractual basis. As Eli A.
Rubinstein, a government researcher, who
served as vice chairman of the advisory committee later wrote, "what is of special relevance
to public concern in the entire research effort is
that a high-level appointed committee of behavioral scientists completed a major research
program whose conclusions have policy implications for the television industry."[19]

The report that resulted was designed for review by at least three constituencies including
social scientists, the broadcast industry and
political leaders. The initial results of the
document, as Douglass Cater and Stephen
Strickland have written in a fascinating study of
the politics of the Surgeon General's report:

> . . .perhaps predictably, tended to confirm the
> fears of all three groups. Written in a social-
> sciencese which made it almost incomprehensible

to the layman, the Report displayed a caution which angered a number of critics, including some of the social scientists who had helped carry out the research. Nonetheless, to the discomfort of the industry, the Surgeon General's committee unanimously found "preliminary" and "tentative" indications of a "causal relation" between televised violence and aggressive behavior. To the dismay of some policy-makers, the Committee members were unable to conclude how many children were likely to be affected and what should be done about it.[20]

The research program was ambitious and tried not only to build on previous results of television research (of which there were a considerable number) but also attempted to develop refined techniques and measurements in effects study. Content analyses of television programs were commissioned as were studies of television personnel attitudes. But, the central work of the Advisory Committee dealt with effects that were measured both in simulated laboratory situations and in field studies involving real-life situations. In a sense, the researchers were trying to bring more specificity and form to the earlier studies of such researchers as Wilbur Schramm, Jack Lyle, and Edwin Parker who had concluded in 1961 that: "For *some* children, under *some* conditions, *some* television is harmful. For *other* children under the same conditions, or for the same children under other conditions, it may be beneficial. For *most* children, under *most* conditions, *most* television is probably neither particularly harmful or beneficial."[21]

Cater in a thoughtful review of the Surgeon General's report indicates that the product of some of the commissioned laboratory experiments was new evidence that enhanced understanding and eliminated some conventional beliefs about children and television. The field studies helped scope-out relationships between television viewing and aggressive behavior, for example. As Cater and Strickland put it, "the new research heightened the realization that television was a powerful instrument for affecting the interest, feelings, attitudes, beliefs and behavior of its viewers."[22]

That television content should be a matter of public concern had long been accepted by members of Congress and officials in government agencies. Especially sensitive to the role that television might play in the lives of children who were seen as vulnerable pawns being bombarded by many self-serving messages from the television industry and advertising, concerned persons in the public sector were looking for guidelines for public policy. What they got was a mixed bag of results.

The report told them that the average household logs more than six hours of television each day, and that children make their program choices quite early. It also told them that television could have a considerable impact on social learning, but that there was little interaction between and among family members watching together. Television also had the capability of provoking family arguments in instances where parents tried to control the amount or type of viewing. Some of the studies included in the report made more powerful cases than others for causal relationships between viewing and the tendency for violence in young viewers. Researchers associated with the studies and with the advisory committee worried that the tiny, fragmented pieces of research they had commissioned might not add up to compelling information for policymakers.

After assessing the many studies carried out by researchers, the committee fashioned a carefully worded and somewhat compromising statement that set forth their conclusion:

Thus, there is a convergence of the fairly substantial experimental evidence for short-run causation of aggression among some children by viewing violence on the screen and the much less certain evidence from field studies that extensive violence viewing precedes some long-run manifestations of aggressive behavior. This convergence of the two types of evidence constitutes some preliminary indication of a causal relationship, but a good deal of research remains to be done before one can have confidence in these conclusions.[23]

Even with its qualifications, the report was quite significant, said Ithiel de Sola Pool, who summed it up thus: "Twelve scientists of widely different views unanimously agreed that scientific evidence indicates that viewing of television violence by young people causes them to behave more aggressively."[24]

The report brought a storm of protest both in the academic and political communities as well as in the broadcast industry. Had the researchers asked the right questions? Did their studies simulate real-life situations? Were their findings being interpreted too broadly?

What was really at stake here was *the public interest* and the question of what it was and who should determine it. While it was clear that particular government agencies and elected officials would have the final word in making policy, the private sector would have a great deal to say about those policy decisions. And almost everybody admitted that the researchers had just begun to scratch the surface of knowledge needed to fully understand the impact and influence of television on its viewers. Also at issue was the role of social science research in public policy. How much should it count? What should be the relationship between the findings of communication researchers and policymakers? The Social Science Research Council made an effort to clarify this conflict:

The contribution of the social sciences is not to replace public debate and legitimate political processes but to supplement them by additional information and rational evaluation. . . . The social scientist cannot be given full responsibility with respect to the policy judgments into which his findings enter. The policy-makers responsible for making such judgments would do well, however, to make as much use as possible of the knowledge that the behavioral and social sciences provide. Greater danger lies, not in science, but in the pitting of one man's subjective judgments against another's.[25]

CHILDREN AND ADVERTISING

The Surgeon General's report stimulated a wide range of scholarly activity concerned with media effects. One category of research that would later develop as a scholarly arena in its own right was children and advertising. The Surgeon General's scientific advisory committee commissioned several studies that raised questions about the potential harmful effects of television advertising on children.

This research coincided with considerable public discussion about children and advertising. Decrying the manipulation and exploitation of children by product advertising, several consumer groups and government agencies called for regulation and control of advertising directed to children. In 1971, both the Federal Communications Commission and the Federal Trade Commission held hearings to probe the charges of those concerned with the problem. While some critics favored an outright ban on advertising to children, a compromise was reached and the National Association of Broadcasters proposed a code of self-regulation. This, however, did not terminate the discussion. Various consumer groups, public interest lobbies, and parent's organizations (to name only a few) have continued to scrutinize television advertising aimed at children. And frequently spokesmen involved in the controversy have looked to research and researchers for evidence.

Fortunately, a number of communications researchers with keen interest in consumer behavior, especially how children learn to make buying decisions, were on the scene. These researchers employed a variety of social science tools to probe questions perplexing the public. Some used content analysis to ascertain what kinds of commercials with what kinds of appeals were being directed to children. Other researchers, wanting to learn more about the impact of the commercial message on the child himself or his parents, used both field experiments and survey research to probe for answers. Consumer behavior specialist Scott Ward outlined three areas of research in a paper prepared for the Surgeon General's report. They included (1) commercial watching behavior—to what extent do children pay attention to commercial messages, (2) effects on cognitive development—which explored a whole range of influences on children's thinking processes including discriminating fantasy from fact, and (3) effects on interpersonal behavior—especially what influence does the child exert on the parent's buying decisions as a result of television advertising.[26]

Ward, in a summary of a whole program of research on children and television advertising, revealed findings that emphasize the complexity of this area of communication research:

1. Young children's reaction to television advertising reflect stages in cognitive development.
2. "Selectivity" in viewing commercials increases with age, but processes of commercial watching are highly complex.

3. Mothers perceive that television advertising influences their children, and they estimate commercials' effects by the frequency which their children attempt to influence purchases.
4. Adolescents hold negative attitudes toward television advertising and there are only slight differences between black and white adolescents in attitudes.
5. Adolescents acquire consumer attitudes and skills from television advertising. Such consumer learning occurs as a function of the quality of television advertising use, more than the quantity of media use.[27]

Interestingly, communication researchers who studied these findings linked them with Swiss psychologist Jean Piaget's theory of cognitive development that details children's thinking capabilities at different stages of life. Piaget's work was heuristic, based on clinical observations of children over the years. Researcher Ward and colleagues Daniel B. Wackman and Ellen Wartella were able to study the awareness of ''what a commercial is'' by children in different age groupings as well as the ability of children to distinguish between programs and commercials. They also asked to what extent children liked commercials and thought they were truthful. This research led to some conclusions about the ways in which children process information.[28]

These researchers and others concerned with children and advertising have probed both the negative and positive aspects of these media effects. While the television advertising research was originally motivated by fear, it was later turned around and studied on a more neutral basis and the result has been research findings that not only provide warnings about potentially unhealthy practices but also information that tells us how children learn to buy, important in a free enterprise economy.[29]

RESEARCH AND PUBLIC POLICY

So what of the researcher and research funding in an arena that is so strongly dominated by government and foundation support? Is the researcher a leader or follower? Do public policy concerns that have run along lines of urban disorder, generalized violence, and television effects really represent the most significant concerns for the researcher? To what extent do researchers modify their ideas, temper their enthusiasms to sniff-out the money at the public trough? Or are most researchers simply drawn in to areas where they are already active scholars? These questions have no simple answers and yet some understanding of them is necessary if one is to evaluate the nature and thrust of communication research activity. Some researchers maintain that significant theoretical and applied studies can be mounted with minimal funding and certainly without either government or private sector support. Others would say that truly significant long-term studies require long-term support in hard cash to guarantee a consistent and continuous effort.

SUMMARY AND CONCLUSIONS

For most of its history, mass communication research, especially that aimed at sorting out media effects, has had quite modest funding support from public and private sources. During the 1960s, a time of considerable affluence for research funding generally, mass communication researchers for the most part were not particularly aggressive in seeking support. Just as communication researchers began to gain momentum in their search for support, a new era of relative austerity in public and private support came about. Even so, many researchers have been successful in seeking financial support for their work and they are competing favorably with those from other fields.

This chapter has considered some of the concerns of the public or of particular public and private institutions that have fostered research on the effects of the mass media. Concern about television and its impact as well as concern about the social and political upheaval of the last thirty years have been chief among the stimuli for communication research. Specific dilemmas that have brought about national attention have included race relations and civil disorders, violence, obscenity and pornography, television and social behavior, and the role of advertising in the lives of children. These areas are considered from several perspectives—what motivated the studies in the first place, what were their findings and what role (if any) did they play in public policy.

Although some researchers like Wilbur Schramm and George Gerbner, for example, ''wrote the book'' on the art of grantsmanship years ago, for the most part communication researchers have been slow to learn these lessons. Schools of journalism and mass communication have generally not been among the major recipients of grants from federal agencies and private foundations. This is changing, however, as communication researchers generate information that is useful to business and government agencies. For example, such concerns as the communication aspects of aging, alcoholism, and drug use have attracted financial support.

An obvious source of funding for communication research would seem to be the communications industry. While the industry has provided some funding (for example small grants from the American Newspaper Publishers Association, the National Association of Broadcasters, and the Magazine Publishers Association to name a few) the amount of this support has been niggardly. Perhaps this is because communication researchers have not sufficiently convinced the industry of the value and relevance of their work. This seemed to be changing by the late 1970s, however, as industry problems (for example, declining newspaper circulations) seemed to demand more intelligence about the media consumer—his needs and demands. And happily for the researcher, many of the public policy areas mentioned in this chapter stimulated further research in the same areas, much of it funded by private foundations.

It would be naive to suggest that the findings of communication research should be the dominant force in decision making in the public arena. Research can obviously answer some questions, deliver some new information for consideration by lawmakers and bureaucrats, but it is not a panacea. Increasingly, though, it is an important voice in public policy deliberations in competition with legal, ethical, moral, and political considerations. As research techniques are refined, as broader questions are addressed and as more long-term data are available, research will no doubt play a larger role. At the same time research findings will need advocates and spokespersons to disseminate them to the public-at-large and to key decision makers. The result would be a better opportunity for researchers to help solve many of the theoretical and practical problems that confront our society.

Notes

[1]Gay Talese, "A Matter of Fantasy," *Esquire*, vol. 84, no. 2, (Aug. 1975): 49.

[2]Ibid., p. 151.

[3]Ibid., p. 152.

[4]*Report of the National Advisory Commission on Civil Disorders*, New York Times edition (New York: Dutton, 1968), p. 362.

[5]Ibid.

[6]Ibid., p. 20.

[7]Ibid., p. 389.

[8]*Mass Media and Violence, A Staff Report to the National Commission on the Causes and Prevention of Violence*, Prepared by Robert K. Baker and Sandra J. Ball, (Washington: U.S. Government Printing Office, 1969), p. 152.

[9]Ibid. See contents pages xiv-xxi.

[10]Ibid., pp. 245-46.

[11]Ibid., p. 375.

[12]Ibid., vii.

[13]Ibid., p. 379.

[14]*The Report of the Commission on Obscenity and Pornography*, New York Times edition (New York: Bantam Books, 1970), p. 1.

[15]Ibid., p. 169.

[16]Ibid., p. 286.

[17]Senator Pastore's letter to HEW Secretary Robert Finch, Mar. 5, 1969, reported in Douglass Cater and Stephen Strickland, *TV Violence and The Child, The Evolution and Fate of the Surgeon General's Report* (New York: Russell Sage Foundation, 1975), p. 17.

[18]U.S. Senate Subcommittee on Communication, *Surgeon General's Report by the Scientific Advisory Committee on Television and Social Behavior* (Washington: U.S. Printing Office, 1972).

[19]Eli A. Rubinstein, "The TV Violence Report: What's Next,?" *Journal of Communication,* 24:1 (Winter 1974), p. 82.

[20]Cater and Strickland, *TV Violence and the Child*, p. 2.

[21]Wilbur Schramm, Jack Lyle and Edwin B. Parker, *Television in the Lives of Our Children* (Stanford: Stanford University Press, 1961), p. 1.

[22]Cater and Strickland, *TV Violence and the Child*, p. 55.

[23]Surgeon General's Scientific Advisory Committee on Television and Social Behavior, *Television and Growing Up: The Impact of Televised Violence* (Washington, D.C.: U.S. Government Printing Office, 1972), p. 10.

[24]United States Senate Subcommittee on Communications, *Hearings on the Surgeon General's Report by the Scientific Advisory Committee on Television and Social Behavior* (Washington, D.C.: U.S. Government Printing Office, March 21-24, 1972), p. 47.

[25]National Academy of Sciences Social Science Research Council, *The Behavioral and Social Sciences* (Englewood Cliffs, N.J.: Prentice-Hall, Inc., 1969), p. 93, 128.

[26]Scott Ward, "Effects of Television Advertising on Children and Adolescents," in *Television and Social Behavior*, Eli A. Rubinstein, et al., vol. 4, p. 432-67.

[27]Ibid., pp. 448-9.

[28]Daniel B. Wackman, Scott Ward, Ellen Wartella and James Ettema, "Children's Information Processing of Television Commercial Messages," (Paper delivered at American Psychological Assn., Montreal, Canada, Aug. 30, 1973). *See also,* Scott Ward and Daniel B. Wackman, "Children's Information Processing of Television Advertising," in *New Models for Mass Communication Research*, ed. Peter Clarke, (Beverly Hills: Sage Publications, 1973), pp. 119-46; Ward & Wackman, "Children's Purchase Influence Attempts and Parental Yielding," *Journal of Marketing Research*, Aug. 1972, pp. 316-19; and Wackman and Wartella, "A Review of Research Related to Suggested Guidelines for Premium Advertising," (Paper prepared for Council of Better Business Bureau, Inc., Children's Review Unit, National Advertising Division's Advisory Panel, April 1975).

[29]Scott Ward, Daniel B. Wackman and Ellen Wartella, *Children Learning to Buy: The Development of Consumer Information Processing Skills* (Beverly Hills: Sage Publications, 1977).

"You, the broadcasting industry, have enormous power in your hands. You have the power to clarify. You have the power to confuse. Men in public life cannot remotely rival your opportunities because day after day, night after night, hour after hour, . . .you shape the nation's dialogue."

—Lyndon B. Johnson (1968)

Chapter 3

The Political Impact of the Media

Poised and solemn, Robert Redford and Dustin Hoffman stare out of an advertisement for the popular 1976 film, "All the President's Men." A caption on the page reads, "In 1972, two young men precipitated the greatest Constitutional crisis since the Civil War." The film, based on the book by the same name written by *Washington Post* reporters Bob Woodward and Carl Bernstein, makes a powerful case for the impact and influence of the press on American politics and government. And in the days after the Watergate crisis it was not unusual for a euphoric press to make extravagant claims about itself. For example, Alan U. Schwartz writing in *The Atlantic* in 1977 said, "The power of the media—the press, radio and television, books, magazines, and motion pictures—has grown, almost geometrically in recent decades. Unchecked, it could control the minds, actions, and destiny of our people."[1] This made the heroic exploits of Woodward and Bernstein all the more important, and it is easy to see why the dynamic duo became instant journalistic heroes.

Historians may debate for years the relative importance of investigative journalism in "solving" the Watergate case and hastening the downfall of the government. The press itself was oblivious to other influences, wrote press critic Edward Jay Epstein:

A sustaining myth of journalism holds that every great government scandal is revealed through the work of enterprising reporters who by one means or another pierce the official veil of secrecy. The role that government institutions themselves play in exposing official misconduct and corruption therefore tends to be neglected if not wholly ignored in the press.[2]

But regardless of the debate and its merits, one thing is clear, the press and the public believe that the media have a strong influence in determining the outcome of political and governmental battles. Sorting-out relative influences and factors such as law enforcement agencies, government bureaus and legislative bodies becomes a more difficult proposition.

Witness the Congressional sex scandals of the mid-1970s, for example. Several members of Congress (among them Wilbur Mills, Wayne Hays, Donald Reigle and Allen Howe) were implicated in news stories that suggested personal misconduct. There was considerable coverage of the issue of private morality in public life. And one clear result was the defrocking of two of America's most powerful political figures—Mills and Hays. Would this have happened without press coverage? Did the press initiate the investigation? What influence, if any, did the coverage have on other members of Congress, on political leaders and other influential persons? These are not questions that can be answered by idle speculation, but they do point up the importance of mass communication in America's political life and demonstrate why this is a worthy topic of discussion.

ELECTIONS AS A RESEARCH TARGET

As earlier chapters have indicated politics and elections have often been the setting for communication research aimed at exploring media effects. The pioneering work of Columbia researchers Paul Lazarsfeld and Bernard Berelson frequently centered on elections. Much of what we learned about media effects during the period of minimal media consequences came from election studies. Why so much attention to elections? Many reasons have been advanced. Elections are inherently interesting and colorful. They are regarded as important since they may signal the change of government or the confirmation of an incumbent. Of course, there is another advantage for researchers—campaigns have a somewhat prescribed length and they do end on election day. Thus an election study becomes a manageable entity for the researcher who likes the notion of a beginning and end in his study.

The famous Erie County study of 1940 and subsequent work led to theories of personal influence and selective perception (mentioned in Chapter 1) causing a pullback by social scientists from the idea of all-powerful media. Researchers became more cautious about ascribing massive effects to media in mobilizing public opinion. However, they did not abandon the idea of effects altogether. Researchers investigated such things as opinion-holding. Why, they would ask, do the media affect the holding of this opinion rather than that one? Bernard Berelson lamented this tendency of researchers who concerned themselves with narrow questions, rather than the broader, more generalized effect of holding political opinions at all when he wrote:

The media have a major influence in producing an interest in public affairs by constantly bringing them to people's attention in a context of presumed citizenly concern. The more the media stresses a political issue, the less indecision there is on the issue among the general public. At the same time, however, the communication media may also be promoting in actuality, but without intention, a sense of political apathy among some of its audience.[3]

This, Berelson said, could happen in at least two ways: recreational and diversionary (entertainment) content of the media could minimize political interest, or the media might "increase political apathy simply through presentation of the magnitude, the diversity, and the complexity of the political issues on which the responsible citizen is supposed to be informed."[4]

If the Erie County study was a triumph of interpersonal communication over mass communication, it should be remembered that only one aspect of political communication was being studied. The researchers only wanted to know whether the persuasive preelection campaign actually caused people to change their votes. In the later Elmira study during the 1948 election, persons with high media use patterns were found to be less likely to change their votes. Thus came the notion of reinforcement of existing attitudes and values. The media's main influence was seen as providing information and for this reason its impact on the election was regarded as quite indirect. As the Columbia University researchers turned their attention to other problems, the Survey Research Center of the University of Michigan initiated a series of voting behavior studies that continue today. While the Columbia studies centered on a single community and were conducted in the tradition of community studies with attention to the cultural and political milieu, the Michigan studies were national in scope. "To a large extent," write three leading political communication researchers, "each voter was considered to have an identical social environment; voting was considered to be an individual phenomenon that produced aggregate national effects, not a local one with a community base."[5] In a sense, this was a happy coincidence, since the media were becoming more national, but the Michigan approach was not without its problems. The Michigan studies had a national bias, thus making it difficult to know what kind of political information people were actually getting. Lee B. Becker and colleagues write, "the result was that the potential effects of the media on the voter's cognitive and affective map of politics'— on which the SRC [Survey Research Center] studies focused—was left largely unexplored. Media use was considered an individual political activity, in the same category as attending political rallies and contributing financial support to one of the parties."[6] Thus, the many studies of political behavior conducted during the 1940s, 50s and 60s yielded much useful information about political behavior in the political process, but less attention was given to the role of mass communication. Downgraded in the early studies, media influence was regarded as somewhat peripheral in the political arena. Yet, questions about limited media influence persisted. Among them were questions about the role of editorial endorsements.

EDITORIAL PAGE ENDORSEMENTS

Does the editorial page—and especially candidate endorsements—have an influence on the political process or on individual voters? This is a question that has interested researchers and students of the press for years. And there are dozens of studies at the national and local level that probe this concern. The history of journalism is replete with anecdotes about powerful publishers and their supposed influence on elections. And certainly, politicians have given credence to this view by courting the publishers, hat in hand, asking for support. Sometimes, however, it is difficult to separate folklore from hard evidence and few researchers have been able to successfully determine whether the press leads or follows.

The editorial page with declarations of support for particular candidates and graphic images rendered by editorial cartoonists, not to mention columns and feature material, has persuasion as its avowed purpose. It is not difficult to see why a legend about editorial page influence in elections grew up. For much of the late nineteenth and early twentieth centuries Republicans dominated the White House and the Congress. Newspapers traditionally endorsed Republicans. Indeed, in the twenty-one Presidential elections between 1896 and 1976, American newspapers editorial page endorsements favored Republicans by a large margin except in 1964 when Lyndon Johnson was preferred to Barry Goldwater.

It was during the incumbency of Franklin D. Roosevelt when serious questions about the power of the press were raised with regularity. Roosevelt's victories in the face of regular editorial page opposition made some observers doubt the influence of the press. By 1952, historian Frank Luther Mott would suggest that the press had lost its punch. Mott concluded after studying presidential endorsement patterns that "there seems to be no correlation, positive or negative, between support by a majority of newspapers during a campaign and victory in a presidential canvass.''[7] Of course, Mott was making a gross assessment comparing the won-loss columns of candidates with endorsement patterns in an all-or-nothing manner. That newspaper endorsements might have peripheral or fragmented influence, either positive or negative, was not considered.

Understandably the strong Republican stance of editorial pages led researchers to ask whether there was a corresponding bias in news columns, especially with regard to political coverage. In 1952, Adlai Stevenson, then the Democratic standard-bearer, had charged that America had a ''one party press.'' In a review of more than a dozen studies that have looked at alleged slanting in the news columns, two Indiana University researchers concluded, ''analysis of a substantial body of behavioral research reveals conflicting findings, but many studies suggest moderate bias in the news columns favoring the candidate given editorial endorsement.''[8] But, at the same time, they acknowledged several studies that found essentially equal treatment of candidates.

While claims about the influence of the press in national elections have diminished, there is a prevailing view that press influence is much more potent on the local scene. ''It is probable,'' wrote Curtis D. MacDougall, ''that the press 'batting average' of apparent success would be higher in local than in national elections.''[9] In a 1975 analysis, Bernard Hennessy agrees with some qualification: ''What of the thousands of more obscure state and local candidacies, often run in jurisdictions where only a few communications channels exist—are newspapers under such circumstances, not more influential for election outcomes? The answer seems to be 'yes,' although the evidence is too scanty to be conclusive.''[10]

The problem with obtaining conclusive results is in accounting for the many factors that might be present in a campaign. In a study of California newspapers from the late 1940s to the mid-1960s, James E. Gregg found a high success rate in endorsements of local candidates who were eventually elected to office. And interestingly, the same study revealed that newspaper endorsement of noncandidate election issues (e.g. referendum, initiative) was even more successful.[11] One should not, of course, take research of this kind as the only explanation of the role of political endorsements. Some observers would regard Gregg's conclusions as naive and might suggest that the press tends to be more a follower than a leader in local electoral situations. It must be remembered that the studies cited here pertain to a single election in a single locale. They raise important questions. They do not necessarily provide universal answers. Research is simply too fragmented and uncertain for that.

In another local study, G. Cleveland Wilhoit and a colleague assessed the relationship between newspaper editorial endorsement of a candidate and coverage of the candidate in public opinion poll news. They found with some exception that an endorsed candidate got more favorable coverage in opinion poll news. However, they reported that papers not endorsing a candidate ''treated with greater disparity two political candidates contending for the same office. The finding suggested that a policy on nonendorsement by ''neutral'' papers did not reduce bias in political news coverage.''[12]

Maxwell McCombs in a study of the influence of editorial endorsements agrees that attempts to influence national office are probably ineffective, but suggests the opportunities at the state and local level are more significant. ''At the state and local level," he writes, "there are fewer variables—or at least fewer salient variables—shaping political behavior. In such cases the information and opinion input of the editorial endorsement may be a major and sometimes the only source of orientation for the voter."[13] It was among people making voting decisions at the last minute that the media could have its greatest impact, McCombs observed.

The somewhat shaky evidence and mixed results of research on political effects in endorsement patterns gives support to Walter Weiss's assessment:

> When the effects of the media on the outcomes of political campaigns in an open society are limited to conversions of vote intentions from one party to another, the media seem relatively ineffective. Few people appear to be converted merely through exposure to formal political communications. The available evidence suggests that the preponderance of total media effects is contributed by the reinforcement or substantiation of vote decisions brought about by other factors, such as habitual patterns of voting or social and personal influences.[14]

While this assessment may limit any simplistic cause-effect interpretation of the role of newspaper endorsements, the idea of reinforcement as an effect should not be overlooked. As we have mentioned earlier in another context, reinforcement was a terribly important effect that was raised cogently in the violence studies.

THE ROBINSON STUDIES

Conflicting with the Weiss view and adding new evidence to the notion that endorsement editorials might have some influence in elections were studies by John P. Robinson, which were mentioned briefly in Chapter 1. Robinson's startling findings had a newspaper's "perceived support" for a candidate responsible for as much as a six percent edge in the vote for that candidate. The Robinson findings added fuel to earlier observations about British elections by two political scientists who reported changes in the political preferences of Britons exposed to certain newspapers. Indeed, these researchers were able to "attribute to the press some role in changing the relative strength of the parties in the short run."[15] This was not said without qualification, however. The British researchers allowed that the particular election they studied may possibly have been a special case.

In Robinson's 1968 study using University of Michigan Survey Research Center data, a national sample of voters were asked whether they recognized any political allegiance in the news media. Newspapers were most often seen as the medium that took sides, usually favoring the Republicans. Robinson not only broke down responses for individual media (television, radio, newspapers and magazines), but he also learned the party identification of the voters and for whom they intended to vote in the election. He even divided his sample into weak and strong party identification (for example, weak Democrat, strong Democrat). What he did was provide more refinements in measuring his survey responses, thus yielding more precise data. This differs markedly with the gross measure methods of correlating newspaper support with candidate success since it measures small shifts in voting preference. From his data Robinson could conclude that the largely pro-Nixon coverage (as perceived by the voters and confirmed by the *Editor & Publisher* tally of endorsements) could be associated with some shift of the vote in Nixon's favor. Voting "in the direction of perceived newspaper bias" was most likely among undecided voters who made up their minds late in the campaign. Even when he controlled for other variables and looked for alternative explanations, Robinson could still report that a newspaper's perceived support for one candidate or another could give them as much as a six percent edge. And even though the public "ranked television as its most important and relatively unbiased source of campaign news...far more people report having voted for the candidate espoused by the newspaper than by the other media,"[16] he said.

Why? In a subsequent 1974 article, Robinson explained:

> Prior to national election day, television transmits a continual glut of partisan campaign appeals. In contrast to the editorial endorsements of newspapers, however, television seldom offers its own message to the voters on how they ought to cast their ballots. The newspaper endorsement is a direct message, which appears to reduce objectively the confusing arguments of the campaign to a single conclusion.[17]

Still Robinson and others are careful in their speculations about the press as kingmaker. Even in his 1968 study Robinson acknowledged that the six percent differential was about half as great as that of personal influence; however, the real significance of the six percent margin becomes evident when one considers the history of close elections in the U.S. The media influence is there, but it does not outdistance the persuasive interpersonal efforts of one's peers. The 1968 findings were confirmed in a similar 1972 study. Indeed, "confidence in a linkage between newspaper endorsements and presidential voting behavior was bolstered by...empirical findings."[18]

Robinson makes no dogmatic pronouncements. For example, in an examination of electoral and endorsement data through five presidential elections, he observed some consistency between the two but stopped short of declaring it a "lawful relationship." Robinson was also bothered by the notion of causality—that is, did the newspaper endorsement *cause* the electoral result or simply *reflect* public sentiment? Or, perhaps did both happen? More elaborate tests are needed before one can be very certain about cause and effect relationships, he says. Looking at the potential negative effects of media, Robinson says that the newspaper editorial endorsements might be both *kingmaker* and *kingbreaker*. Yet even accounting for appropriate cautions, two clear themes emerge in the Robinson data:

1) In close elections (1960 and 1968), voting differentials by newspaper endorsements are confined to Independents.
2) In landslide elections (1956, 1964, 1972) voting differentials by newspaper endorsement extend to members of the losing party as well as to Independents.[19]

With little doubt, newspaper's influence on the voter's choice of candidate in presidential elections has remained significant over time.

CHAIN OWNERSHIP AND ENDORSEMENTS

The Robinson studies have provided continued stimulus for investigation into the impact and influence of newspaper editorial endorsements. Recognizing that the readership of editorial pages is not particularly impressive, researchers nonetheless were impressed with the striking influence of the starkly unambiguous political endorsements in elections.

Four University of Minnesota researchers who looked at newspaper endorsement patterns considered a variable Robinson had not—

ownership. Recognizing that the self-reported partisanship of newspapers in America was dropping off, the researchers noticed that this was happening in the face of increased chain ownership of the same newspapers. With fewer newspapers carrying a ''Republican'' or ''Democratic'' designation on their mast-heads[20] and with spokesmen for chains claiming that they had relative autonomy in determining editorial policy (in spite of group ownership), the researchers wondered whether there was more diversity in editorial endorsements.

In a 1974 survey, the *Masthead,* a publication of the National Conference of Editorial Writers, asked editors, managers, and editorial writers in eighteen newspaper chains to write candidly about ''who decides presidential endorsements.'' Almost all of them answered— ''the individual publisher at the local level.''[21] This and other public pronouncement by publishers led the researchers to hypothesize that chain-owned newspapers are not homogeneous in their endorsements of presidential candidates. But the hypothesis did not hold up to tests. In fact, the researchers found that chain-owned newspapers were more likely to endorse than nonchain–owned. In the four elections between 1960 and 1972, ''substantial numbers of chains were homogeneous in their endorsements, that is, 85 percent or more of the papers endorsing a candidate supported the same candidate.''[22] Thus it could be stated that:

> In only the 1964 election did more than one-fourth of the chains exhibit a heterogeneous endorsement pattern. (This) would seem to contradict clearly the proposition advanced by spokesmen for chain ownership, and the hypothesis of this study, that members of chains are quite independent in their political endorsement editorial policies. In general, the vast majority of chains exhibited

homogeneous endorsement patterns in the four presidential years studied.[23]

Against the backdrop of the Robinson studies, the chain-ownership study has even larger meaning and a greater importance in terms of media effects. In light of the increasing number of independent voters in America,[24] persons who are apparently most susceptible to editorial endorsements alongside similar growth patterns among chains, the press may have considerable power. Thus, the study concludes:

> ...it may be that the press system in America plays an important role in maintaining the two-party system. In the face of the enormous Democratic Party registration edge, it may be that the Republican-biased newspaper endorsements could have an increasingly important influence on Independent voters, thus adjusting the balance in partisan politics.[25]

This conclusion is necessarily speculative because there are no earlier baseline data that allow for a comparison.

IS TV POWER A MYTH?

For a number of years now it has been assumed that television plays a decisive role in political campaigns. Gene Wycoff wrote in a 1968 book, *The Image Candidates,* that *the* determining factor in electing a political candidate is his television image. ''Television apparently does more than just present political candidates. Television transfigures candidates into personal images or characterizations that can be quite unique to the medium,''[26] he wrote. Conventional wisdom had it that the celebrated presidential campaign debates between John Kennedy and Richard Nixon in 1960 might have tipped the electoral balance for Kennedy. At the heart of Spiro Agnew's vituperative attack on the news media in 1969 was the assumption that television newscasts have enormous power. And, of course, American television gives massive coverage to election campaigns, often treating them like horse races. But how much influence does television really have on election outcomes?

To begin with campaign managers and candidates think that television has considerable influence and they plan their campaigns accordingly. In a revealing Harvard University conference in 1972, presidential campaign aides, representing all of the primary and general election candidates of that year, told how campaign decisions were made to maximize coverage on the evening television news. James Perry of the *National Observer* expressed a conventional wisdom that "you hear all the time these days that print has lost its influence and doesn't have much impact on a campaign—that what is important is electronic."[27] A Nixon aide, Peter H. Dailey, agreed saying, "it's obvious that television is the dominant element today. The average television set is in use in a house six hours a day."[28]

Thus emerges a popular view that television is the primary source of information about politics and it is from television network news that people get most of their knowledge about election issues. Not so, say two Syracuse University researchers, who declared that "TV power is a myth" in a 1976 book. In an exhaustive study that included detailed content analysis of political commercials and evening newscasts on the three networks as well as 2,000 interviewers with voters at three stages during the campaign, the two researchers Thomas E. Patterson and Robert D. McClure concluded:

> What emerges from this study is that the nightly network newscasts present a picture of politics that is thoroughly lacking in substance. They ignore

major issues. They ignore the candidates personal qualifications for the presidency. In fact, during the 1972 general election, voters got more knowledge of candidate issue positions out of paid political commercials than they did from TV newscasts.[29]

Crowds, hecklers, motorcades, and so forth, despite providing the best visual story on television, often meant a story that was lacking in content. Issue stories tended to feature "talking heads" and this is dull television fare. Thus, network news avoided issues, emphasizing instead campaign hoopla.

In their interviews with voters during the campaign, Patterson and McClure asked about reading and viewing patterns and tried to ascertain how knowledgeable their interviewees were. "Regular viewing of network news had no influence on how much these people learned," the researchers said, and "by contrast, newspapers were far more effective than television in making voters better informed on the issues. The minutes people spent reading their newspapers, unlike the minutes they gave to watching network news, clearly increased their issue awareness."[30]

As their probe into TV advertising indicated, viewers are influenced most prominently by television when there is variation in the message in short takes. Television news fare, on the other hand, produced a dulling sameness for the viewer. The two researchers conclude that image is not enough and that voters are mostly influenced by the policies and actions of a candidate and how they see those characteristics as affecting them personally. This finding flies in the face of an all-powerful television dictating public tastes and preferences on the basis of positive television exposure. If the work of Patterson and McClure is accurate "the common assumptions by candidates, politicians and reporters about the political impact of the media are almost 180 degrees off target,'' writes Warren Weaver of the *New York Times*.[31] To be sure the book sent shock waves through the television industry.

In another study Patterson and McClure found that television news was not an efficient communicator of political information but that ''when television news breaks into regular entertainment programming to report a greater than bulletin-length story, the salience of that issue or event to the viewer is sharply and uniquely affected.''[32] The usual story that preempts other programming (such as Richard Nixon's trip to China) and is treated with continuity and depth can have a significant impact on voters' perceptions. Patterson and McClure and other researchers have reported that while a television viewer may remember quite well a candidate's face from television coverage, they may know nothing about him. Thus, it was that they found:

> Newspapers succeed where television news fails because newspapers can clearly demonstrate the significance they attach to a given story. Newspapers have at their disposal the traditional means of indicating emphasis and significance—long stories, short stories; stories with pictures, stories without pictures; large headlines, small headlines; front page, back page; above the fold, below the fold. Thus the print medium gives readers a *strong, lasting, visual* indication of significance.[33]

Though this study, as others, is carefully qualified, the authors lament the lack of continuous political communication research, that which could generalize beyond election campaigns.

POLITICAL RESEARCH DIRECTIONS

Researchers concerned with political communication make few dramatic claims. Their work is carefully stated and usually alternative explana-

tions are advanced. Little seems to be known with any certainty. This should not be cause for alarm, however, says Davis Bobrow, ''to say that we know little is, of course not to say that we know nothing.''[34] Bobrow calls for more discriminating judgments in political research. What is known about the political effect of the media? Bobrow says a considerable amount. For example:

> 1) Aspects of mass communications that decisions by political actors can affect: message content, media personnel and technology, cultural level or messages, and availability of media output.
>
> 2) Aspects of the political system that mass communication can affect: who gets what from whom, when, how, why, with what effect, and with what response?
>
> 3) Mass communicators, political officials, and individual and group publics engage in purposeful decision-making that leads them to seek or avoid some effects and not others; different preference priorities determine which of a variety of possible effects will be sought and achieved.[35]

Forest P. Chisman has suggested that research linking politics and mass communication is evolving in three important directions, namely, (1) there is less emphasis today on isolated individuals as receivers of political communication and more emphasis on the social and interpersonal context of media use; (2) there is increasing emphasis on the individual as a user of mass media wherein the person is an active participant, rather than a passive part of the mass; (3) there is a shift away from the media as attitude change agents and more emphasis on the media as they structure the information environment. Thus, in the first area we have co-orientation research, in the second, uses and gratifications and in the third, agenda-setting.[36]

In an article aimed at political communications researchers Garrett J. O'Keefe proposes a number of directions and objectives for future research. Some of them were:

- —the nature of political influence
- —factors in voter decision-making
- —political uses of media during campaigns
- —campaign media content
- —cognitive effects of campaign media
- —perceptions of campaign issues and candidates images
- —interpersonal communication and political campaigns
- —voter typologies and communication behavior
- —political parties and communication behavior
- —political socialization and communication behavior.[37]

O'Keefe and others have reported that the survey instrument, coupled with content analysis may be the most commonly used method of political communication research. And he suggests further that impressionistic studies that search out the feeling tone of the political milieu might also be helpful. And, of course, studies using literary or historical methods might be illuminating as well. There seems to be a need for more coordination of studies and for continued explorations over time. It is to that end that the Committee on Mass Communications and Political Behavior of the prestigious Social Science Research Council is dedicated. Studies funded and proposed by this group look not only at societal relationships of media and politics, but at communicators themselves in the context of their media organizations.

Although studies of the political impact of mass media are quite limited and narrowly-drawn, this approach is not without its critics. After all, writes the British researcher Colin Seymour-Ure, "media are so deeply embedded in the system that without them political activity in its contemporary forms could scarcely carry on at all."[38] Seymour-Ure would have researchers find a wider conception of effects by considering (a) the nature of media effects, (b) the production of those effects and (c) the political context of effects. In a sense this is happening to some degree as one considers the various approaches to research summarized in this book. In this section of the book we have considered studies that probe the nature of media effects. In the next section we examine the internal processes of the mass media that in fact "create and produce" those effects. What we fail to do is consider in a substantial way the political context of effects. The student is directed to books specifically concerned with political communication and political behavior that spell out the full dimensions of that most complex field. Of course, a number of the studies cited here do speak generally to the issue of political context.

SUMMARY AND CONCLUSIONS

When one digs into the swirling mass of data about the political impact of the media, there are many tentative conclusions that can be reached. Politicians probably overstate the importance of television and underestimate the potential of print. The public tendency to get most of its information from television doesn't necessarily hold for subdivisions of that public—say, for example, potential voters. Refinements in social science instruments have yielded important new information and insights about the role of mass communication in electoral campaigns, conflicting somewhat with the minimal effects thesis of thirty years ago.

Research probing the political impact of the mass media has attracted considerable interest for many years. In this chapter we explain why elections are so frequently a topic for communication research. Early studies of political communication and their projection of a media with minimal effects are reviewed. Specific attention is directed to studies of editorial-page endorsements and their influence or lack of it. The work of researcher John P. Robinson, which is making people ask "can the mass media affect political behavior after all?," is reviewed. Other sections of this chapter probe chain ownership and political endorsements and new research that is raising important questions about the actual power of television in politics. Finally, several new directions in political communication research are examined.

Interest in the political impact of the media both among scholars and practitioners has never been higher and it will continue to accelerate. The desire of people to gain and keep power and in that process to know and understand the role of the media is not likely to diminish now or in the immediate future. Students of political communication need to look for comparability in studies, to link and build upon present knowledge in order to interpret the new findings that continue to spill out of journals, conferences, and books.

Notes

[1] Alan U. Schwartz, "Danger: Pendulum Swinging, Using the Courts to Muzzle the Press," *The Atlantic*, February 1977, p. 30.

[2] Edward Jay Epstein, "Did the Press Uncover Watergate," *Commentary*, July 1974, p. 21.

[3] Bernard Berelson, "Communications and Public Opinion," in *Mass Communications*, ed. Wilbur Schramm (Urbana: University of Illinois Press, 1960), p. 539.

[4] Ibid., p. 540.

[5] Lee B. Becker, Maxwell E. McCombs and Jack M. McLeod, "The Development of Political Cognitions," in *Political Communication*, ed. Steven H. Chaffee, vol. 4, Annual Reviews of Communication Research (Beverly Hills, Ca.: Sage Publications, 1975), p. 32.

[6] Ibid., p. 33.

[7] Frank Luther Mott, "Has the Press Lost Its Punch?" *The Rotarian*, Oct. 1952, p. 13. A useful contemporary view of the role of the press in political campaigns is found in Edwin Emery, "Changing Role of the Mass Media in American Politics," *The Annals of the American Academy of Political and Social Science*, Sept. 1976, pp. 84-94.

[8] G. Cleveland Wilhoit and Taik Sup Auh, "Newspaper Endorsement and Coverage of Public Opinion Polls in 1970," *Journalism Quarterly*, Winter 1974, p. 654.

[9] Curtis D. MacDougall, *Understanding Public Opinion* (Dubuque, Iowa: William C. Brown, 1966), p. 509.

[10] Bernard Hennessy, *Essentials of Public Opinion* (North Scituate, Mass.: Duxbury Press, 1975), pp. 162-63.

[11] *See* generally, James E. Gregg, "Newspaper Editorial Endorsements and California Elections, 1948-62," *Journalism Quarterly*, 42 (1965), p. 533.

[12] Wilhoit and Sup Auh," Coverage of Public Opinion Polls in 1970," p. 658.

[13] Maxwell E. McCombs, "Editorial Endorsements: A Study of Influence," *Journalism Quarterly*, Autumn 1967, p. 545.

[14] Walter Weiss, "Effects of the Mass Media of Communication," in *Handbook of Social Psychology*, ed. Gardiner Lindzey and Elliot Aronson, vol. 5 (Boston: Addison-Westley, 1969), p. 176.

[15] David Butler and Donald Stokes, *Political Change in Britain* (New York: St. Martins Press, 1969).

[16] John P. Robinson, "Perceived Media Bias and the 1968 Vote: Can the Media Affect Behavior After All?," *Journalism Quarterly*, Summer 1972, pp. 239-46.

[17] John P. Robinson, "The Press as King-Maker: What Surveys from the Last Five Campaigns Show," *Journalism Quarterly*, Winter 1974, p. 588.

[18] Ibid., p. 593.

[19] Ibid., p. 592.

[20] *See* Table 6-1, "The Self-Reported Partisanship of Daily Newspapers in America, 1944, 1960 and 1972," in Hennessy, *Essentials of Public Opinion*, p. 160.

[21] Robert T. Pittman, "Yeah, What About That Monopoly of Opinion?," *The Masthead*, Fall 1974, p. 61.

[22] Daniel B. Wackman, Donald M. Gillmor, Cecilie Gaziano and Everette E. Dennis, "Chain Newspaper Autonomy as Reflected in Presidential Campaign Endorsements," *Journalism Quarterly*, Autumn 1975, p. 419.

[23] Ibid.

[24] This is documented regularly by major opinion polls. *See*, for example, George Gallup, "GOP Membership Least in 35 Years," *Minneapolis Tribune*, Sept. 21, 1975, p. 13A.

[25] Wackman, Gillmor, Gaziano, and Dennis, "Chain Newspaper Autonomy," p. 420.

[26] Gene Wyckoff, *The Image Candidates: American Politics in the Age of Television* (New York: The MacMillan Co.), p. 216.

[27] Ernest R. May and Janet Fraser, eds., *Campaign '72, The Managers Speak*, (Cambridge, Mass.: Harvard University Press), pp. 253-54.

[28] Ibid., p. 254.

[29] Quotation from Thomas E. Patterson and Robert D. McClure, "Political Campaigns: TV Power is a Myth," *Psychology Today,* July 1976, p. 61. The book referred to is by the same authors and is titled, *The Unseeing Eye,* New York: G. P. Putnam, 1976.

[30] Ibid., p. 62.

[31] *See* Foreword by Warren Weaver, Jr., in Patterson & McClure, *The Unseeing Eye, The Myth of Television Power in National Elections* (New York: G. P. Putnam's Sons, 1976), p. 18.

[32] Robert D. McClure and Thomas E. Patterson, "Print vs. Network News," *Journal of Communication,* Spring 1976, p. 26.

[33] Ibid.

[34] Davis B. Bobrow, "Mass Communication and the Political System," in *Mass Communication Research: Major Issues and Future Directions,* ed. W. P. Davison and F. T. C. Yu (Praeger, New York, 1974), p. 109.

[35] Ibid.

[36] Forest P. Chisman, "New Directions and Developments," *Journal of Communication,* Spring 1976, p. 91.

[37] Garrett J. O'Keefe, "Political Campaigns and Mass Communication Research," in Chaffee, *Political Communication,* pp. 129-159.

[38] Colin Seymour-Ure, *The Political Impact of Mass Media* (London: Constable, 1974), p. 62.

"...there is no doubt that the media have an effect on society."

—Herbert Gans (1974)

Chapter 4

The Popular Culture Perspective

Each spring a group of college and university teachers with varied backgrounds and even more varied interests gather in convention to discuss pulp fiction, comic books, television commercials, fast foods—even beer cans. And this is only a small sample of the wide-ranging fare on the program of the Association for Popular Culture, a youngish academic organization, whose members have been called intellectual scavengers and trivia freaks.* To be sure there is in this convention and its people more than a modicum of rebelliousness and even a bit of put-on. For the most part, though, these students of popular culture are serious. They will be the first to admit that the things they study (for example, the novels of Jacqueline Susann) may not have recognized aesthetic, artistic or literary merit. But, they maintain, these things are important—important because they appeal to large numbers of people in their everyday lives. To Ray Browne, one of the field's leading commentators, "popular cul-

ture is all those elements of life which are not narrowly intellectual or creatively elitist and which are generally though not necessarily disseminated through the mass media."[1] Adds David Madden, "it is anything produced by or disseminated by the mass media or mass production or transportation, either directly or indirectly, and that reaches a majority of the people."[2] Popular culture study is a contemporary outgrowth of the earlier and more elitist mass society-mass culture/mass behavior debate that raged in the pages of intellectual journals for more than thirty years. In both popular culture study and the mass culture critique there are many assumptions about the impact and influence of the mass media.

In a thoughtful review of popular culture research, the Japanese sociologist Hidetoshi Kato has written:

> . . .popular culture research is concerned with the "content" and "effect" aspects of communication, especially mass communication. Indeed, often, mass media can be seen as one of the most decisive factors shaping the popular culture of a society. For example, the belief systems and behavior patterns of the younger generation in many societies today are strongly affected by the messages they prefer to receive (or are forced to receive) either directly or indirectly through mass media. Popular culture research *is* a form of communication research.[3]

As we have suggested in earlier chapters, social scientists are not the only ones interested in media influence and impact. Although some students of popular culture and mass culture

*A more balanced view comes from Albert Kreiling of the University of Illinois who writes: Currently, the most active interest in the subject (popular culture) centers in the Popular Culture Association, whose members generally display an optimistic fascination with popular artifacts and entertainment in contrast to the anxious pessimism of the earlier critics. The current wave of interest has resulted in some interesting and valuable studies, and it is perhaps too early to pass judgment upon the body of work as a whole. Still, it can be fairly said that so far the movement lacks coherent objectives, a solid intellectual foundation for its investigations and a penetrating set of intellectual questions. (Kreiling, "Toward a Sociological Approach to Popular Culture," Assn. for Education in Journalism, Carleton University, Ottawa, Canada, Aug. 18, 1975.)

might use social science methods in their research, they are, for the most part, humanists
who are more comfortable with the historical
method and with literary criticism. Using different methods, though still logical and systematic, they come to different conclusions
about media effects. Some contemporary students of popular culture seem to generalize
quite extensively from somewhat fragmented
studies and the more elitist mass culture critics
deal with broad social currents and make pronouncements about the whole society. The
popular culture perspective embraces a great
many approaches to the study of media influence. Some scholars have contented themselves
with content-analytic studies and have made assumptions about the impact of certain content
on certain audiences. Others have examined
heroes in popular culture, assuming that the
success of historical or social heroes tells us
something about the society that responds to
them. Still others are interested in the study of
images. Images (of women or racial groups or a
hundred other subjects) are examined for their
intrinsic value and as they relate to the mass
audience. Technology and its impact on human
communication through mass communication
has also been another recurrent theme in the
popular culture critique of effects. The Canadian media critic Marshall McLuhan, for
example, is a leading proponent of this view.

While social scientists might dispute the nature of ''proof'' that the humanists accept in
their examination of effects, some might agree
that popular culture study provides a much
broader, more macroscopic view of the relationship between mass media and society. This
chapter explores some (though certainly not all)
of the media effects themes in the popular cul-
ture/mass culture literature and attempts to put
them in context with other communication research.

THE MASS SOCIETY
MASS CULTURE CRITICS

The critics of mass society, who have written
with continuity since the nineteenth century
about the authoritarian impulses of urbanization
and industrialization, see the mass media as
manipulative vehicles. The result is a threat to
democracy and a debasement of individual
values and rationality. In an eloquent essay,
Ernest van den Haag made this viewpoint clear:

> All mass media in the end alienate people from
> personal experience and, though appearing to
> offset it, intensify their moral isolation from each
> other, from reality and from themselves. One may
> turn to the mass media when lonely or bored. But
> mass media, once they become a habit, impair the
> capacity for meaningful experience. Though more
> diffuse and not as gripping, the habit feeds on it-
> self, establishing a vicious circle as addictions
> do.[4]

Pushed along by the massiveness of society, the
individual becomes more and more dependent
on mass communication to stay in touch. This,
the mass society critics say, leads to dehumani-
zation and depersonalization as people are
mobilized and manipulated by mass media. It
was once hoped that the mass media would
''enlarge and animate'' public discussion and
debate, but lamented C. Wright Mills, there is
''reason to believe that these media [mass
media] have helped less to enlarge and animate
the discussion of primary publics than to transform them into a set of media markets in mass-
like society.''[5] Observing that so few social
realities can be seen first-hand, it is natural that
the ''pictures in our heads'' come from the
mass media, says Mills. This would cause no

particular problem if the media offered truly diversified messages, he says, but media fare produced for the most part by large monopolies, offers instead a dulling sameness. The result, Mills asserts is:

> (1) the media tell the man in the mass who he is—they give him identity; (2) they tell him what he wants to be—they give him aspirations; (3) they tell him how to get that way—they give him technique; and (4) they tell him how to feel that he is that way even when he is not—they give him escape. The gaps between the identity and aspiration lead to technique and/or to escape. That is probably the basic psychological formula of the mass media today. But as a formula, it is not attuned to the development of the human being. It is the formula of a pseudo-world which the media invent and sustain.[6]

The conclusions of mass society critics have been based on various heuristic probes of culture. When they have looked at inventories of culture as an ultimate human product, the critics have been appalled by the content that appeals to the masses. Commentary of the effects of mass culture on society was a natural outgrowth of concern over commercialization and popularization and it has "been deplored for longer than the mass media have been in existence,"[7] one critic wrote. Popular culture, which may include media as well as consumer products and various entertainments, is directed to the masses by the economic and political forces of society. The critics' attacks on popular culture (often with specific reference to the role of the media) may be based on various concerns—sometimes artistic, sometimes psychological and social ones. Herbert Gans in a 1974 analysis, *Popular Culture and High Culture,* says the popular culture/mass culture critique has had four major themes:

1. *The negative character of popular culture creation.* Popular culture is undesirable because, unlike high culture, it is mass-produced by profit-minded entrepreneurs solely for the gratification of a paying audience.

2. *The negative effects on high culture.* Popular culture borrows from high culture, thus debasing it, and also lures away many potential creators of high culture, thus depleting its reservoir of talent.

3. *The negative effects on the popular culture audience.* The consumption of popular culture content at best produces spurious gratifications, and at worst is emotionally harmful to the audience.

4. *The negative effects on society.* The wide distribution of popular culture not only reduces the level of cultural quality—or civilization—of the society, but also encourages totalitarianism by creating a passive audience peculiarly responsive to the techniques of mass persuasion used by demogogues bent on dictatorship.[8]

Gans acknowledges that many of these conclusions cannot be demonstrated empirically in a way that would satisfy social scientists yet they are central to the observations of many thoughtful scholar-critics. It should be emphasized that these conclusions are the result of broad, philosophical analysis, of historical probing and of personal observation. For the most part the popular culture-mass culture theorists over a period of years traced the impact of popular culture (such as media fare) on the more traditional elements of high culture. They saw a bastardization, a weakening of elite culture as the mass media democratized so many experiences for the public. These critics are making societal evaluations against the backdrop of aesthetic and cultural standards. Their concern is not with the impact of media on a single individual but on the whole fabric of society itself. They are working at a much higher level of analysis (a societal level) than are survey researchers who probe attitudes and opinions (and work at an individual level). The work of these scholar critics should be evaluated in terms of the assumptions they set forth and the evidence marshalled to support them. Some of these commentators build powerful cases (on occasion tied to a particular philosophical critique, for example, Marxism) and at other times they are more fanciful, less persuasive.

But it should be clear that they are not straw men to be sneered at. They count among their numbers some of our most distinguished intellectuals. Their concerns are often political, intellectual, and artistic freedom, creativity and the creation of an environment where culture in its highest form flourishes. These are things that are very real, but which are not easily measured by the tools of social science. The scholar-critics are asking large, societal questions and finding evidence in their own interpretations of the sweep of history.

Naturally such an approach, which sometimes borders on the dogmatic is not without its detractors. Countercriticism has assailed the popular culture/mass culture analysis as elitist and one-sided. E. A. Shils, for example, said the negative stream of criticism was the reaction of European exiles who didn't know how to cope with American society. And it was true that many of the critics were refugees from the nations of Europe that were consumed by totalitarian forces during the 1920s and 1930s. Shils also took issue with the notion that popular culture should be held responsible for the deficiencies of popular taste.[9] Others who like Shils were less pessimistic than earlier critics joined the debate and found cause for optimism both in high and popular culture. And those who conducted cross-cultural studies cautioned against the sweeping societal assumptions of mass culture theory. The critics often spoke in global terms, but for the most part, they were talking about American society and American media.

Even though it was somewhat ideological, the debate engendered by the critics in the 1950s and beyond provided considerable stimulus for thought about the media and its impact. This was particularly relevant as television emerged as a major media force. In their philosophical assessments, the critics provided hypotheses for further study, oftentimes focusing on situations that could be tested-out at least in part. More importantly, the critics, in looking at effects, fashioned ideas about how the media operates. This was not inconsistent with many determinist economic views. At best, the popular culture debate was stimulating; at worst, it was simplistic. And while there was a tendency to distinguish mass society/mass culture critiques from social science research on similar matters, the distinction was often overblown. There are some clear links between mass society theory and social science research, as Denis McQuail has observed:

> The concern with the persuasive power of the media, with measuring the great size of the media audience, with searching out socially-harmful consequences are all consistent with, if not directly inspired by, mass society theory. The image of the isolated individual at the mercy of the mass media is common to both traditions.[10]

Of course, in many areas there is not much specific empirical evidence to support the contentions of the mass society theorists.

Another link between the *popular culture* and empirical traditions is *uses and gratifications* study, which was introduced in Chapter 1. Scholars identified with both of these approaches have a shared interest in understanding the relationship of the audience to media content. Some uses and gratifications researchers have actually translated popular culture speculations into research questions and have subjected them to empirical test. For example, popular culturist warnings about escapism and reassurance in the media as well as the role of the media as a substitute for interpersonal contact have been studied by the uses and gratifications scholars.[11] There are some fundamental differences, however:

> . . .commentators on popular culture often (a) suppose that the character of audience appeals may be identified from a close reading of content alone, and/or (b) imply that media output generated a powerful demand for the very qualities that it then satisfies and/or (c) project an essentially unflattering view of the audience's dependence on mass communication.[12]

Of course this is an elitist position. Some uses and gratifications researchers have suggested a more neutral stance as they relate surveys of audience appeals to detailed examinations of content. Thus, they are able to get at some of the same questions posed by the popular culture/mass culture students without making value judgments about the audience. The uses and gratifications people who work in this area examine the content of communication and try to present it dispassionately in the context of survey data about audience needs and wants. This accomplishes some of the same things that the popular culture scholars want to without resorting to their elitist, moralistic tone.

One researcher who takes a somewhat different view is Charles Wright who looks at mass media from a functional perspective. Functions, Wright says, are really the consequences of "routine, regular and standardized components of communications."[13] And functions in such a scheme were distinguished from the intended uses of the information by the audience. "Thus, a network might intend that a television situation comedy attract a large number of viewers in order to provide an audience for the sale of its sponsor's products; but the program might have the consequence (among others) of making bigotry a socially acceptable topic for public observation, discussion and laughter."[14] Linking uses and gratifications research with media functions (i.e. informing, influencing, etc.), Wright says this will give us a clue as to how well the media is meeting people's communication needs.

It should be remembered that as long as the critics insisted on the use of such terms as *mass culture* and *mass society* there were strong negative assumptions about media and media content. After all, the mass was seen as an undifferentiated crowd and its addiction to mass culture was regarded as dangerous. As Bernard Rosenberg wrote, "mass culture threatens not merely to cretinize our taste, but to brutalize our senses while paving the way to totalitarianism."[15]

Certainly not all of the mass culture scholars accepted Rosenberg's pejorative characterizations. Some were less global in their assessments and more concerned with the interrelationships between and among different levels of culture—high, middle and low-brow, for example. There were also other analytical frameworks that were used to assess the impact of various media and culture artifacts. All this went well beyond the earlier, simplistic notion that there was only high culture and popular culture, the latter having a negative effect on the former. In a much more refined and recent analysis, Gans has pointed out the differences between the creators of popular culture and its users. And he suggests that the term "popular culture'' is preferable to ''mass culture'' because it lacks a negative connotation. Not all would agree, but this seems to be the contemporary trend.

In a perceptive paper that distinguished between popular culture and mass culture, Don Dodson contrasted two popular rock groups of the 1960s—the Jefferson Airplane and the Monkees. The Jefferson Airplane evolved ''naturally'' from the San Francisco rock scene where ''rock was participatory [and] the bands, not yet controlled by business agents and record companies, had direct contact with their audience.''[16] By contrast, the Monkees were created for a television series. Dodson explains:

> The Jefferson Airplane and the Monkees exemplify sharp differences. One group grew out of a close knit community; the other rolled off an assembly line. One had creative autonomy; the other had none. One wrote its own songs; the other did not. Lumping the two under the same category, whether it is called ''popular'' or ''mass,'' blurs real contrasts in the way they worked. Similar differences demarcate artists working in almost every genre of entertainment.[17]

Arguing that the old distinctions between and among people (such as class, age, racial and ethnic background) are breaking down, Gans says that the concept of *taste publics* might be more useful for social analysis. In suggesting these taste publics and cultures (high culture, upper-middle culture, lower-middle culture, low culture, and quasi-folk low culture) Gans offers some distinctions that may prove useful in media analysis of popular culture. Explaining, he writes:

> . . .the major source of differentiation between taste cultures and publics is socioeconomic level or class. Among the three criteria that sociologists use most often to describe and define class position—income, occupation, and education— the most important factor is education (by which I

mean, here and everywhere, not only schooling but also what people learn from the mass media and other sources), and for two reasons. First, every item of cultural content carries with it a built-in educational requirement, low for the comic strip, high for the poetry of T. S. Eliot. Second, aesthetic standards and tastes are taught in our society both by the home and the school. Thus, a person's educational achievement and the kind of school he or she attended will probably predict better than any other single index that person's cultural choices.[18]

The study of popular culture (through taste cultures and publics) greatly enlarges our understanding of media which is, of course, one of the main aspects of popular culture. The Gans' typology expands on the concerns of the sociologist and helps to analyze artistic and literary characteristics, thus presenting a fuller and richer picture of media, both popular and elite.

IMAGES AND HEROES IN POPULAR CULTURE

Not all of the study of popular culture and popular media from a humanistic perspective deals with large, societal questions. Some studies have narrowed their scope to limited issues and problems from which general observations can be made. Two such areas are the study of heroes and the study of images.

Hero Study and the Media

The process by which obscure men and women become celebrities, heroes, or public figures is one of the enigmas of contemporary mass society. That the mass media are at least a conduit in the process cannot be doubted, but whether they have a predominant influence on the perceptions of people who respond to a public figure or popular celebrity cannot be determined so easily. One modest step toward such understanding has been attempted by scholars who have studied the images of public people in mass media content. In a now-famous study Leo Lowenthal examined biographies in popular magazines by looking at four periods from 1900 to 1941. Believing that a biography was a means by which "an average person is able to reconcile his interest in the important trends of history and in the personal lives of other people,"[19] Lowenthal sorted out American heroes along political, business-professional, and entertainment lines. His assumption was that the kinds of heroes who are featured in American magazines (over the long sweep of history) says something about American values and tastes. He found that "idols of production" in the fields of business, politics, and industry were more dominant in the early years of the twentieth century while "idols of consumption," persons from entertainment, the arts, and sports moved ahead by World War II. It is assumed, of course, that magazine content somehow reflects reader interest and thus public values. There is, of course, no hard evidence that this is the case.

Hero study traces its origins to an 1885 essay by the historian Thomas Carlysle who emphasized the role of forceful personality in history. Through the years other scholars have also examined the hero or public personality. The rise and fall of heroes and the diffusion of information about them has pointed toward study of popular culture and the mass media. Even though historians long ago abandoned the "great man" theory of explaining the development of civilization, studies of the hero have remained popular vehicles for grapling with popular culture. Sidney Hook, Eric Bentley, Gerald W. Johnson, and Marshall Fishwick are

among the scholars who have written about heroes. One relatively recent hero study by Theodore Green traced magazine biographies from 1787 to 1918. His main finding: a diminished role for individualism in American society during the period of his study.

Students of heroes and celebrities are wont to believe that these figures have a considerable impact on people in their everyday lives. This is doubly important, they say, when the media are involved. Richard Schickel in a study of Douglas Fairbanks, Sr. as the first true movie star has written that "the media are anything but neutral, reportorial entities or a simple transmission belt for ideas. And that qualification implies that, to a greater degree than we allow ourselves to support, the quality of celebrity 'acting' while in view of the media is a large—perhaps the largest—factor in determining national goals."[20] Celebrities, says Schickel, command our attention by commanding the attention of the media.

Thus image-making and hero study come together, as Schickel remarks: "In short, what Fairbanks and the entire first generation of stars had to do, besides play their roles, was to serve as transitional figures in an era of revolutionary change in the media, change that was both creator and creation of a similar revolution in mass sensibility. What happened in this period was that the public ceased to insist that there be an obvious correlation between achievement and fame."[21] The apparent psycho-social functions for heroes that can be studied in the context of media effects are evident.

Not unrelated to hero study is the concept of social typing, which is seen in the work of sociologist Orrin Klapp. Heroes to Klapp are symbolic leaders who both reflect and influence society. But perhaps more important is the process that creates them—and this process presupposes considerable activity by the media. There is, Klapp suggests, a dialectic involved in becoming a human symbol:

1. Social typing is a cooperative process in which a person has the initiative of hitting the first ball as in a tennis game.
2. People (the audience) return cues to him and give him a view of his "image."
3. All shots, however, are not returned. There is both perceptual and functional selection. People see only what interests them and respond only to images that "do something" for them.
4. The actor can accept or reject the cues returned, but he cannot make a shot from a position different from where he was when the ball came to him; that is, he cannot project a totally different image.
5. Indeed, even if he disliked what is happening, he may not be able to prevent the game from going in a direction he does not choose (he develops image trouble); his lack of cooperation may make matters worse, and he may lose the game.
6. But he can always capitalize on an existing situation; he can play it up, do trick shots, elaborate on the gag or try to improve or change the trend, so long as he works within the general framework in which the public will play ball and within the dimensions and rules of the court.
7. His status—the symbol or image that emerges—is always a product of the game and cannot be surely set in advance. He may become a star, a hero, a laughing stock, a villain, or a scapegoat, but he must wait until the game has been played to find out.[22]

This dialectic is useful in describing the role of the media in marshalling the public image of many divergent public figures from Charles A. Lindbergh to Howard Hughes. In Lindbergh's case Americans needed a clean, young man as a popular hero to cleanse the unpleasantness of the Harding scandals. In Hughes' case the image problem is well-explained by the Klapp

paradigm. Here the public figure with a playboy-industrialist image sought privacy at a time when interest in him was high. Thus, his fettish for privacy changed his image to eccentric and recluse and brought him more publicity and less privacy than he might have had under normal circumstances. Studying heroes and symbolic leaders who are known to the public mostly through their appearance in the mass media is one way to study the media and their role in shaping public perceptions.

Image Study

Closely related to hero study is image study, which involves the perceptions of one group or class of another. For example, there have been hundreds of studies in the foreign policy field such as Harold Isaacs' *Images of Asia: American View of China and India.* Indeed, Americans' preoccupation with what other nations think of them has spawned a whole library shelf of studies. Daniel Boorstin dealt with images and their creation in his useful book, *The Image or What Happened to the American Dream,* which introduced the concept of pseudo-events. Boorstin's analysis had particular utility in explaining the process of communication in modern public relations practice. The pseudo-event, he said, had the following characteristics:

(1) It is not spontaneous, but comes about because someone has planted, planned or incited it. Typically, it is not a train wreck or an earthquake, but an interview.
(2) It is planted primarily (not always exclusively) for the immediate purpose of being reported or reproduced. Therefore its occurrence is arranged for the convenience of the reporting or reproducing media. Its success is measured by how widely it is measured. . . .
(3) Its relation to the underlying reality of the situation is ambiguous. Its interest arises largely from this ambiguity. . . .
(4) It is usually intended as a self-fulfilling prophecy. . . .[23]

Image studies have varied widely. Some have been concerned with intellectuals' images of an issue or problem; others have looked for prevailing images among the masses. Image studies have often followed critical contemporary subjects and trends. For example, during the late 1960s there were a number of studies of the images of Black Americans in the news media. Later, scholars stimulated by the ecological and consumer movements, looked at coverage of these areas from an image standpoint.

Contemporary interest in feminism has stirred interest in images of women in a wide range of media outlets from advertising and films to magazines and newspapers. Image studies usually isolate a particular kind of content or subject matter and examine it thoroughly. The best of these studies usually provide some context with other issues and interests so that the part can be seen in connection with the whole. For example, a study of the image of Black Americans in the comic strip would best be done in the context of other minority persons.

Image studies are by no means confined to the popular culture field, nor are they necessarily the domain of humanist scholars. Many social scientists have also been concerned with images and image study. And many students of images, regardless of their scholarly orientation, use such social science methods as content analysis in their research.

Image study, says Ithiel de Sola Pool, is really the study of representations. "The representations a person chooses to use helps define one's own identity and gives a person a sense of identity,"[24] he says. In a review of major contributions to image study, Pool noted similarities in the writings of such figures as Sigmund Freud, Walter Lippmann, Robert Abelson, and Harold Isaacs, all of whom were concerned with representations. Freud in his *Interpretation of Dreams* generalized from dreams to larger and wider representations of images. He helped identify universal symbols in the mental set of people. Pool says that Walter Lippmann's *Public Opinion* was really a popularization of Freud. Indeed, Lippmann makes reference to Freud in this book that introduced the notion of stereotypes or "pictures in the mind." Later the dynamics of images are seen in the research of such cognitive psychologists as Fritz Heider, Theodore Newcomb and Robert Abelson. In a sense, the work of these scholars pointed up the different strategies available in the creation of stereotypes. Finally, says Pool, Isaacs in looking for national stereotypes demonstrates the enormous complexity and variety of images. The four traditions assessed by Pool, while widely varied in direction and purpose, have some common threads and provide instructive lessons for students interested in images and image-making capacity. The similarities that Pool finds in these writings help to define images that he says are simplified representations that are quasi-logical and acquired early in life. These images or representations are strongly defended against change and are not easily disproven by evidence. They are visual and descriptive and usually have easily portrayed features. They are emotionally laden and emotionally charged, often expressed in pairs of terms (for example, patriotism and chauvinism). There is a good and bad side to almost every image.[25] To Pool the most important thing about an image is what it tells us about the identity of the individual or groups of individuals that hold it.

How do stereotypes or images maintain themselves? Two sociologists suggest a process:

Once the stereotype has become a part of the culture, it is maintained by *selective perception* (noting only the confirming incidents or cases failing to note or remember the exceptions), *selective interpretation* (interpreting observations in terms of the stereotype: e.g. Jews are "pushy" while gentiles are "ambitious"), *selective identification* ("they look like school teachers. . . ."), and *selective exception* ("he really doesn't act at all Jewish.") All of these processes involve a reminder of the stereotype, so that even the exceptions and the incorrect identifications serve to feed and sustain the stereotype.[26]

Arthur Asa Berger in a study of American images in European comic books asserts that stereotypes have functions for the individual while they may be disfunctional for the society in general. Berger notes six important functions of stereotypes:

1. Stereotypes rationalize group prejudice.
2. Stereotypes create group cohesion.
3. Stereotypes separate people from one another.
4. Stereotypes reinforce certain types of behavior.
5. Stereotypes enable people to interpret the world and process information.
6. Stereotypes most commonly deal with social roles and related matters.[27]

The author in a study that tried to combine image study with hero study examined the emergence and decline of Marshall McLuhan as an intellectual celebrity. Articles by and about McLuhan appearing in popular magazines were traced over a nine-year period. The study demonstrated how certain types of magazines influenced others in disseminating information about the Canadian media guru. In addition, the social typing models of Klapp and Boorstin (mentioned earlier) were applied.[28] In another study, the author looked at images of children in American popular magazines at the turn of the century (1901-05) and in the 1970s (1971-75) to see what the publications were saying about children and childhood. The

image of the child, while based on reality as Pool suggests, was only partly factual.[29]

Image study is particularly useful in ascertaining how the mass media pictures a particular subject or issue. As McCombs and Shaw have suggested in their work on agenda-setting, this kind of information may shape the reader/citizen's thinking. Image study also has implications for a better understanding of the internal dynamics of media organizations, since selections are involved in determining how images will be shaped and which ones will be emphasized.

GENERAL McLUHANACY

No student of popular culture ever got more attention for his views on the mass media and its effects than Marshall McLuhan. Though his opinions and analyses have less currency today than they once did, McLuhan in several provocative books brought about the biggest stir that the media-effects debate has ever experienced. Looking at communication as a central theme in the history of civilization, McLuhan came to several conclusions. One of the most controversial was that the *process* of media, the very being of television, was far, far more important than its content. Or, as he put it in his well-known aphorism: "the medium is the message." McLuhan saw *form* as more important than *content* and thus dismissed the dire warnings of most of the mass culturalists. "In a sense," says Professor Jean Ward of the University of Minnesota, "McLuhan pulled the rug out from under the mass culture/mass society debate. He was telling them they had missed the point, that content was not debasing society after all."[30] McLuhan distinguished between levels of involvement of people with media. He introduced such terms as *hot* and *cool* to differentiate between those media with heavy content that repell the person (newspaper) and those that require the individual to "participate" in making the image (such as putting together dot patterns on a television screen). Thus television was regarded as a cool or involving medium. McLuhan was interested in an orchestration of the senses and believed that media helped fulfill one or more of the basic sensory functions of the human body. Thus the telephone became an extension of the ear; television an extension of the eye. This was in line with McLuhan's view of history which he divided into three periods: (1) the tribal or preliterate period when the senses were free and unconstricted by communication technology; (2) the Gutenberg or individual stage when movable type caused people to communicate by the written word and to read and act in a "lineal-sequential" fashion, reading from right to left, etc. (This, he says forever shaped western logic and thinking.) Finally, there is the (3) neotribal or electronic stage when the senses are called upon in a different way and when different sensations are experienced.

McLuhan's books and articles were what he called "probes." They stimulated discussion, raised questions and proposed solutions. Perhaps because they ran counter to the scientific method and because he contradicted himself at times, they came under almost immediate attack. McLuhan himself complicated matters by sometimes joking and leading the reader astray in almost incomprehensible prose.

If the effect of the media in modern society had lost its currency in the wake of Joseph Klapper's 1960 book, *The Effects of Mass Communication,* which carried the notion of minimal consequences and was seen by some

commentators as an apology for television, which he said had no negative effects, McLuhan's writings opened it up fully once again. The television industry, advertising executives, and others immediately championed McLuhan as a wise and learned critic who had the good sense to see the importance of their medium. As an author, consultant to industry, and popular lecturer, McLuhan took his message to quite a wide audience. In an eloquent essay about McLuhan, James W. Carey wrote: "It is unfortunate, I think, that some of the daring and exquisite insights McLuhan has into communication process are largely vitiated by his style of presentation, his manner and his method. The meaning of McLuhan is not in his message, his sentences, but in his person as a social actor, in himself as a vessel of social meaning."[31] Of course, McLuhan's greatest contribution may have been in advancing a thoughtful critique of communication and communication process. For the most part, McLuhan's theories were the observations of a literary man. They were not based on scientific data. Yet in the body of McLuhan's work may reside many hypotheses that could be researched by social scientists.

Some critics believe that McLuhan is the creator of a cultural myth about media and especially television. They say that there is little real evidence for his conclusions while admitting that they are certainly intriguing. A quite shrill McLuhan critic is writer-director Jonathan Miller who declared that McLuhan "offers no actual truth from what I read: perhaps McLuhan has accomplished the greatest paradox of all, creating the possibility of truth by shocking all of us with a gigantic system of lies."[32] That is undoubtedly much too harsh a verdict for McLuhan who did so much to propogate the discussion of media effects. In spite of his own difficulty in communicating clearly, he managed to excite a dialogue that put the media high on the agenda of public discussion. Like many of the other strains of effects analysis we have considered in this book, McLuhan is not a lone figure who simply appeared in the 1960s, but part of a longer, continuing tradition. McLuhan was strongly influenced by the economic historian Harold Innes who wrote the *Bias of Communication* and his colleagues Edmund Carpenter, Harley Parker, and others. He owes a debt to the intellectual currents in literary criticism which shaped his analysis.

THE POPULAR CULTURE MOVEMENT

In 1967, about the time that interest in McLuhan and his theories of mass communication peaked, a small, scholarly journal started in Bowling Green, Ohio. *The Journal of Popular Culture,* edited by an English professor named Ray B. Browne provided a forum for individual studies of popular media, entertainment, consumer goods, and other so-called "artifacts" of popular culture. Studies of mystery novels, western films, modern dance, pop architecture, and other topics filled the journal. Two years later in 1969, The Popular Culture Association, which is mentioned earlier in this chapter, was organized. This group provided an annual forum for presentation of research and discussions about popular culture. The mood of the Association and the journal was sometimes antiacademic. The popular culture scholars scorned the usual pretentiousness of academic meetings and declared their interest in the full range of popular culture fare from consumer products and fast foods to dime novels and

comic strips. They expressed the belief that the popular culture scholar should be interested in those things that are a part of average people's everyday life and consumption patterns. Those engaged in the popular culture movement were sometimes so closely focused on isolated subjects that they found it difficult to make the more sweeping analyses of the mass culture scholars. Some critics called studies of particular magazines or consumer products research by reductionism. Such critics have accused the popular culture scholars of studying fragments and ignoring the whole. Similarly, there has been considerable criticism of the lack of rigor in popular culture scholarship. The popular culturist reliance on literary criticism as a scholarly method and their emphasis on the consequences of content rather than audience perceptions is also worrisome. What, if anything, does all this tell us about the mass media? It provides some creative clues about the uses and gratifications of particular media; it gives us insight about the manufacture of the media message (or content), and it suggests reasons for the public's consumption of popular culture. The popular culture movement is optimistic in its approach and avoids the negative elitism of earlier critics.

SUMMARY AND CONCLUSIONS

The various popular culture critiques of mass media have considerable utility. They are global and move into wide-ranging areas of analysis. They are not asking about the impact of a particular message on a particular audience at a particular time, but are instead making bold pronouncements about media in the context of culture and society generally. In this chapter we have pointed out many of the advantages and pitfalls of this approach. And we have noted other relationships: popular culture scholars are framing important questions that can be pursued by literary critics and historians or by the more empirically minded uses and gratifications researchers. They raise issues about the nature and consequences of messages.

The material in this chapter contrasts dramatically with that presented in the first three chapters. With some exceptions we are discussing research that is the work of scholars who prefer historical and literary methods to those of the social sciences. They deal at a broader level and come to different conclusions. This chapter reviews the role of mass communication research in the popular culture field. It discusses the mass society/mass culture critics and their prognostications about mass communication—the negative effects that they saw media having on society. The relationship of popular culture to uses and gratifications study is also considered as are two approaches to research on media impact in popular culture—image study and hero study. The important popular culture theorist and media analyst Marshall McLuhan is discussed. Finally, the Popular Culture Association and movement is also treated.

Popular culture study has yielded much thoughtful material about images of individuals and groups as they emerge in media content. Image and hero studies are helpful in understanding public perceptions and the potential impact of modern movements and personalities. As with other media study this kind needs to be considered in context. Lacking the rigor of social science evidence, it nevertheless has much utility in considering alternative explanations about the mass media in society.

Notes

[1] Ray B. Browne, "Popular Culture: Notes Toward a Definition," in *The Popular Culture Explosion,* ed. Ray B. Browne and David Madden (Dubuque, Iowa: William C. Brown Co., 3rd Printing, 1973), p. 207.

[2] David Madden, "Why Study Popular Culture?," in Brown & Madden, *The Popular Culture Explosion* p. 4.

[3] Hidetoshi Kato, *Essays in Comparative Popular Culture, Coffee, Comics and Communication,* no. 13, (Papers of the East-West Communication Institute, Honolulu, 1976), p. 5.

[4] Ernest van den Haag, "Of Happiness and of Despair We Have No Measure," in *Mass Media and Mass Man*, ed. Alan Casty (New York: Holt, Rinehart & Winston, 1968), p. 5.

[5] C. Wright Mills, "Some Effects of Mass Media," in Casty, *Mass Media and Man* p. 32.

[6] Ibid., p. 35.

[7] Denis McQuail, *Towards a Sociology of Mass Communications* (London: Collier-Macmillan, 1969), p. 23.

[8] Herbert J. Gans, *Popular Culture and High Culture* (New York: Basic Books, 1974), p. 19.

[9] E. A. Shils, "Mass Society and Its Culture," in *Culture for the Millions? Mass Media in Modern Society,* ed. N. Jacobs (Princeton, N.J.: D. Van Nostrand Co.), pp. 288-314.

[10] McQuail, *Towards a Sociology of Mass Communication*, pp. 54-55.

[11] *See* discussion in Elihu Katz, Jay G. Blumler and Michael Gurevitch, "Uses of Mass Communication by the Individual," in *Mass Communication Research, Major Issues and Future Directions,* ed. W. Phillips Davison and Frederick T. C. Yu (New York: Praeger, 1974), p. 18.

[12] Ibid.

[13] Charles R. Wright, "Functional Analysis and Mass Communication Revisited," in *The Uses of Mass Communications, Current Perspectives on Gratifications Research,* ed. Jay G. Blumler and Elihu Katz (Beverly Hills: Sage Publications, 1974), p. 209.

[14] Ibid.

[15] Bernard Rosenberg, "Mass Culture in America," in *Mass Culture—The Popular Arts in America,* ed. Bernard Rosenberg and D. M. White (New York: The Free Press, 1957), p. 9.

[16] Don Dodson, "Differentiating Popular Culture and Mass Culture," (paper read at Assn. for Education in Journalism Ottawa, Canada, Aug. 18, 1975), p. 11.

[17] Ibid., p. 19.

[18] Gans, *Popular Culture and High Culture,* pp. 70-71.

[19] Leo Lowenthal, "Biographies in Popular Magazines," in *American Social Problems,* ed. William Petersen (Garden City, N.Y.: Doubleday, 1956), p. 71.

[20] Richard Schickel, *His Picture in the Papers, a Speculation on Celebrity in America, Based on the Life of Douglas Fairbanks, Sr.* (New York: Charterhouse, 1973), p. 10.

[21] Ibid., p. 7.

[22] Orrin E. Klapp, *Symbolic Leaders, Public Dramas and Public Men* (Chicago: Aldine Publishing Co., 1964), pp. 34-35.

[23] Daniel J. Boorstin, *The Image or What Happened to the American Dream* (New York: Atheneum, 1962), pp. 11, 12.

[24] Ithiel de Sola Pool, "Overview of Image Study," in Comparative Popular Culture Seminar—Images of America, East-West Communication Center, July 29, 1976, Honolulu.

[25] Ibid.

[26] Paul B. Horton and Chester L. Hunt, *Sociology* (Englewood Cliffs, N.J.: Prentice-Hall, 1968).

[27] Arthur Asa Berger, "Unflattering Definitions, Significant Stereotypes of Americans in European (French and Italian) Comics," (Paper at 1976 Comparative Popular Culture Seminar).

[28] *See also,* Everette E. Dennis, "Post Mortem on McLuhan: A Public Figure's Emergence and Decline as Seen in Popular Magazines," *Mass Communication Review,* April 1974, pp. 31-40.

[29] Everette E. Dennis, "One View of America:

Children and Childhood in Periodical Literature, 1901-1905 and 1971-1975,'' (paper read at 1976 Comparative Popular Culture Seminar): *see also* Dennis and Michal Sadoff, ''Media Coverage of Children and Childhood: Calculated Indifference or Neglect,'' *Journalism Quarterly,* Spring 1976, p. 47.

[30]Jean Ward, Lecture at University of Minnesota School of Journalism and conversation with the author, Aug. 13, 1976.

[31]James W. Carey, ''Harold Adams Innes and Marshall McLuhan,'' (Paper read at Association for Education in Journalism convention, Iowa City, Iowa, Aug. 28-Sept. 3, 1966, p. 37).

[32]Jonathan Miller, *Marshall McLuhan* (New York: Viking Press, 1971), p. 124.

Part 2

Looking Inside: The Media As Social Institutions

"Newspapers seem to come from a colossal sausage machine which grinds out words in digestible packages to suit each region of the nation."

—*James Aronson in*
Packaging the News *(1971)*

Chapter 5

The Press As A Social Institution

While the relationship of the press to the larger society has stimulated considerable interest, much less attention has been paid to the internal operations of the news media. But that is changing. The disdain that journalists have for conniving bureaucrats and organization people diverts scholarly and public concentration from the organizational dynamics of the press itself. So often the staff of a new publication is so concerned with the product being produced that the niceties of management seem submerged if not forgotten. However, in recent years, sometimes for technological reasons (electronic newsrooms require smooth organizational procedures) and sometimes for philosophical reasons (aligning practice with preachment) interest in the press as an organization has accelerated.

Take *Ms.* magazine, for instance. While some publications preach egalitarian values in their editorial columns, their own staff organization may be little more than a dictatorship. This was the case with the muckraking magazines at the turn of the century and also with the underground papers of the counterculture in the 1960s.[1] However, this was something the entrepreneurs and journalists who started *Ms.* wanted to avoid. If the magazine was to profess feminist values, it should also live them, the founders believed.

Few publications have been as vigilant as *Ms.* in aligning principles with practice. *Ms.,* a magazine for and about women, began on an idealistic note in 1972 as an advocacy publication standing unequivocally with the ideals of the women's movement. Journalistic activist Gloria Steinem, one of the magazine's founders, and her colleagues saw the new publication as a vehicle to help women "explore this new world" in which sexual and social roles were changing.

As with other new publications the first priority was getting financial backing and assembling a staff. A pilot issue of the magazine appeared in December 1971 as a supplement to *New York*, for whom Steinem then worked. Between December and July 1972 when the magazine began publication in earnest on its own, "the work got done and decisions got made,"[2] a staff report indicated. In an effort to keep the magazine's internal dynamics congruent with its professed philosophy, the staff gave considerable thought to its organization. As a staff member put it:

> Feminist philosophies often point out that a hierarchy, military or otherwise, is an imitation of patriarchy, and that there are many other ways of getting work done. We didn't approach the idea so intellectually, but we did arrive at the same conclusion from gut experience. As women we have been on the bottom of hierarchies for too long. We knew how wasteful they really were.[3]

Pledging to remember this, the staff considered ways to produce a magazine that was good for women both in its content and in the way it was run. Even as the staff grew from four (in January 1972) to 36 by early 1973, an effort at a kind of modified office democracy was maintained. The staff was quite varied, ranging from Pat Carbine, a former editor-in-chief of *McCall's*, to a woman without journalistic experience who once worked as a cab driver. Yet, as Ms. Carbine later recalled, there was an effort to involve everyone in decision making as far as that was practical. "When a major decision is to be made, we ask everyone within earshot for their opinion,"[4] she said. Individual motivation seemed to be central to the operation of the staff. There was no set working hours, perhaps because of the idealistic dedication of the staff, "there is always someone in the office at 8 a.m. and till past 10 at night,"[5] Ms. Carbine said.

Men in the magazine industry chuckled when *Ms.* announced that it would have no secretaries. Work was assigned to individuals on the basis of what they felt they could do best. For example, Ms. Carbine said, "the woman who types our manuscripts does it because she is a good typist and takes pride in her work—but she also writes articles."[6] At *Ms.*, a magazine owned, controlled and staffed by women, organizational responsibilities were dispersed across the staff, although persons with the most experience and recognized competence seemed to have more voice in decision making (and presumably they were paid more, too).

This case example from *Ms.* demonstrates the importance and relevance of a media organization's management practices and posture. Although *Ms.* was a relatively small organization, all media can be seen in their organizational and business sense. "Mass news," as sociologist John Johnstone has written, "is very much an organizational phenomenon, and with increasing centralization in the industry and increasing complexity in newsroom technology, it is likely to become even more so."[7]

Mass communication organizations have institutional characteristics that have developed along with the economic, social and political history of the country. But the media are more than a business, as two commentators explained: "Consideration of the press as a social institution forces the student of newspaper influence to face this paradox: the newspaper is cast in a dual role because it is both a private profit enterprise and a means of communication on which the public relies for social intelligence."[8] And, of course, the special protection guaranteed to the press by the First Amendment makes the picture even more complex. Douglass Cater in a book by the same name called it the "fourth branch of government," suggesting a political role and governmental role that distinguishes it from other corporate enterprises. William L. Rivers believes that the press became "the other government"[9] during the Watergate period, exercising even more influence and authority than it usually does. Something else also distinguishes the media from other institutions because they have direct access to the people. They need not go through the governmental, economic, religious or even family structure, but can communicate with individuals directly without filtering their messages through other agencies or institutions.

THE MEDIA AS SOCIAL SYSTEMS

Students of information theory (introduced by C. E. Shannon in 1948) have made mathematical forays into media organizations, looking at such things as receivers, transmitters, and codes of communication. The media organization might be seen as a system or network wherein decisions are made. Stafford Beer explains: "If we liken the system to an electric circuit, then the existence of power in some portions of the communication network is a form of information reaching the elements concerned, and will switch it on or off. This is fundamentally a *decision-making* process."[10]

The organizational components of a newspaper or broadcast station can also be seen as a social system. Various departments from advertising to circulation and editorial interact with one another. There are operating rules and procedures, norms by which the personnel of the organization are governed. And, in the end, the system is judged and measured by how well it works. Problems in the system are seen as dysfunctions. Something isn't working smoothly and slows the organization's activities. Looking at the newspaper or broadcast station as a system has considerable value as the material in this chapter notes, however our knowledge about the newspaper as a social system is still a bit primitive. Such was sociologist Robert E. Park's observation in his classic discussion of the life cycle of newspapers, "The Natural History of the Newspaper." While it was true, he wrote, "that we have not studied the newspaper as the biologists have studied...the potato bug"[11] we have been inclined to "regard them [social institutions] as sacred and to treat any fundamental criticism of them as a sort of blasphemy."[12] Park suggested a closer look at the institutions that are the press.

In a well-known study quoted elsewhere in this book, sociologist Warren Breed examined the newspaper as a formal organization wherein policy was made at one level and conformed to at lower levels. "Ideally," Breed wrote, "there would be no problem of either 'control' or 'policy' on a newspaper in a full democracy. The only controls would be the nature of the event and the reporter's effective ability to describe it."[13] But, in practice it doesn't work out that way:

...we find the publisher does set news policy, and this policy is usually followed by members of his staff. Conformity is not automatic, however, for three reasons: (1) the existence of ethical journalistic norms; (2) the fact that staff subordinates (reporters, etc.) tend to have more "liberal" attitudes (and therefore perceptions) than the publisher and could invoke the norms to justify antipolicy writing; and (3) the ethical taboo preventing the publisher from commanding subordinates to follow policy.[14]

Seeing *policy* as the center of the operating forces that keep the news organization on an even keel, Breed advanced six reasons to explain why the stability of the organization was maintained. They were (1) institutional authority and sanctions, exercised by management, (2) feelings of obligation and esteem for superiors by staff, (3) mobility aspirations—the desire to get ahead, (4) absence of conflicting group allegiance, (5) the pleasant nature of the journalistic activity—the fact that staffers liked their work and (6) news as a value—the fact that there are certain agreed-upon notions of news judgment. These six factors, Breed said, work to promote conformity in the newspaper organization.

Years later another scholar underscored Breed's view. "The news organization's policy is perhaps the single most important determinant of which of the day's events are defined as news,"[15] John Dimmick wrote. Dimmick is one of a number of scholars who have studied newsroom decision making, especially as it relates to the selection of news and the interaction between reporters and their sources. Some of these "gatekeeping" and "gatekeeper" studies are mentioned in the next two chapters. They make useful application of some of the principles of communication theory to the study of the internal dynamics of the press.

THE PRESS AS A LIVING SYSTEM

Management scientist Chris Argyris prefers to think of the internal operations of a newspaper as a "living system." And he is interested in how people deal with each other within such a system. What do management people say to each other in small meetings and in personal conversations? This, he says, is more important than any description they might give of their "management strategy." As Argyris puts it, "if we are to learn about the capacity of a system to scrutinize and renew itself, we need to observe the participants consciously struggling to consider changing their system, and (ideally) we need to watch them experimenting with actual changes."[16] Every "living system" has its own characteristics and the newspaper that Argyris studied was no exception. The paper called *The Daily Planet* by Argyris (but identified in other sources as a thinly-disguised portrait of the *New York Times*) was characterized as (and by):

1. A living system based on high competition and low trust.

2. Win-lose dynamics, wherein individuals concentrate more on "winning" than on cooperating with each other.

3. Evaluation and control rather than diagnosis and innovation.

4. Resistances to exploring risky issues and new ideas.

5. Little additiveness in problem solving, that is no continuing dialog with continuity among employees.

6. The view that group meetings were a waste of time.

7. Deep pessimism about changing human nature and increasing organizational effectiveness.

8. Avoidance of interpersonal, group, and intergroup conflict.

9. Withholding information that may be threatening.

10. Secrecy in management decisions.

11. Illusive commitments to decisions whereby people would express agreement with a decision when they really didn't agree at all.

12. The tendency to centralize decision making.[17] The Argyris study has both theoretical and applied value. At a theoretical level it fits in with the literature of organizational theory and contributes to our understanding of organizational behavior. At an applied level it has immediate implications for the management of the newspaper involved. In fact, Argyris was hired to lead a task force that attempted to implement some of the proposed changes. For newspapers generally, especially large metropolitan dailies, there was much of direct relevance in the study. Argyris's "living system" is a quite practical application of system theory to newsroom management problems.

The work of management scientists like Argyris complements research findings in the sociology of organizations as they relate to the news media. Organizational studies were slow in coming (compared with effects analyses) because there was a market demand for audience studies that identified such variables as occupational stratification, income, sex, age, and others in studies of short term effects of mass media.[18]

NEW EMPHASIS ON INNER WORKINGS

Denis McQuail's seminal book, *Towards a Sociology of Mass Communications* was published in 1969, about the time that more attention was given by researchers to the inner workings of mass communication organizations. The new study built on the earlier work in "gatekeeping," which was based on Harold Lasswell's description of the communication process as "Who? Says What? In Which Channel? To Whom? With What Effect?"[19] For years the study of channel and control analysis were virtually ignored. The gatekeeper studies while they did shed light on such factors as news selection, social control of the newsroom, and professionalism of the communicator fell short in an important respect: they failed "to explicitly inquire into relations between the organization of the mass media and the communicator,"[20] writes Taeyoul Hahn in a doctoral dissertation. Hahn and others have accurately observed that studies of the internal workings of the press done in the period before mid-1970 were either in the gatekeeper tradition, which involved tracing behavioral norms or in another tradition, sometimes called control analysis. Often control-analysis studies had to do with legal-governmental constraints on the press. Some studies of economic influences (e.g. advertiser pressure) also fell into this category.

Of course, serious students of media sociology must look beyond those materials specifically related to the press. In studying the press as an organization, scholars can examine various approaches to the study of organization such as bureaucracy, closed system, open system, and a structural approach. Similarly, there are organizational types that are suggested in the work of leading sociologists.

Of special interest to media sociologists are what Hahn calls "strains in the dual structure of the press."[21] This is the curious professional versus bureaucratic nature of the press, as was

mentioned earlier in this chapter, which is both a business and a profession. Essentially, there are two very different organizations co-existing under one roof: a business operation and an editorial operation. That there should be serious and deeply felt conflicts between these two entities is quite natural. The business-oriented, profit-oriented advertising manager lives alongside the editor and reporter who are guided more by professional values and demands. As Hahn has observed: "Potential for conflict within an organization increases with the variety of professions or occupations it incorporates. Since professional members of the organization . . .develop stronger identification with their organizations, constraints may be placed on organizational outcome preferences. Professionals and bureaucrats vie for power in organizational decision-making."[22] The result is a whole series of power and goal conflicts within the organization. While social science studies documenting these conflicts are few, there are a number of anecdotal books and memoirs that enhance our intelligence in this area. Although these materials are not our concern here because they are not scholarly inquiries *per se,* students should be aware of them as rich sources for research ideas. Many of the memoirs of editors and reporters from the *Autobiography of Lincoln Steffens* to Woodward and Bernstein's *All the President's Men* deal with power and goal conflicts within the organization. Perhaps even more striking are such accounts as Fred Friendly's *Due to Circumstances Beyond Our Control,* describing why he left CBS News when economic constraints seemed to outweigh professional values, or Otto Friedrich's *Decline and Fall,* which traces editorial and business conflicts in the last days of the *Saturday Evening Post.*

PUBLISHERS AND THEIR POWER

Newspaper publishers and broadcast owner/managers have also been the focus of power-goal studies. Sociologist Arnold Rose once observed:

> The business community has ties of ownership and friendship with the press, as well as the opportunity to exercise cruder pressure on the press through allocation of advertising (although the trend in smaller cities toward having only one newspaper company continues, this pressure is less effective.) There can be little doubt that those who own and manage most of the newspapers of the United States are more pro-business than they are supportive of any other segment of the population.[23]

One researcher asked whether a newspaper editor-publisher's role within the community was in conflict with his ability to adhere to professional values. J. K. Hvistendahl in a study of Iowa editors found that about 50 percent of the community publishers he interviewed were in their community's power structure.[24] An occupational bias in the publisher's circle of acquaintances was pointed up in a three-state study conducted by Lewis Donohew. A sample of publishers acknowledged that persons from the business community were most likely to influence them.[25] Clarice N. Olien and colleagues George A. Donohue and Phillip J. Tichenor studied the relationship of power status of the publisher in the community and conflict reporting. Their findings were mixed: in larger, more heterogeneous rural communities publisher status was positively correlated with conflict reporting. This was unlike smaller communities where it was negatively linked.[26]

Ben Bagdikian has observed that "in weekly papers, the editor-publisher polarization varies widely, but there is little doubt that most weeklies avoid controversy and act as volunteer bulletin boards for surface events."[27] Of course, many of the studies and commentaries on publisher power go beyond the newsroom and probe the relationship of high level media personnel in the social and economic life of their community. To what extent the press does or does not represent and reflect the structure of the community may depend on the integration of media leaders into the life of the local community.

In his landmark study of the *Community Press in an Urban Setting*, Morris Janowitz attempted a large scale, systematic examination of the community publisher and his audience. Janowitz noted that the community publisher is expected to maintain close contacts with local business people.[28] The conflict on goals and power between the journalistic and business objectives of the press were noted in a study of "The Weekly Newspaper's Leadership Role As Seen by Community Leaders." This study by Alex S. Edelstein and J. Blaine Schultz found two types of community editor-publishers: the journalistic editor who was professionally-minded, concerned with holding up a mirror to the community; and the community editor who played down controversy and was more of a cheerleader for the community than a critic of it.[29]

Edelstein in another study with Otto N. Larsen found that the weekly newspaper is an important "facilitative" agent in contributing to a community's sense of itself.[30] There are (as this discussion indicates) a number of studies that deal with the role of the publisher-manager within the media organization as well as within the community. Studying the publisher is important since this figure is a vital controlling mechanism within the press.

In a study of managing editors of all evening general circulation daily newspapers in the

United States David Bowers asked the news executives about publisher influence on news coverage. Some of his findings: publishers who reside in the community are more likely to be involved in news decisions than those quite distant from the operation, quashing the idea that absentee publishers set down rigid editorial standards for their papers; the larger the paper, the less likely the publisher is to exert much influence; publishers tend to be most active in those areas of news that might affect revenues; and more expressed than implied directions came from the publisher in instances where specific news stories were involved.[31] Unfortunately there has not been enough systematic research on a large enough scale to clearly focus, let alone effectively probe, the many questions inherent in the business-professional conflict.

From what research does exist it is clear that there is a constant struggle, sometimes subtle, sometimes overt, between the business and editorial entities of media organizations. And often, journalists representing professional values must acquiesce to business interests as represented by the publisher who is the ultimate boss. Perhaps this is what Upton Sinclair had in mind when he offered this strident admonition to fellow journalists: "The Brass Check is found in your pay-envelope each week—you who write and print and distribute our newspapers and magazines. The Brass Check is the price of your shame—you who take the fair body of truth and sell it in the marketplace, who betray the virgin hopes of mankind into the loathsome brothel of Big Business."[32]

STRUCTURAL CONTROL OF THE PRESS

Research on the structural control of the press, whether by direct publisher intervention or by the nature of the news organization itself, is somewhat fragmented. There are bits and pieces of data in the research, mostly flowing from study of single newspapers or groups of editors over a short period of time. And the methods used by the researchers vary from participant-observer techniques, wherein one puts great trust in the observational powers of a single social scientist who presents what is essentially a case study, to survey research interviews and management science analyses of organizational problems and communication.

An ambitious and highly-instructive study of structural control was conducted by Hahn who has been previously mentioned in this chapter. A comparative study that examined the dual-structure of the press in metropolitan newspapers in Milwaukee, Wisconsin and Seoul, Korea, the Hahn research looked at differences between bureaucrats (business staff persons) and professionals (news executives, editors, and reporters). Hahn confirmed some things already imbedded in the literature and made some new observations as well. His findings:

1. Value and goal conflicts occur between journalists and business personnel in news organizations.
2. There are power conflicts between the newsroom and business departments, each seeking greater voice in making decisions on important issues.
3. Journalists tend to lose in the conflict with business management or with the organization itself because top business management has the greater power in organizational decision-making.[33]

Hahn did not stop with these hand-wringing findings. Instead, he asked, "what can be done?" He looked for remedies that would remove obstacles to professional functioning in the press. He suggested greater journalistic participation in management and ownership, the infusion of stronger professional values both in the newsroom and the business office, better intra-organizational communication such as ombudsmen, consultative committees and other activities that would enhance internal communication. Three major influences control the press, Hahn says. They are business, professionals, and the government. "The press," he says, "must be analyzed not only in relation to political power but also in relation to business power. In studying the structure of the press, therefore, attention must be given to the trilateral relationship of the government, the journalist and the industry, rather than to a bilateral press-government conflict."[34]

JOURNALISTIC AND BUSINESS RELATIONSHIPS

The Hahn study complements a descriptive examination of business-journalistic relationships within the press by J. Edward Gerald. In a thoughtfully provocative 1963 book, *The Social Responsibility of the Press,* Gerald provided an intellectual background and basis for more unity in studies of the press. Gerald traced the history of journalism, both in its reportorial-journalistic aspects and in terms of business development. He intertwined the history of journalism with the history of business, pointing out common interests and unified purposes. But Gerald recognized that there are two general concepts of professional organization of the press. The one most widely explored, he said, "assumes that the ethics of journalism and business are in conflict and that journalists must organize to protect themselves from the spirit of the counting room."[35] But this is not the only approach:

> The other concept is that the whole institution, business and communication combined, should

undertake professionalism. Although less often found in scholarly consideration, this concept accepts the unity of communicators and their business partners, rather than seeking to make them opponents within the same firm. The whole-institution proposal offers the best opportunity for long-term success. It is the only kind of professionalism we have at this time. The omission of government from any part of the relationship is deliberate, and eliminates any possibility that professionalism would be considered an abridgement of freedom of the press.[36]

The traditional professional model gives journalists a negative power, to resist management encroachment on freedom of expression. The Gerald model, however, is more positive offering the possibility of joint leadership of a positive nature. Recognizing the interrelationships between business and journalism within the same organization seems essential to understanding how media institutions operate. While there may often be conflicting elements in newsroom operation whereby editors fight for more news space in the face of advertising demands, the fact remains that for the most part the organizations function with a minimum of conflict and with much cooperation.

SUMMARY AND CONCLUSION

"The mass media of communication are social institutions that serve the society by gathering, writing and distributing the news of the day. They take their character principally from our political and economic institutions, offering information and entertainment in the marketplace to uncoerced buyers,"[37] Gerald has written.

Treating the press as a social institution is a quite useful way to study its internal dynamics. After a brief consideration of the relationship between editorial goals and organizational structure at *Ms.* and other publications, this chapter reviews the literature of scholars who have examined the media as a social system. In a similar vein is the work of management scientist Chris Argyris who considers the press a "living system." Research focusing on the inner workings of media is reviewed and the matter of structural control of the press is examined.

An important step toward a full understanding of the relationship of this institution (the press) to the society at large (discussed in earlier chapters) is to understand its internal workings. Beyond the formal table of organization that every newspaper and broadcast station has, are many informal practices and nuances of management style. Human organizations do not run like machines, but are, instead, susceptible to various strains and pressures that sometimes slow down, sometimes speed up the inner workings. Always there is an influence, large or small, from economic realities, governmental influence, and other internal threats. But, perhaps more importantly, there is the human process of interaction whereby editors and reporters and business managers play their roles in the organizational drama. After a long period of lack of interest, communications scholars are taking a look at the inner workings of the press. They are probing that age-old notion, so eloquently stated by Sir Winston Churchill who said, "first we shape our institutions, then our institutions shape us." This chapter and the two that follow it are concerned with the internal dynamics of the press and its ultimate impact on the product of communication.

Notes

[1] For a fuller discussion of this concept, *see,* Everette E. Dennis, "Utopian Values in Journalistic Content and Organizational Structure," *Journal of Popular Culture,* Spring 1975, pp. 724-34.

[2] "A Personal Report from *Ms.,*" *Ms.,* July 1972, p. 5.

[3] Ibid.

[4] Patricia Carbine, speech to the Minnesota Press Club, Feb. 22, 1973.

[5] Ibid.

[6] Ibid.

[7] John W. C. Johnstone, Edward J. Slawski, and William W. Bowman, *Newspeople and Networks, A Sociological Portrait of the American Journalist* (Urbana, Ill.: University of Illinois Press, 1976), pp. 10-2, 3 of a preliminary mass.

[8] George L. Bird and Frederick E. Merwin, eds., *The Newspaper and Society* (New York: Prentice-Hall, 1942), p. 77.

[9] William L. Rivers, "The Other Government: The New Media and Ethics," *Social Responsibility: Journalism, Law, Medicine,* vol. 2 (Lexington, Va.: Washington & Lee University, 1976). *See also,* Tom Bethell, "The Myth of an Adversary Press," *Harper's,* Jan. 1977.

[10] Stafford Beer, *Cybernetics and Management* (New York: John Wiley, 1959) p. 11.

[11] Robert E. Park, "The Natural History of the Newspaper," in Wilbur Schramm, *Mass Communications* (Urbana: University of Illinois Press, 1960), p. 22.

[12] Ibid., pp. 22-23.

[13] Warren Breed, "Social Control in the Newsroom," in Schramm, *Mass Communications,* p. 178.

[14] Ibid.

[15] John Dimmick, "The Gate-Keeper: An Uncertainty Theory," *Journalism Monographs,* no. 37, (Nov. 1974): p. 14.

[16] Chris Argyris, *Behind the Front Page, Organizational Self-Renewal in a Metropolitan Newspaper* (San Francisco: Jossey-Brass, 1974), p. 2.

[17] Ibid., *see* pp. 1-32.

[18] Taeyoul Hahn, "Structural Control of the Press: An Exploration in Organizational Analysis," (Ph.D. dissertation, Univ. of Minnesota, 1972), p. 9.

[19] *See* generally, Harold D. Lasswell, "The Structure and Function of Communication in Society," in *The Communication of Ideas,* ed. Lyman Bryson (New York: Harper & Row, 1948).

[20] Hahn, "Structural Control of the Press," p. 12

[21] Ibid., p. 37.

[22] Ibid., p. 67.

[23] Arnold M. Rose, *The Power Structure: Political Process in American Society* (New York: Oxford University Press, 1967), p. 111.

[24] J. K. Hvistendahl, "Publisher's Power: Functional or Dysfunctional?," *Journalism Quarterly,* Autumn 1970, pp. 472-78.

[25] Lewis Donohew, "Publishers and Their 'Influence' Groups," *Journalism Quarterly,* Winter 1965, pp. 122-13.

[26] Clarice N. Olien, George A. Donohue and Philip J. Tichenor, "The Community Editor's Power and the Reporting of Conflict," *Journalism Quarterly,* Summer 1968, pp. 243-52.

[27] Ben H. Bagdikian, "Professional Personnel and Organizational Structure in the Mass Media," in W. Phillips Davison and Frederick T. C. Yu, *Mass Communication Research, Major Issues and Future Directions* (New York: Praeger, 1974), 126.

[28] *See* generally, Morris Janowitz, *The Community Press in an Urban Setting: The Social Elements of Urbanism* (Chicago: University of Chicago Press, 2d ed. 1967).

[29] Alex S. Edelstein and J. Blaine Schulz, "The Weekly Newspapers Leadership Role as Seen by Community Leaders," *Journalism Quarterly,* 40, 1963, pp. 565-74.

[30] Alex S. Edelstein and Otto N. Larsen, "The Weekly Press Contribution to a Sense of Urban Community," *Journalism Quarterly,* 37, 1960, pp. 489-98.

[31]David R. Bowers, "A Report on Activity by Publishers in Directing Newsroom Decisions," *Journalism Quarterly,* Spring 1967, pp. 43-52.

[32]Upton Sinclair, *The Brass Check: A Study of American Journalism,* (Pasadena, Ca.: Published by the author, 1920), p. 436.

[33]Hahn, "Structural Control of the Press," pp. 205-06.

[34]Ibid., p. 213.

[35]J. Edward Gerald, *The Social Responsibility of the Press* (Minneapolis, Mn.: University of Minnesota Press, 1963), p. 173.

[36]Ibid.

[37]Ibid., p. 3.

"The news has become a part of our lives. It is more than a luxury, a diversion. It is a permanent enlargement of our consciousness."
—*Tiffany Blake,* Chicago Tribune
editorial writer in Collier's *(1911)*

Chapter 6

The Journalistic Enterprise— The Product

Inseparable from any consideration of journalists and their work is the study of their product, that is, the news or content of the news media. Although Marshall McLuhan once denigrated the importance of media content, recent research (cited earlier in this book) suggests that much of the media's impact is informational, dependent on the nature of its content. Thus, studies of media content and the forces shaping it are gaining renewed significance.

Smiling a half-smile, Will Rogers used to tell his audiences: "All I know is what I read in the papers." Rogers had no idea how much this statement would grow in importance for future generations as news coverage of distant lands and phenomena accelerated. But in spite of the recognized importance of the informational function of the media (as distinguished from entertainment) scholars have paid scant attention to it. Recognizing this Robert Darnton writing in *Daedalus* criticized the failure of communication researchers to understand the relationship between reporters and their work: "The context of work shapes the content of news and stories also take form under the influence of inherited techniques of storytelling. Those two elements of newswriting may seem contradictory, but they come together during a reporter's breaking-in when he is most vulnerable and most malleable."[1] These comments notwithstanding, there has been some concern in recent years with the nature of the journalist's product,

both in the print and electronic media. Scholars with varying viewpoints and methods have probed the nature of news and news content. Of course, it is impossible to separate news-gathering *practices* from the resultant product or *content* of news. This chapter takes note of some of these scholarly explorations. The research discussed here is less likely to be quantified than that discussed in earlier chapters. There are, however, some exceptions.

What have scholars sleuthing through journalistic content been concerned about? First, there have been continual efforts to define news and its properties. This helps us understand how journalists and journalistic managers (i.e., editors) set priorities, how they decide what gets covered and what doesn't. Additionally, the more we know about news and news judgment, the more we know about the division of labor within the journalistic organization and the allocation of other resources. Studying what *is there* as far as news coverage goes, also tells us *what isn't*. Omissions in coverage, both in terms of subject matter generally and sources specifically, have also interested researchers.

Secondly, the largely descriptive mission of the researchers who study news and news definition leads quite naturally to a philosophical analysis of "objectivity," both as a journalistic ethic and as a craft attitude that governs news organizations and their operation. Objectivity is both a journalistic form (a writing style) as well as a method of news gathering. Research in this area has ranged from philosophical analysis to historical trend analysis and studies of reporter attitudes.

Thirdly, objectivity as a subject for study is closely linked to various changes in journalism. Since the mid-1960s there has been an agonizing argument over the "New Journalism," a journalistic movement and an approach to content that has inspired much controversy. The New Journalism lends itself to much of the same kind of study mentioned above.

Finally, there is in the contemporary journalistic marketplace a preoccupation with investigative journalism, which in its more high-minded formulations is equated with an adversary relationship between press and government; in its less-attractive features it is sometimes decried as gossip. Researchers here have tended toward comparative analysis of different kinds of coverage as well as historical inquiry about precedents for similar activity.

THE NATURE OF NEWS

Time was when news defintions were relegated to reporting textbooks. Terms like significance, prominence, timeliness, proximity, and others were attached in a laundry-list fashion as the definition of news. Those who engaged in this quite useful descriptive exercise tried to isolate abstractions from what they saw in the newspapers and on newscasts, to move from the specific to the general seeking a meaningful codification. In an articulate restatement of the traditional definition of news Mitchell V. Charnley wrote, "news is the timely report of facts or opinion that hold interest or importance, or both, for a considerable number of people."[2] Agreeing, Curtis D. MacDougall observed:

Scholarly attempts to define news, for which the reporter is supposed to have a nose, correctly emphasize the fact that it is the account of an event, not the event itself. At any given moment billions of simultaneous events occur throughout the world. Someone dies, is born, gives a speech, attends a meeting, takes a trip, commits a crime and so on ad infinitum. All of these occurrences are potentially news. They do not become so until some purveyor of news gives an account of them. The news, in other words, is the account of the event, not something intrinsic in the event itself.[3]

A perceptive essay by Raymond and Alice Bauer reinforces this view. "The concept of 'news' which dominates our reporting media dictates that an event is news only if it is discontinuous with preceding events and if it is relatively recent in occurrence."[4]

In all the attempts at news definition, it is generally agreed that news evolves from a quite dynamic process and is the direct result of interplay between sources and reporters, reporters and editors, media organizations and their audiences. The news, scholars say, is the end product of many tactics and strategies of media personnel. Leon V. Sigal in a study of the relationship between reporters and their sources thinks of news as the interaction of individuals and information:

Four bargaining games run concurrently; those among newsmen inside their organizations, among reporters on the beat, between the reporter and his sources news, and among those sources, mostly officials in various government positions. Outcomes in one game, can affect outcomes of the others. From the standpoint of bureaucratic politics, then, news is an outcome of the bargaining interplay of newsmen and sources.[5]

As the previous definitions of news indicate, those interested in this pursuit come from varied backgrounds. Some are journalism educators and communications researchers, others are sociologists and political scientists. As one ex-

amines their work in the area of news definition, it is clear that they have similar concerns:
the actors and their product. Additionally, historians of journalism and mass communication
have demonstrated how technology, news
gathering methods, and writing conventions
have had an impact on the definition of news.
Combining the here-and-now interests of
sociology with the long-term perspectives of
history, sociologist Bernard Roshco says the
changing concept of news is due to a basic shift
in the content of the American news media,
which moved from *reprinting* in its early days
to *reporting* in the modern era.

Roshco's study, an important and insightful
analysis, moves well beyond the typical critic's
lament that "certain stores have been covered
incompletely, or incorrectly, or unfairly, or not
at all," which is at the center of many critiques
of news definition. Roshco asks two questions:
"(1) how do the relationships the press maintains with other institutions determine what it
defines as news, where it seeks news, and how
it presents news? and (2) how is the news content of the American press shaped by the dominant values of American society?"[6] Focusing on the origin of the message rather than its
effect, Roshco takes the reader on an orderly
trip into the sociology of news. Borrowing from
the sociology of knowledge, he relates the conflict over news definition to the relationship between the concepts of "acquaintance-with"
versus "knowledge-about." News, he says,
can be defined as "timely acquaintance with"
since "knowledge-about" requires more
abstract formulations. As he puts it, "usually
ones becomes acquainted-with through personal
experience; whereas one acquires knowledge-
about through formal education or systematic
investigation."[7]

Conscious of the realities of the newsroom,

Roshco asserts that news is concerned with describing signals, rather than analyzing their significance. And yet, while acknowledging the
difference between the journalist and the scholar, he makes it clear that news should be enhanced by knowledge-about lest it provide
"only superficial understanding of what is
being reported."[8]

In developing the concept "from reprinting
to reporting," Roshco casts the history of journalism in a sociological context. Technological
innovations, he maintains, altered definitions of
timeliness and enlarged the range of information with which the press could become ac-
quainted. News can only be understood in
terms of the "newsmaking" process, he concludes. Further, one must know and understand
the norms of the press that "grew out of the
interplay between two interdependent, but
sometimes conflicting, needs; a need for a constant supply of salable news, a need for stable
relationships with news sources whose personal
or institutional interests might, on occasion, be
at odds with those of the press."[9]

In addition to studying news definitions in
the context of newsmaking, some scholars have
been more concerned with the functions of
news. Wilbur Schramm, for example, using
Freud's pleasure and reality principles, distinguished between immediate and delayed reward
news. As he put it:

> In general, the kind of news which may be ex-
> pected to furnish immediate reward are news of
> crime and corruption, accidents and disasters,
> sports and recreation, social events, and human
> interest. Delayed reward may be expected from
> news of public affairs, economic matters, social
> problems, science, education and health. News of
> the first kind pays its rewards at once. . . .News of
> the second kind pays its rewards later.[10]

Todd Hunt in a study of contemporary news
patterns found it useful to discuss event-cen-

tered news and process-centered news. The first was "current, probably less than 24 hours old. Uninterpreted at most, terms are explained and casual events are briefly summarized in order to offer the reader a context."[11] The second was "not necessarily current. It is written when the editors find a writer is able to integrate and describe ongoing events in a meaningful and complete way."[12] Expanding on Hunt's analysis, Arnold Ismach says, "the inescapable observation is that most news is event-centered. It is typically about a recent happening, and is generally uninterpreted, with minimal context, unrelated to other situations and events. This contrasts with what has been termed process-centered news—interpretative presentations of conditions and situations in society that are related in broad context and over time."[13] Adds Ismach:

> This latter category [process-centered news] is not an academic invention, an ideological improbability nurtured in an ivy tower. It is an approach increasingly occupying the public affairs reporter, fostered by progressive news organizations, large and small.[14]

News definitions are also governed by the medium. Newspaper news and television news, while they have some important similarities, are also dramatically different. Finding major differences in the structure, voice, and content of newspaper versus television news, Paul Weaver wrote: "The television news emphasis on spectacle, its reliance on the single omniscient observer, and its commitment to the notion of a unified, depiction of events, all make TV an extraordinarily powerful mobilizer of public attention and public opinion."[15] Weaver found newspaper news providing a great deal of precise information that gives the reader more choice.

Why are scholars interested in news defini-

tion? Many reasons can be advanced: it helps keep track of the content of the media, helps explain what is there and why. News definition, after all, is simply the process of selecting particular items for exposure while others are discarded. News definition is a good vehicle by which one can study the sociology of journalism since it explains something about the *product* of the complex process of newsmaking. Finally, defining news in terms of its functions and purposes gives some insight into its impact and effect on individuals and society. Definitions of news and the study that goes with them, whether it is based on content analysis, organizational study, or psychological variables, helps us understand why the media is what it is. Such definitions and their operational nature cannot only help unravel an epistimological confusion, but are important in analyzing the continuing criticism of the press, much of it based on content. Many of contemporary journalism's controversies come back to the question of news definition. As Ismach reminds us, "the objectivity versus interpretation debate was just a preliminary bout in a related but much more basic battle: the redefinition of news."[16]

THE ASSAULT ON OBJECTIVITY

For years now journalists and critics of the press have debated about the ethic of objectivity, which some commentators have called the occupational ideology of the American press. So too have scholars been concerned about objectivity. Understanding the basis of objectivity, which implies fairness, impartiality, and balance, is an important dimension of media sociology. While there has been much controversy over whether objectivity can really exist in any kind of pure state, there can be little doubt that it has been regarded as a fundamental linchpin of American journalistic practice. Historians of the press tell us that objectivity was a natural outgrowth of a reform movement in journalism. It was a kind of collective journalistic response to the partisanism of earlier generations and to the sensationalism and irresponsibility of the 1890s. Objectivity or unbiased and emotionally detached journalism was equated with professionalism as the newspaper press began to move away from the journalism of reform and advocacy by the 1920s. Bernard Roshco in a scholarly analysis of objectivity suggests that the concept has a controlling influence in the relationship between reporters, editors, and sources. And, objectivity, he said, had considerable utility. For example:

1. Easily employed guidelines for selecting and evaluating news content facilitated rapid processing and publication of a wide variety of news stories.
2. Giving sources the responsibility for supplying content freed reporters from the need for extensive knowledge about subject-matter.
3. Making technique rather than substance the basis of judging role-performance helped insulate reporters—and their media—from charges of error, bias and other forms of unprofessional performance.
4. Because reporters were usually interchangeable, an editor could assign the same reporter to cover many kinds of news. The easily recruited and trained general-assignment reporter, rather than the specialist in a particular field, became the backbone of the news-gathering operation.[17]

Scholarly commentary on subjectivity in news judgment begins with Walter Lippmann's discussion of the subject in his *Public Opinion,* a book that incidentally noted that no social scientist to that date (1922) had attempted to study the press. The first detailed study of news-re-porting, Leo Rosten's doctoral dissertation in 1937, mentioned objectivity in its queries directed to news-reporters. By 1955, a dissertation titled, ''The Concept of Objectivity in Journalism in the United States'' by Ronald Shilen of New York University had appeared.

There is a tendency in the 1970s to look upon the assault on objectivity as a phenomenon of the 1960s, the legacy of the new journalism and of advocacy reporting during that period. However, much earlier, in the 1930s and 1940s, the professional literature was not without articles questioning and analyzing the concept.[18] And, during the 1950s, when Senator Joseph McCarthy made his now-famous speech accusing State Department employees of Communist Party membership and sympathies, objectivity and the transmission-belt nature of much of contemporary journalism was under attack. Certainly, the turbulent events of the 1960s had an impact on the discussion, though. The racial riots in urban centers for which the press and the people were unprepared, student unrest, and the public response to the Vietnam War, were among the factors that incited scholarly interest in the nature of news and the concept of objectivity.

As Gaye Tuchman has written, ''to a sociologist, the word 'objectivity' is fraught with meaning. It invokes philosophy, notions of science, and ideas of professionalism. It conjures up the ghosts of Durkheim and Weber, recalling disputes in scholarly journals concerning the nature of a 'social fact' and the term 'value free.' ''[19]

There is in journalists, Tuchman and others have observed, a strong belief, perhaps even an article of faith, that it is possible to separate fact from opinion. It is as if reporters were seeing themselves as an extension of Sergeant Joe Friday (Jack Webb in the old ''Dragnet'' series on television) saying, ''just the facts, ma'am, just the facts.''

The idea of the separation of fact from opinion in newspapers developed in the nineteenth century with the rise of the editorial page. It became an article of journalistic faith that opinions were to be placed on the editorial page where they were clearly labeled and understood to be position statements whereas the news was to be more detached and objective in its presentation of factual material. One national publication, *Newsweek,* was so enamored with the idea of separating fact from opinion that this became the theme of its advertising for a period. The discussion of fact and opinion grows more complex as one considers the infusion of journalistic analysis and interpretive reporting that has blurred old definitions. While there may be a clear distinction between a straight news story and an editorial, new modes of reporting make it all more difficult to discern.

It was always recognized, of course, that there was a subjective element in the process of selecting news. Tuchman says objectivity is a ''strategic ritual'' that protects journalists from the risks of their trade. What is objectivity from the journalist's point-of-view? It is the gathering of facts in an unbiased, detached, and impersonal manner with the purpose of meeting deadlines and avoiding libel suits and other problems. There are, Tuchman says, in addition to verifying ''facts,'' at least four strategic procedures that enable the journalist to claim objectivity:

1. *Presentation of conflicting possibilities.* Journalists must be able to identify ''facts,'' even though some truth-claims are not readily verifiable.
2. *Presentation of supporting evidence.* There are occasions when the journalist can obtain evidence to support a truth claim. Supporting evidence consists of locating and citing additional ''facts,'' which are *commonly accepted as ''truth.''* This insistence upon supporting ''facts'' is pervasive. . . .
3. *The judicious use of quotation marks.* The newsmen view quotations of other people's opinions as a form of supporting evidence. By interjecting someone else's opinion, they believe they are removing themselves from participation in the story, and they are letting the ''facts'' speak. . . .
4. *Structuring information in an appropriate sequence.* Structuring information in an appropriate sequence is also a procedure to denote objectivity which is exemplified as a formal attribute of news stories. The most important information concerning an event is supposed to be presented in the first paragraph, and each succeeding paragraph should contain information of decreasing importance.[20]

What research on objectivity suggests is that it is part of the belief system of the journalist, a guiding philosophy and part of the definition of news itself. Scholars who study this concept do so to learn more about the workings of the press and the nature of its content. Notions of objectivity explain why stories are written the way they are, why certain information is included in a particular order and why some information is omitted altogether. In short, it is one more way that explains how reporters do their work and something of the product that results. There is, of course, a substantial literature in the professional magazines and trade journals that confronts the merits and liabilities of the objective mode. Examining that debate is not our purpose here.

THE NEW JOURNALISM

Closely tied to the debate over objectivity is scholarly interest in the New Journalism, a term that grew up in the late 1960s and which was applied to many different journalistic approaches and activities. Just when interest in the New Journalism began is not clear, but one of the most vivid portrayals of it came in the late 1960s when Norman Mailer read about his antics at a Washington D.C. peace march in the pages of *Time*. Decrying the superficiality of *Time's* coverage, Mailer decided to respond with a 300+ page nonfiction novel, *Armies of the Night*. "Now we may leave *Time* in order to find out what happened," he declared. Various commentators soon described such writers as Tom Wolfe, Truman Capote, Gay Talese, and Jimmy Breslin as practitioners of the New Journalism. Simply defined, this kind of New Journalism was the use of fiction methods by journalists—a kind of literary journalism that employed dialog, interior monolog, extensive description and scene-setting.

The New Journalism was by no means a quiet or subtle movement. Its practitioners immodestly claimed that the New Journalism was "dethroning the novel" as literature's main event, outdistancing the old journalism and replacing objectivity as a guiding philosophy. One writer (Truman Capote) even went so far as to claim that he had created a new art form. With such broughaha it was no wonder that researchers interested in the media would isolate the New Journalism for study.

Some like the author and William L. Rivers wanted to put the New Journalism in context and examined it in relation to the various aspects of dissatisfaction with existing styles and standards that seemed to be a part of the journalistic world in the late 1960s and early 1970s. thus we saw the New Journalism of Tom Wolfe & Company as one aspect of a wide range of activity. This form was called the New Nonfiction and was treated along with advocacy jour-

nalism (which had a mostly political tone) and alternative journalism (which was a kind of modern muckraking found in small alternative journals). The approach used in two books with which the author was associated (*The Magic Writing Machine*, 1971; and *Other Voices: The New Journalism in America*, 1974), was to sort out the various journalistic activities that people were calling "New Journalism" and to offer a typology. Thus, it was possible to work out definitions and descriptive accounts of each type of journalistic activity whether it was the precision journalism form that used social science methods or the new nonfiction form that used literary methods. We took the practitioners at their word and tried to examine their work in a distinterested way. The result was a descriptive account of contemporary journalistic history.

Michael Johnson, a literary scholar, examined both form and content of New Journalism in a highly selective, but useful 1971 book, *The New Journalism*. Treating the underground press, artists of nonfiction, and changes in established media as reflected in content, Johnson offered a normative analysis. New Journalism in his view represented an improvement if not an elevation in contemporary journalistic practice, which he saw as impoverished and in need of change.

Tom Wolfe, high priest of the New Journalism, is also a trained scholar with a Ph.D. in American Studies from Yale University, so his own account of the New Journalism's birth in a book also called *The New Journalism*, attracted considerable public and scholarly attention. With a brilliant flair, Wolfe took on the old journalism with an essay that tried to define New Journalism and relate it to realism in literature. Wolfe saw the New Journalism as a modern articulation of realism, an approach contemporary novelists and short story writers had mostly rejected. While entertaining and insightful, Wolfe's discussion was dismissed by some critics for its self-indulgent "me and my pals make history together" nature.

By far the most disciplined discussion of the New Journalism came in a 1974 study by James E. Murphy who attempted to explicate an operational definition of the New Journalism by reviewing the by-then growing literature on the subject and by observing the New Journalism form firsthand. Although lacking a solid link with the literature of media sociology, Murphy nonetheless related the New Journalism form to journalistic practice. His conclusions:

1) New Journalism is not new as a technique; the novelty lies in the high *degree* to which the techniques are utilized today, their conscious use, and in the notoriety which their current utilization has gained.
2) New Journalism is a distinctive genre only to the extent that all those who use or have used fictional techniques in reporting may be said to form a distinctive group.
3) New Journalism is literary because of its application of the techniques of dramatic literature to nonfiction; it is journalism because it uses those techniques in news reporting.
4) The distinction between fiction and nonfiction, epistemologically shaky at best, should in no way be called on to justify any distinction between literature and journalism, or literature and non-literature.
5) Elements of subjectivity and intensivity or their opposites in writing or reporting are matters of degree and should not be judged by either-or criteria.[21]

Through the 1960s and 1970s, the scholarly literature about the New Journalism continued to grow. Several were collections of New Journalism writing with critical essays by the editors. One of the best of these was found in a book, *The Reporter as Artist,* edited by Ronald Weber. Weber, a professor of American Studies, perceptively analyzed the claims of the New Journalists, especially Tom Wolfe, and treated the New Journalism, both in its artistic and journalistic contexts. His knowledge of American literature, reflected in his essay, makes this analysis especially useful. A more traditional view that put New Journalism in the context of magazine article writing was found in a lucid book by Andre Fontaine, *The Art of Writing Nonfiction.* Few commentators of the period had a better sense of form than Fontaine, and this is evident in his forthright examination of New Journalism as a magazine article form.

Seeing the New Journalism as an aspect of popular culture, Marshall Fishwick assembled a collection of original essays that traced interrelationships of the two. As Fishwick put it, "my plea is for such attention [scholarly] both to popular culture and the New Journalism—and especially to the role style plays."[22] The two, New Journalism and popular culture, Fishwick noted, have many of the same problems, especially lack of clear definition, but at the same time there is a considerable amount of "internal similarity and intertwining."[23] Expanding, Fishwick writes:

1. Both are subversive, challenging the status quo and Establishment in various guises.
2. Both utilize "the puts"—and putdowns and put-ons. Figures as different as Will Rogers, W. C. Fields, Jimmy Breslin, Art Buchwald, Bob Dylan, Hunter Thompson and Fritz the Cat put down the pretentious, seeing in, under and around.
3. This is not done in the name of morality but of entertainment. Popular culture is unabashedly commercial. . . .
4. The key word is "in." The reporter doesn't want to observe the story, but to get *inside* it. Without the "in" sound, you're out. "In" remains a mystery.
5. Such transience breeds tension and turmoil. Some of our most popular entertainers commit suicide: Marilyn Monroe, Janis Joplin, Jimi

Hendrix, etc. Even the major journals of the New Journalism, *(Herald Tribune, Look, Ramparts)* disappear.

6. In place of objectivity, a new cult of specificity. Hard, tangible exploitable images and insights make reputations and money. Said Paul Tillich: "God is in the details."

7. Style is crucial. When a singer or writer has "real style," we can overlook or forgive almost anything. Who cares what Bing Crosby or Frank Sinatra sings—or what subject Tom Wolfe or Gay Talese write on? "It ain't Whatcha Do, It's the Way that You Do It."[24]

In his comparisons, Fishwick uses the methods of literary criticism. He tries to put New Journalism content in the context of popular culture activity generally and find similarities. The Fishwick collection is eighteen rather diverse essays by communications researchers, literary scholars, sociologists, and others. They range from philosophical accounts to a quite practical study of what professional journalists think of New Journalism.

In a study that examines the New Journalism as literature, *Fact & Fiction, The New Journalism and the Nonfiction Novel* (1977), author John Hollowell tries to determine the nonfiction novel's place in contemporary writing and the changes in the writer's relationship to history that this reflects.

The literature about the New Journalism is primarily literary and historical. It chronicles the new trend as a development in American journalism. Some of the studies are more concerned with the forces that brought the movement about while others stick closer to the content and style of New Journalism writing. By the early 1970s, Theodore Peterson would write waggishly that books about the New Journalism had become something of a home industry. Whether this literature will be more than an obscure footnote in the future is dependent on the extent to which the movement has a lasting influence on American journalism. A few sociological studies have touched on New Journalism, but none in a substantial way. Though it began with a bang, the long term influence of New Journalism, both as style and substantive content in print media, may be a more subtle thing to study. Content analytic studies examining the changing nature of news content as well as surveys of reporters and editors are already yielding answers to these questions.

INVESTIGATIVE AND ADVERSARIAL JOURNALISM

As talk about the New Journalism subsided, there was considerable public and scholarly discussion about investigative journalism—the result, in part, of the explosive revelations of reporters during the Watergate period. Where the New Journalism was more concerned with style and form (although it delivered highly contemporaneous content), investigative reporting focused almost exclusively on content and the impact of that content on governmental operations. That the press should be a watchdog of government, an adversary, had long been a cornerstone of journalistic philosophy. In fact, the notion is so well established that it is quickly socialized into a reporter and becomes a deeply held craft attitude. Even though the press had engaged in notable skirmishes with government throughout history, the adversarial concept was more platitude than practice during much of the Cold War period and beyond. During the 1960s with unrest over Vietnam and rather blatant credibility problems in the national government, journalistic consensus, like social and political consensus, crumbled. Reporters were less likely to overlook governmental transgressions for the sake of national unity and more likely to report on them.

For some reporters this was nothing new. Sleuthing investigators like Clark Mollenhoff and Jack Anderson were seasoned professionals. Both had brought continuous embarrassment to government officials and bureaucrats by exposing conflicts of interest and occasional corruption. Anderson, who was trained by and conditioned to the journalistic moralizing of the late Drew Pearson, was a part of a continuing tradition of Washington exposé that found new life during the massive growth of government during the New Deal. It had earlier roots, of course, paralleling political reform movements, accelerating during the lurid and shocking "Yellow Journalism" of the 1880s and 1890s. It may have reached its highest form in the meticulous work of the Muckrakers at the turn of the century when painstaking investigation was combined with solid literary style.

The preoccupation with investigative reporting in the 1970s focused initially on the adventures of Bob Woodward and Carl Bernstein chronicled in their best-selling book, *All the President's Men,* and drew on the combative relationship between the press and government during the early years of the Nixon administration. Major skirmishes in that accelerating hostility were the Agnew attacks on the press that began in 1969; Jack Anderson's revelation on the Bangladesh papers, which embarrassed Henry Kissinger and transformed Anderson from journalistic pariah to Pulitzer Prize winner; publication by the *New York Times* and *Washington Post* of the Pentagon Papers and the resultant litigation; and the heavy use of subpoena power by the Department of Justice. Against this backdrop came the mounting Watergate story, a two-and-a-half-year saga of cor-

ruption in high places. The efforts of Woodward and Bernstein and others who investigated the Watergate affair differed in at least one respect from earlier exposès. It was not a single exposè, but a series of exposès, some fueled by journalistic enterprise, some stimulated by the courts and other government agencies. This continuity of coverage was not always a positive factor, though. Sometimes it was prolonged and suspenseful coverage of nonevents such as the delivery of evidence to the judge in the case, John Sirica. As John L. Hulteng has written in an analysis of Watergate journalism:

> This is crescendo journalism; it reflects a desire to keep the story alive, to build mounting suspense, to add on pressure. The news magazines and the TV networks have used this countdown technique—a kind of ever more portentous drum-roll of ominous developments—at several stages of the Watergate investigations, and in reporting on periodic opinion pooling results.[25]

But beyond its prolonged nature there was nothing to distinguish Watergate coverage from earlier exposès of government scandal and corruption. Journalists and journalistic organizations are fond of celebrating the heroic exploits of their colleagues and Woodward and Bernstein became instant journalistic celebrities. As they were honored for what was clearly careful and courageous reporting, there was a tendency to overstate their innovations and impact and to embellish its importance. Warning against this tendency, Edward Jay Epstein wrote:

> A sustaining myth of journalism holds that every great government scandal is revealed through the work of enterprising reporters who by one means or another pierce the official veil of secrecy. The role that government institutions themselves play in exposing official misconduct and corruption therefore tends to be neglected if not wholly ignored by the press.[26]

In an essay in the *Public Interest* magazine, Paul Weaver observed that "traditionally, American journalism has been very close to, dependent upon, and cooperative with official sources."[27] But in recent years, he says, "a small but significant and still-growing segment of the journalistic community has begun to revise this relationship by assuming a posture of greater independence and less cooperativeness."[28] Weaver sees this trend making the press "freer but also less informative and possibly more partisan."[29] To Weaver and other scholar-critics the movement toward an adversarial journalism is romantic and seen by its adherents as a heresy:

> The current "heretical" movement in American journalism is defined by the fact that it takes the mythical part of the "orthodox" tradition—the fiction of the autonomous, investigative, adversary press—for the whole of that tradition. It presents itself as an effort to make our press live up to what it always said it was: a journalism that is autonomous instead of interdependent, original instead of derivative, and in an adversary instead of cooperative relationship with government and officialdom.[30]

Attempting to demolish what he regards as an adversary myth in contemporary journalism, sociologist Irving Kristol says, "adversary journalism today is rooted, not in political principle, but in a kind of joyful schizophrenia."[31] While boasting that they are a rigorous watchdog of government, "journalists today are overwhelmingly in favor of ever greater concentration of power in government—Federal, state and local—while in their daily adversary proceedings, they create an even greater distrust and suspicion of government."[32] While Kristol's statement may represent an articulate conservative critique of the press, it confuses the debate over adversarial-investigative reporting because the focus of most reporters is on the performance of public officials, rather than the nature of public policy itself.

Offering a more useful unraveling of the investigative-adversary concept is Mitchell V. Charnley, author of a widely-used textbook of journalistic reporting:

> I think it is a mistake to equate "watchdog" and "adversary." Good reporting can investigate government and, I suppose, when the implications or the conclusions of the reporting are adversely critical, it might be called adversary. But good reporting can also watch-government and find it golden, and I believe an objective *attitude* is still the ideal attitude for a reporter. Adversary reporting, as a term, seems to be to mean that the reporter says in advance: "I am out to find things that are adverse." That is to say, things that are deprecatory, derogatory, pejorative. Such adjectives should come after the fact rather than before.[33]

What the debate over adversary journalism clearly demonstrates is that it helps to define the nature of press-government relationships, but does little to advance the state of the art in either information-gathering techniques or the quality of writing. Thus, the adversarial-investigative considerations cannot supplant the New Journalism when it comes to studies of the journalistic product. Investigative reporting should be recognized for its contributions to the public intelligence on public affairs. In an age of increasingly sophisticated methods of acquiring information in other fields, students of journalistic practice have found that investigative reporting and studies of it yields little that is useful in understanding the journalistic product. For the most part scholars who have looked at investigative reporting have been concerned with the way that reporters do their work. The results of that work—the actual copy and stories—have been largely ignored. Comparative studies of the exposè over time have not been attempted.

The post-Watergate period has stimulated considerable interest in the activities of the press in probing the lives of public officials. A second Woodward-Bernstein book, *The Final Days,* was replete with personal references to Richard Nixon and his family. This aroused some ire in the trade press. Similarly, journalistic investigations of former Congressmen Wilbur Mills and Wayne Hays, both of whom were involved in sex scandals, led to a generalized concern about the prevalence of gossip in the news media. Alexander Cockburn of the *Village Voice* wrote extensively about this and *Newsweek* devoted a cover story to the subject. The contention was, in part, that the suspicions stimulated in the Watergate period, had led to some petty applications in daily journalism.

SUMMARY AND CONCLUSION

This chapter has presented an overview of some key issues with regard to media content. We have not touched on the many studies of omission of content, often a central criticism of the press. Yet, it follows that omissions are related to the same factors discussed in this chapter, for example, news definition, objectivity, and others. A knowledge of news judgment and news decision helps to understand the operational role of objectivity and also to get a notion of how both the New Journalism and adversarial journalism challenge the traditional posture. Studies of the content of communication, the ultimate journalistic product, is an important window on journalistic practice.

Notes

[1] Robert Darnton, ''Writing News and Telling Stories,'' *Daedalus,* Spring 1975, pp. 192-93.

[2] Mitchell V. Charnley, *Reporting,* 3rd ed. (New York: Holt, Rinehart & Winston, 1975), p. 44.

[3] Curtis D. MacDougall, *Interpretative Reporting,* 5th ed. (New York: Macmillan, 1968), p. 12.

[4] Raymond A. Bauer and Alice H. Bauer, ''America, 'Mass Society,' and Mass Media,'' *Journal of Social Issues,* July 1960, pp. 50-51.

[5] Leon V. Sigal, *Reporters and Officials: The Organization and Politics of Newsmaking* (Lexington, Mass.: D. C. Heath, 1973), p. 5.

[6] Bernard Roshco, *Newsmaking* (Chicago: University of Chicago Press, 1975), p. 3.

[7] Ibid., p. 14.

[8] Ibid., p. 14.

[9] Ibid., p. 23.

[10] Wilbur Schram, ''The Nature of News,'' *Journalism Quarterly,* Sept. 1949, p. 260.

[11] Todd Hunt, ''Beyond the Journalistic Event: The Changing Concept of News,'' *Mass Comm Review,* April 1974, p. 26.

[12] Ibid.

[13] George S. Hage, Everette E. Dennis, Arnold H. Ismach and Stephen Hartgen, *New Strategies for Public Affairs Reporting* (Englewood Cliffs, N.J.: Prentice-Hall, 1976), pp. 20-21. This chapter was written by Ismach.

[14] Ibid., p. 21.

[15] Paul H. Weaver, ''Newspaper News and Television News,'' in *Television as a Social Force, New Approaches to TV Criticism,* ed. Douglass Cater (New York: Praeger Publishers, 1975), p. 93.

[16] Hage, Dennis, Ismach, and Hartgen, *Public Affairs Reporting,* p. 19.

[17] Roshco, *Newsmaking,* p. 42.

[18] Kenneth Stewart, *News is What We Make It,* (Boston: Houghton-Mifflin Co., 1943).

[19] Gaye Tuchman, ''Objectivity as Strategic Ritual: An Examination of Newsmen's Notions of Objectivity,'' *American Journal of Sociology,* vol. 77, no. 4, p. 660.

[20] Ibid., summarized from pp. 665-670.

[21] James E. Murphy, ''The New Journalism: A Critical Perspective,'' *Journalism Monographs,* no. 34, May 1974, pp. 35-36.

[22] Marshall Fishwick, ed., *The New Journalism* (Bowling Green, OH: Popular Press, 1975), p. 5.

[23] Ibid., p. 3.

[24] Ibid., pp. 3-4.

[25] John L. Hulteng, ''Nixon, Watergate and the Press: The Whole Story Needs to be Told, but Not Oversold,'' *The Oregonian,* April 21, 1974, Forum Section, p. 1, Portland, Oregon.

[26] Edward Jay Epstein, ''Did the Press Uncover Watergate?,'' *Commentary,* July 1972, p. 21.

[27] Paul H. Weaver, ''The New Journalism and the Old—Thoughts After Watergate,'' *The Public Interest,* Spring 1974, p. 68.

[28] Ibid., pp. 68-9.

[29] Ibid., p. 69.

[30] Ibid., p. 75.

[31] Irving Kristol, ''Is the Press Misusing Its Power?,'' *(More),* Jan. 1975, pp. 26, 28.

[32] Ibid.

[33] Personal letter to the author from Mitchell V. Charnley, Feb. 18, 1975.

"...the impact of the journalist on public opinion is one of the strongest motivating forces in our society. He acts and reacts through an information system of unmatched delicacy, complexity and power."

—*John Hohenberg in*
The Professional Journalist
1969

Chapter 7

Journalists At Work

It may be that one of the legacies of Watergate is a new image for the journalist. "Bob Woodward remembers well the Friday when the phone rang and the voice said, 'We've got to talk. Tonight.' Woodward said, fine, come by at nine. A taxi dropped the man off at the curb and Woodward greeted the rumpled figure who was broken, footsore and full of questions."[1] The figure was not "Deep Throat," but Robert Redford who would later be responsible for bringing the adventures of Woodward and Bernstein to the silver screen.

If anything the film, which won critical acclaim, enhances the image of the journalist. As an enthusiastic critic put it:

> To some extent, all movies deal with images, real or literary, that preexist in the public's mind and with which their own fictions constantly risk colliding. But approaching "All The President's Men"...is like finding oneself in a hall of mirrors, a Pirandellian riddle. (This holds true, incidentally, even if you are *not* familiar with the city room of the *Washington Post* which has been reproduced down to the books in Ben Bradlee's office and the paper in the waste baskets!)[2]

Certainly the film image of the two reporters who are portrayed as hardworking professionals stands in sharp contrast to earlier film images, notably the rough and tumble journalism of Chicago in the 1920s, which is seen in the classic play/film "The Front Page."

Interest in reporters and reporting is high, sometimes because of inherent interest in the subjects they write about, sometimes because of the vigor with which reporters pursue their stories. Take Geraldo Rivera for example. In 1971, Rivera, a tall, modishly dressed, twenty-eight-year-old lawyer turned reporter, was working for WABC-TV in New York City. One of his assignments took him to an institution for the mentally retarded on Staten Island. Appalled by the conditions he saw, Rivera produced a series of hard-hitting reports that carried a strongly moralistic and reformist tone. The graphic images of human suffering that emerged from Rivera's reports had an impact: thousands of citizens wrote letters both to the television station and to public officials. The governor and state legislature responded by promising to improve conditions in the institution. As for Rivera, he became "the hotest young TV newsman in the country and the No. 1 idol of the New York Puerto Rican community from whom he sprang."[3] He also won several journalistic awards. The rest of the news media also carried the story, but after Rivera's initial revelations.[4] When asked why so much attention was paid to him and his station and this story, Rivera reflected:

> Aside from the fact that we were there first with the most...it was because I refused to give the State of New York any credit for doing anything good, because the good it was doing was so small compared to the bad it was doing. The other stations all succumbed to the "tell the other side of the story" syndrome. They gave the politicians equal time.[5]

Rivera who later became more of an entertainer

than a newsman was expressing views that ran counter to the mainstream of American journalism. Rivera became a celebrity, which Daniel Boorstin once described as a person who is "well-known for his well-knownness." If traditional journalistic values (and those most often conveyed to the public) embraced notions of fairness, accuracy and objectivity, Rivera was calling for an unabashed investigative advocacy. And Rivera was right in his perceptions of how traditional journalists, whether in newspapers or on television, would have covered the Willowbrook story. While exposing the shocking conditions through their own investigation and in interviews with staff persons, patients, and their parents, the traditional journalist also would have interviewed hospital officials and governmental authorities to get "their side of the story." And chances are that the resultant story would have been less sharply defined, more ambivalent than Rivera's. Rivera's dramatic example reveals his own values and in a sense places them in the context of the journalistic mainstream.

Stories like Rivera's and others have been partially responsible for renewed scholarly interest in the journalist. Amazingly, until recently very little was known about the journalist. Although there are many images of journalists in films, short stories, and novels, not to mention the many nonfiction accounts, no one has ever been sure how representative they were. Ask any journalist to describe his colleagues and he'll do so readily. When liberal politicians have complained about the conservative bias of American newspaper editorial endorsements, they have often been assured that the working press is liberal, leaning toward the Democratic party. But, there was never much evidence of this. Journalists are quite insulated, working within their own news organizations, having little contact with other reporters on the local scene, let alone nationally. And who was to say that reporters in one city were like those in another? Certainly such an assumption would not be good social science. Increasing intelligence about reporters and reporting was generated by the journalism review movement in the late 1960s and early 1970s. National and regional conferences associated with that movement also contributed. Reporters outside of such select groups as governmental press corps and specialists got to know each other.

No doubt these activities in addition to the return to a concept of a powerful media, which was accentuated by the conflict between press and government during the Johnson and Nixon administrations accounts, in part, for the renewed scholarly interest in the news media and its practitioners, especially reporters. That interest has been expressed by communication researchers, sociologists, political scientists, and management scientists among others.

JOURNALISTS AND THEIR WORK

Not until the late 1970s was there a national sociological profile of the American journalist, although there were studies of particular groups of journalists prior to that time that were illuminating. In the 1930s, for example, Leo Rosten produced his landmark study of the Washington press corps.[6] Rosten examined the pressures on reporters in Washington. His study was replicated twenty-five years later by William L. Rivers.[7]

Rather than looking specifically at reporters and their work, most of the early studies looked at newsroom operations. The several gatekeeper studies, for example, looked at decision making in the newsroom with specific emphasis on what got-in and what was kept-out of the newspaper.[8] For the most part these studies were of telegraph editors, rather than reporters. They demonstrated the role of bias in news selection and the highly subjective nature of the editing process, generally. Several of the studies involved sociological observation of a single gatekeeper. As David Manning White concluded in one of the earliest studies:

> It is a well-known fact in individual psychology that people tend to perceive as true only those happenings which fit into their own beliefs concerning what is likely to happen. It begins to appear (if Mr. Gates is a fair representative of his class) that in his position as gatekeeper the newspaper editor sees to it (even though he may never be consciously aware of it) that the community shall hear as a fact only those events which the newsman, as the representative of his culture, believes to be true.[9]

Our understanding of journalists and their work is enhanced by research from different sources, and different research traditions. And, once again, we are talking about different levels of analysis. At the intra-individual level there are studies of reporters' lifestyles. These range from individual case examples of reporters working under deadline pressure to general inventories of reporters and their values. Other studies are concerned with small group behavior. For example, the Supreme Court press corps and other specialist reporters have been the subject of research. Still others examine organizational level problems, viewing reporters and their work in a larger societal context such as studies of reporters and officials. Keeping the levels of analysis in mind is important in making sense of research and in determining how far it can be applied, how broadly generalized.

There has been a tendency for some commentators to blur these studies together, confusing the research and in the process, the reader. On several occasions in this book we refer to *gatekeeper* and *gatekeeping* studies. They are *not* the same thing. Gatekeeper studies focus on individuals. They take into account different variables and postulate different sorts of relationships than do gatekeeping studies, which are concerned with either groups of people within a news organization or the organizations themselves.

Jerry J. Waxman made this distinction in a study of local broadcast gatekeeping in natural disasters.[10] Waxman found it more useful to study the gatekeeping process, which considered influences and pressures both within and outside the news-organization. He found this approach preferable to the "static psychological approach" of the gatekeeper studies that often see the gatekeeper (or editor) as somewhat passive. For Waxman's purposes in studying the news organization under crisis conditions of natural disasters it was important to study the relationship between the broadcast station and public awareness. In this instance the researcher obviously made the right choice. A gatekeeper study here would have yielded less appropriate information and would not have answered satisfactorily Waxman's questions about the broadcast station's community relationships. But in other circumstances, given different research questions, especially those focusing on the individual gatekeeper as a decisionmaker, the gatekeeper studies would, of course, be more appropriate.

There is a paucity of scholarly inquiry into the life of the journalist but that does not mean there isn't considerable intelligence on the topic. The several general histories of journalism spend a good deal of space on leading reporters and editors. There are scores of memoirs of editors and reporters from the mid-nineteenth century to the present, many of them never mined in any systematic way for their perceptions of the newsroom. Several doctoral dissertations trace, in part, the history of reporting. Notable among these is Thomas Reilly's study of the origins of modern reporting in the Mexican War.[11] Similarly, Frederick Marbut's *News from the Capital* chronicles the story of Washington correspondence.

This chapter reviews mostly social science findings about journalists, beginning with the gatekeeper studies, continuing through contemporary reporter-source studies, management studies, and ending with case examples drawn from studies of legislative and judicial reporting.

INSIDE THE NEWSROOM

Wilbur Schramm in a memorandum on gatekeepers talked about the "message" and the "chain." That, he says, is what communication is all about. A message is developed, and it moves to its potential audience through a chain of activity. And, concludes Schramm, "the gatekeeper, saying 'yes' or 'no' to messages that come to him along the chain, obviously plays one of the most important roles in social communication."[12]

In a now-classic study of social control in the newsroom, sociologist Warren Breed observed professional norms that have an impact on the journalist. Some, he said, were *technical* norms having to do with writing, editing, and reporting. Others were of an *ethical* nature relating to the obligation of the journalist to his audience. Breed discovered that a major socializing influ-

ence on the journalist was something called "policy." Although he saw "policy" as a covert phenomenon, Breed wrote:

> Every newspaper has a policy, admitted or not. One paper's policy may be pro-Republican, cool to labor, antagonistic to the school board, etc. The principal areas of policy are politics, business, labor; much of it stems from considerations of class. Policy is manifested in "slanting." Just what determines any publisher's policy is a large question . . .however, the publisher has much to say in both long-term and immediate policy decisions. . . .Finally, policy is covert, due to the existence of ethical norms of journalism; policy often contravenes these norms. No executive is willing to risk embarrassment of being accused of open to commands to slant a news story.[13]

"Gatekeepers," John Dimmick has written, "are uncertain which events are to be defined as news."[14] That uncertainty is reduced by a number of factors including "policy," news-definitions promulgated in the newsroom, opinions of sources of news, monitoring another newspaper as a check and balance, and other factors. "The hypothesis that an organization's news policy is a means of reducing the gatekeeper's uncertainty is supported by the findings of several studies,"[15] Dimmick says.

How much can one generalize from the gatekeeper studies, many of them conducted at single newspapers in the 1950s and 1960s? Did the notion of "policy" carry over to television newsrooms in the 1970s, for example? Daniel Garvey in a study of social control in the television newsroom tried to find out. Garvey wanted to see whether Breed's 1955 conclusions would have any application to the selection of television news in 1970. In addition, he wanted to establish a quantitative basis for studying social control. Garvey noted that Breed reached his conclusions through interviewing a relatively small number of journalists. "The faith one puts in Breed's conclusions depends on how accurately one believes his observations reflect the actual state of affairs in journalism."[16]

Garvey's study involved summaries of news items from television newscasts that were rank-ordered by news room employees. Although he had some difficulty getting full cooperation from as many stations as he might have wished, Garvey's study yielded some important findings. In stations where a manager played an open and active role in news policy, it was found that the longer an individual worked for a station the greater was his agreement with management about news. In spite of the somewhat independent posture that many newspersons take, Garvey found that the actual items used in a news program conformed more to the choices of the manager than to those of any member of the news staff. This study "suggests a more direct role by management than Breed indicated."[17] However, the station manager was not all-powerful. In some instances the views of news directors tended to prevail over the choices of the manager.

Garvey would conclude that "a phenomenon of policy absorption such as Breed posited does exist in television news."[18] However, he cautioned that policy was by no means universal and that studying it involved consideration of several complex variables.

What are the major influences on the journalist and his work? Dimmick's listing, drawn mainly from the gatekeeping literature seems most useful. They are (1) opinion leaders within the group in which the journalist works, (2) consensus within the newsroom group, (3) reference institutions such as the AP daily budget and the *New York Times,* (4) the policy of the organization, (5) news sources and their interaction with reporters and (6) the attitudes and values of journalists.[19]

WHO ARE THE JOURNALISTS?

In addition to the intriguing interactions of personnel in the newsroom, some scholars and commentators wanted to know more about the characteristics of individual journalists. An early study that began to build a demographic base was an inquiry into "How the Newsman Lives," conducted by David L. Grey and J. Edward Gerald. In interviews with journalists in four midwestern cities in 1964 it was found that the average journalist was a middle-aged man (median age, 49) who was likely to be married and a college graduate. The Gerald-Grey study, a convention paper, like several others at the time focused on the satisfaction of journalists with attention to their salaries, fringe benefits, and working conditions. The emphasis on "satisfaction" in the 1960s would seem irrelevant by the 1970s when journalistic jobs were scarce indeed. In any event, the Gerald-Grey study yielded salary information that began to chip-away at the long-held image of the newsman as an underpaid (or poorly-paid) individual.

Merrill Samuelson studied job satisfaction in the newsroom at a time when there was a "brain drain" away from journalism. Newspaper managers wanted to know how to attract and keep good people because, as Samuelson noted, "newspaper work has traditionally served as an apprenticeship for careers in business and politics."[20]

Other researchers including Jack McLeod and Searle Hawley looked at professionalism among newspersons. Studies of professionalism in journalism are severely hampered by the continuing debate as to whether journalism is a profession at all. The literature of professions from the sociology of work suggests that the professional (1) works in a closed group and shares certain values and norms with his co-workers, (2) works primarily for the satisfaction he derives from his work and secondarily for the monitary rewards, (3) prestige, honors and other types of recognition are more important to the professional than to the nonprofessional, (4) the professional's allegiance is to his profession rather than to his organization and (5) the professional wants autonomy in his work.

Those who study professionalism often find a conflict between staff members whose orientation is professional (usually called *cosmopolitans* by the sociologists) and those whose orientation and loyalty is to the organization (designated as *locals*). In a comparative study McLeod and Hawley contrasted responses of journalists at the Milwaukee *Sentinel* and *Journal* with white collar employees at the same papers. Journalists in the study were more likely to identify with cosmopolitan values while the nonjournalist employees were usually locals in orientation. The journalists "tied general evaluation [of the news] to responsibility and objectivity...showed greater homogeneity within their group...showed a greater tendency to want implementation of professional values...and tended to hold a more critical attitude toward their paper than did the other groups."[21] And the professional orientation of journalists is improving, McLeod and Hawley concluded, "Some 88 percent of our editorial respondents felt that performing 'an essential service to the community' was 'quite important' or 'extremely important' to them. This is a prerequisite to the professionalism of jour-

nalism."[22] The increasing professionalization of journalists has been a persistent theme in the literature from the mid-1960s to the present.[23]

THE JOHNSTONE STUDIES

While studies conducted at a few newspapers or broadcast stations in a particular region of the country had advantages over the fragmented findings of individual case studies, the need for a broader-based national study was still evident. Happily, John Johnstone, a sociologist, and two colleagues at the University of Illinois, Chicago Circle obliged with the most ambitious study of journalists to date.

The work of Johnstone and colleagues was the first large scale national study of practicing journalists in the United States. And its yield was a comprehensive sociological portrait of "the occupational group most directly responsible for the day-to-day informational needs of our society."[24] The researchers drew a sample of nearly 1,500 journalists from a nearly-complete population list of all news-editorial employees in the United States, which was derived from extensive contacts with media organizations through phone calls and personal visits. No attempt to assemble such a list had ever been accomplished.

The study probed several areas, including the demographic characteristics of journalists, their education and training, career mobility in the field, the division of labor within journalism, the journalist as a professional, definitions of journalistic responsibility, rewards and satisfactions in news media journalism, as well as a treatment of journalists in the alternative media.

What were Johnstone's findings? Here are some of them:

Size of the manpower pool in the news media

in the U.S.—69,500, seventy-five percent of it in print, 20 percent in broadcasting and 5 percent in the wire services.

Location—disproportionately located in urban areas, heavy concentrations in the Northeast, especially New York City.

Age and sex composition—Median age 36.5 compared with 39.2 in the overall civilian labor force; 79.7 percent male, 20.3 percent female, well below the averages for other labor force employment.

Social origins—Anglo-Saxon, 39.0 percent; German, 17.5 percent; Irish, 13.6 percent; Scandinavian, 5 percent; French, 4.0 percent; all the rest below, 4.0 percent, including Negroes at 3.9 percent and Jews, 3.2 percent. The social origins are clearly Anglo-Saxon or European. Blacks and Hispanic-Americans have small numbers in the media.

Parents occupations—The vast majority come from white collar backgrounds (61.9 percent).

Education and training—27.9 percent have some college, 39.6 percent have college degrees; 10.5 percent, some graduate training; 8.1 percent, graduate degrees.

Fields of study—27.5 percent, communications; 35.3 percent, general liberal arts; and 3.2 percent in all other fields.

These truncated findings do not reflect the refinements in Johnstone's data, which considered journalists by region of the country, medium and age, as well as other variables.

The Illinois researchers also had a unique opportunity to look at the professional values of American journalists. They found that:

> Within journalism the quest for relevance revolves around old themes—objectivity versus subjectivity, detachment versus advocacy, observer versus watchdog.[25]

Perhaps the most insightful data was yielded in a question that asked the journalists to rate the importance of eight different aspects of news media performance. See Table 7.1 below.

TABLE 7.1

PERCENTAGE OF AMERICAN JOURNALISTS EVALUATING EIGHT NEWS
MEDIA FUNCTIONS AS "EXTREMELY IMPORTANT"

Media Functions	*Percent (N = 1,313)*[a]
1. Investigate claims and statements made by the government.	76.3
2. Provide analysis and interpretation of complex problems.	61.3
3. Get information to the public as quickly as possible.	56.4
4. Discuss national policy while it is still being developed.	55.9
5. Stay away from stories where factual content cannot be verified.	52.8
6. Concentrate on news which is of interest to the widest possible public.	39.1
7. Develop intellectual and cultural interests of the public.	30.5
8. Provide entertainment and relaxation.	16.7

[a]In this and subsequent tables, the "elite" and "rank and file" strata are combined into a single sample weighted by their probabilities of selection. All calculations are computed from the weighted cases, but the reported *N*'s are the unweighted case bases.

—source, John W. C. Johnstone, Edward J. Slawski, and William W. Bowman, "The Professional Values of American Newsmen," *Public Opinion Quarterly*, Winter 1972-73, p. 527.

The data suggest some leaning toward a more participatory journalism with quick transmission of facts and careful verification. This may reflect some changes in journalistic norms, but could also be the product of journalistic thinking during a period of considerable activity in the newsroom (covered later in our discussion of press criticism). Johnstone's data were collected late in 1971 at the height of the journalism review and media criticism trend. Johnstone and colleagues conclude that especially noteworthy is:

> . . .how very much modern newswork is a collective enterprise, and how very intricate is the process by which occurrences in the real world come to be translated into news stories. As participants in modern life, we are able to directly apprehend just a tiny fraction of the events which shape our lives: yet to realize that only some proportion of those whose full-time occupation it is to report these events to us are involved firsthand in their observation and evaluation is an even more startling revelation. It is important, then, to know that so many journalists devote the major share of their time and energy to processing and transmitting information structured by others: awareness of this fact should better enable us to evaluate the information the media provide. Mass news is very much an organizational phenomenon, and with increasing centralization in the industry and increasing complexity in newsroom technology, it is likely to become even more so.[26]

A LOCAL APPLICATION

Intrigued by Johnstone's findings, two journalism professors in Minneapolis assisted a local newspaper, the *Minneapolis Star* in conducting a survey of newspaper and television reporters in Minneapolis and St. Paul. This study, conducted in August 1975, attempted to draw a profile of metropolitan newspaper and television reporters that included politics, religion, and attitudes on a wide range of social issues in addition to summarizing basic demographic data. Questionnaires went to nearly a total population of full-time reporters in the area (151) and there was a response rate of sixty-two percent. A summary of the findings:

> Reporters in the Twin Cities are well-off financially and are highly educated. They're cynical. They have little confidence in those who run several of society's institutions. They have a low regard for public school performance.
>
> About half don't attend church, and one in four is an avowed athiest or agnostic.
>
> They tend to be more liberal and independent in political attitudes than the general public.
>
> They're more likely than the public to think marijuana smoking in moderate amounts is not harmful.
>
> They prefer city living to the suburbs more than most people.[27]

Like Johnstone and colleagues, the Minnesota researchers compared the reporters to others in the general population, or in the case of this study to recent public opinion data for citizens of the Twin Cities. The Minnesota study also made comparisons between its metropolitan reporters and Johnstone's reporters derived from a national sample. In sum, the metropolitan area reporters were generally younger, better educated, more likely to be trained specifically in journalism, more likely to belong to professional organizations. The metropolitan reporters tended to come from higher socioeconomic backgrounds than did the national reporters. The Minnesota study also compared newspaper and television reporters. As much as anything, studies of this kind provide an inventory of information about reporters and raise new questions for inquiry. As the researchers commented:

The profile of reporters on metropolitan news organizations that emerges from this study presents some striking contrasts with reporters nationally, and also presents an anomaly. The respondents displayed a strong concern with the quality of their own work, and with the performance of their news organizations—indications of professionalism. Yet only a relatively small percentage were members of professional organizations, other than unions.[28]

While it is something of a cliche in research to say that "further research is needed" to build a basis for greater understanding, nothing could be more true in reviewing demographic studies of journalists. Work in this area is just beginning and such important variables as time, the national mood, working conditions, the economy, and others are likely to make data about reporters fascinating to watch in the years ahead.

MANAGEMENT STUDIES: BEHIND THE FRONT PAGE

Even though newspapers and broadcast stations are similar to other organizations and social institutions, they also have some unique characteristics. They have been slow to adapt to modern management techniques and greatly resemble their nineteenth century predecessors, more than do other business organizations. As newsrooms transform themselves into the world of modern, electronic technology, new management systems are necessary. And as a result progressive managements have sought assistance in bringing about this change.

One newspaper that did this was the *New York Times*. Quietly, and without fanfare, the *Times* hired Harvard management expert Chris Argyris to study their paper and make recommendations. Argyris did this and later wrote a book titled, *Behind the Front Page,* which discussed the internal managerial problems of a fictitious newspaper, *The Daily Planet*. Argyris, in this thinly-disguised portrait of the *New York Times,* said his purpose in writing the book was to create newspapers that are self-examining and self-regulating. Additionally, he thought that his study would be a step toward enhancing organizational health of newspapers, which have not been models of smooth management. Like other critics of the press, Argyris pointed out that newspapers, so quick to investigate and analyze the rest of society, are reluctant to discuss or deal with their own internal problems which they regard as "private," not public.

Although it was hardly his main concern, the Harvard management specialist also examined the types of reporters he found on the metropolitan newspaper. There were, he said, three types of reporters: traditional reporters, reporter-researchers, and reporter-activists. The traditional reporters' "first commandment is to be objective and get the facts. . . . The reporters who adhere to this concept strive to present the news as objectively as possible."[29] By contrast, the reporter-researcher is the one who no longer finds inverted pyramid news coverage particularly challenging even under time pressures. Argyris continued:

> They sought to do more interpretive news. They wanted to dig beneath the surface of events to find the critical but half-hidden forces that were shaping events. (For example, one reporter did a thorough analysis of societal trends and pressures for urbanization and pressure creating dry rot in our cities).[30]

The reporter-researchers impose analytical abilities and concepts upon reality of the news to give it deeper meaning. Add to this mix the reporter-activist who wishes to use journalism to bring about social change or shake up the world. Argyris saw the reporter-activists as angry, young men. He said they are more critical than constructive. Argyris makes no secret of the fact that he includes Geraldo Rivera in the reporter-activist category.

The basic differences that Argyris observed among reporters was the way they conceptualized their role as reporters and the amount of time and personal resourcefulness they brought to their work. While the reporter-activist might demonstrate his empathy for people in a more overt way, he really doesn't differ fundamentally from the traditional reporter or the reporter-researcher in the way he gathers news and writes it. True, there are differences in tone and point-of-view, but the old journalistic form with its short paragraphs and information organized in a descending order of importance remains intact.

The Argyris study is applied research. His purpose was to observe and describe the organizational operations of the newspaper with an eye toward improvement and revitalization. His probe based on a sample of one but generalized more broadly, discovered "dry rot" in the American press and he concludes his book with a prescription:

> If the processes of organizational entropy we found in the *Planet* are found in other newspapers (and I believe they will be), then newspapers everywhere should want to create and institutionalize procedures for self-examination and processes for self-renewal. Without such processes, and given the protection of the Constitution, newspapers may find their freedom increasingly curtailed or managed by outside institutions.[31]

Although Argyris generalizes quite broadly about newspapers on the basis of a limited study, his work is especially valuable for other reasons. Unlike some researchers who know lit-

tle about corporate issues and management outside of the communications industry, Argyris has vast experience looking at other kinds of business entities. He puts his study of a metropolitan newspaper in this larger context and makes his recommendations on the basis of good management practices while still recognizing the special nuances of the newspaper, which is not quite the same as any other business. Argyris illuminates the conflicts in the media organization between professional and business values. He demonstrates through his observational analyses the impact that these forces have on staff relationships and behavior. Relationships change; roles change.

The author in a conversation with a Japanese communication researcher, Shin-Chi Ito of the University of Tokyo learned that changes in roles and responsibilities of particular newspaper personnel are the subject of research in that country. Ito has postulated that concentration of media ownership and growth of the corporate organization has diminished the influence of the editor. And he reportedly found evidence (as yet unpublished) of this in several countries—including the United States.

Just how the issues of management influence on staff organization and resultant editorial product should be studied is not agreed upon. David Rubin, in a review of Argyris' book in (MORE) raises an important question:

> It is hard to argue with Argyris' bottomline logic that the criteria for effective management at IBM are the same as those at the *New York Times* or any other large news organization. And yet it is difficult to shake the skeptical—maybe irrational—feeling that even if news people are "ineffective" managers, perhaps they must and should be if one accepts the notion of a socially responsible press.[32]

Whether Rubin is talking about the traditional

conflict between profits and social responsibility is not important. What he suggests is a different basis to evaluate some of the questions that Argyris raises. The management studies like those of Argyris use different criteria in reaching their analyses than do others in forthcoming chapters that return to the same conflict (business vs. professional values) but in a different context and at a different level of analysis.

OFFICIALS AND REPORTERS

Some illuminating data are found in the several studies of the relationships between reporters and public officials. This has been an active area for media researchers, sometimes because of the small size of a particular public press corps, sometimes because of the obvious links that a study of this kind provides to other fields. Political scientists with little general interest in the news media, for example, are greatly concerned about the way the press covers Congress or the Supreme Court.

Much like William Porter who in a widely-quoted article described news organizations as bureaucracies,[33] Leon V. Sigal in a book entitled *Reporters and Officials* demonstrated how news is the result of bureaucratic politics. "One may consider a newspaper a hierarchical organization in which the bureaucratic players (publisher, editors, reporters, copy desk) engage in a constant bargaining process over assignments, beats, deadlines, space allocations, budgets and the other factors that will ultimately determine what appears in print and in what form."[34] Sigal's study was based on observations in the newsrooms of the *New York Times* and *Washington Post*.

To Sigal the reporter is an organization man

[or woman] who is guided by journalistic conventions and craft attitudes. "Organizational processes and bureaucratic politics," he says, "account for more of news content, than, say the political proclivities of individual newsmen. In short, what newsmen report may depend less on who they are than on how they work."[35]

Sigal's study reveals a press vulnerable to manipulation by government. While "newsmen resist, even resent, blandishments of officials to play along with them, [they often] fall prey to the more insidious temptations of becoming insiders, having influence."[36]

There are a number of studies that trace relationships between reporters and officials at the state level. Delmer Dunn, in *Public Officials and the Press* observed the ways in which reporters determined news values. Reporters, he says, are unsure that their evaluation of a story is correct "because there are no concrete criteria upon which to base his evaluation."[37] The result is reliance on other reporters to "validate" his decision. Two Iowa social scientists, Charles Wiggins and J. Paul Yarbrough, studied officials and reporters as actors in the state legislative system. The reporter, they conclude, plays a "critical linkage function in the two-way lawmaker-constituent communication process. . . ."[38] Wiggins and Yarbrough, like several other researchers who have studied legislative-press relations, concern themselves with legislators' views of the press and vice versa. Theirs is a sophisticated study that views several different types of reporters and legislators. The reporters are viewed in isolation since they are away from their newsrooms while covering a legislative session. While the various studies of legislative-press relations use different methods and reach different conclusions, they are similar to the extent that they validate the agenda-setting hypothesis, suggesting an important informational (if not persuasive) role for the media. And, of course, public perceptions of government are largely a product of the news media and its reporters.

Some rich historical and anecdotal evidence about the legislature and the press in the national context is found in William L. Rivers, *The Opinion Makers* and Robert O. Blanchard, *Congress and the News Media*. These critical relationships will no doubt continue to attract scholarly interest.

THE PRESS AND THE COURTS

Courts in general and the Supreme Court of the United States in particular have also caught the eye of scholars interested in official-journalistic contacts. The Supreme Court with its vast influence on American life (and its tiny press corps of less than ten persons) is a particularly attractive target for study. In spite of the seemingly manageable nature of research on press coverage of the high court, there are many constraints that make the task more difficult, though.

While much of the scholarship on the press and the court has been prescriptive, tending toward improved coverage, some has also had theoretical implications. David L. Grey, for example, treated the court as an information system in his landmark study *The Supreme Court and the News Media*. Information about the court and its work is tightly controlled, flowing mostly out of court decisions that are shrouded in secrecy until formal action is taken. Grey also did a study of a "typical" court reporter operating under deadline pressure. A compromise reporter whose work fell between the exhaustive reports of the *New York Times*

and the terse bulletins of the wire services was observed and from his work some conclusions were drawn:

(1) the reporter knew at all times how many cases remained undecided by the Court, although he had to guess which cases the court would decide on a particular day.
(2) news selection depended largely on what events transpired on a given day and the reporter had to decide how much "weight" to give a particular story.
(3) reporters made an effort to stay informed of the operations of their competition, often as to a specific story. This enabled the reporter to validate his news sense and gain peer reinforcement.
(4) the reporter acknowledged that he exercised a conservative news judgment. He preferred to be on the safe side, understating, rather than overstating what the Court had decided.[39]

A study by Chester A. Newland identified major constraints on press coverage at the Court and suggested improvements in bureaucratic techniques and court procedures.[40] Other studies examine public opinion and the court, but have little specific relevance to the press. Grey saw the court as a communicator, but it was Seth Goldschlager who was the first scholar interested in news executives' perceptions of Supreme Court coverage. In a survey of 143 managing editors of daily newspapers, Goldschlager found that news executives desired more legal trend stories and interpretive coverage; however, these desires were at variance with the perceptions that reporters had of their editors' wishes.[41]

The author in a 1974 study sought information that would provide a profile of the Supreme Court reporter, a reportorial assessment of Court coverage, and an indication of attitudes about the public information policies and practices of the Court. One of the conclusions of this survey of reporters at the Court (both the regulars and those who cover the institution less frequently) was:

> The average reporter at the Supreme Court is a relatively young, well-educated individual who has had several years of media experience before coming to the Court. Tenure at the Court is rather short. Most of the reporters queried were pleased with their own performance and that of their colleagues. Most were also gratified with the treatment their stories received in their own publications or newscasts. Newspapers and wire services were rated the highest by the performance indicators, while the news magazines and broadcast news received lower ratings.[42]

Studies of court and legislative reporting are quite fragmented and noncomparable. But, they are useful because they treat the reporter in some isolation, yet still in a real-life situation.

SUMMARY AND CONCLUSION

For the most part studies of news media personnel have been concerned with reporters and editors. On occasion, business staff members are also studied, but studies of other personnel groups and influences are almost nonexistent. Communicator studies are gaining increasing popularity in Europe and Asia as well as in this country and they will provide an important link in understanding the functioning of the press. The research evidence reviewed in this chapter indicates once again that investigators have been somewhat fragmentary and scattered in selecting targets for study. But increasingly, a broader collection of data is providing a basis for fuller conclusions.

In this chapter we have considered the changing image of the journalist and the studies that chart that change. After brief consideration of investigative journalism, we review studies of journalists and their work that have been conducted by communication researchers. These include gatekeeper and gatekeeping studies and observations of newsroom interaction, especially at times of decision. Sociological data that explores the demographic characteristics of journalists is also examined both from a national and a metropolitan perspective. Consideration is also given to management science studies of news organizations and studies of specialist journalists—those that cover politics and government as well as those who cover the courts.

Notes

[1]Chris Hodenfield, "Redford, Hoffman haunted Post newsroom for film, found they weren't the only actors," from *Rolling Stone* service, in *Minneapolis Star,* April 14, 1976, p. 1B.

[2]Molly Haskell, "Journalism Goes to the Movies," *Village Voice,* April 12, 1976, p. 131.

[3]"Penthouse Interview, Geraldo Rivera, TV Newsman," *Penthouse,* March 1973, p. 56.

[4]This statement often made in conjunction with Rivera's work is slightly misleading. The Willowbrook story had been the subject of several print and broadcast exposes for nearly twenty years. *See* Everette E. Dennis, "Journalistic Primitivism," *Journal of Popular Culture,* Summer 1975, pp. 126-27.

[5]"Penthouse Interview," p. 57.

[6]Leo Rosten, *The Washington Correspondents* (New York: Harcourt, Brace, 1937).

[7]William L. Rivers, "The Correspondents After 25 Years," *Columbia Journalism Review,* Spring 1962, pp. 4-10.

[8]*See,* for example, David Manning White, "The Gatekeeper: A Case Study in the Selection of News," *Journalism Quarterly,* Fall, 1950, pp. 383-90; Paul B. Snider, "Mr. Gates Revisited: A 1966 Version of the 1949 Case Study," *Journalism Quarterly,* Autumn 1967, pp. 419-27.

[9]David Manning White, "The 'Gatekeeper': A Case Study in the Selection of News," in *People, Society and Mass Communications,* ed. Lewis A. Dexter and David M. White (New York: The Free Press, 1964), p. 171.

[10]Jerry J. Waxman, "Local Broadcast Gatekeeping During Natural Disasters," *Journalism Quarterly,* Winter 1973, pp. 751-58, passim.

[11]Thomas Reilly, "American Reporters and the Mexican War," (Ph.D. dissertation, University of Minnesota, 1975).

[12]"The Gatekeeper, A Memorandum," in Wilbur Schramm, ed., *Mass Communications* (Urbana: University of Illinois Press, 1960), p. 177.

[13]Warren Breed, "Social Control in the News-room," *Social Forces,* May 1955; also in Schramm, *Mass Communication* pp. 179-80.

[14]John Dimmick, "The Gate-Keeper: An Uncertainty Theory," *Journalism Monographs,* No. 37, p. 8.

[15]Ibid., p. 16.

[16]Daniel Garvey, "Social Control in the Television Newsroom," (Ph.D. dissertation, Stanford University, 1971). Quotation from a summary of the study prepared by Garvey, p. 1.

[17]Ibid., p. 2.

[18]Ibid., p. 3.

[19]Breed, "Social Control in the Newsroom," pp. 10-24.

[20]Merrill Samuelson, "A Standardized Test to Measure Job Satisfaction in the Newsroom," *Journalism Quarterly,* 39, 1962, p. 29.

[21]Jack M. McLeod and Searle E. Hawley, Jr., "Professionalism Among Newsmen," *Journalism Quarterly,* 41, 1964, p. 537.

[22]Ibid., 577.

[23]*See* for example, McLeod and Hawley, "Job Satisfaction in the Newsroom," J. Edward Gerald, *The Social Responsibility of the Press* (Minneapolis: University of Minnesota Press, 1963); James W. Carey, "The Communications Revolution and the Professional Communicator," *Sociological Review,* monograph no. 13, (University Keele, 1969); Rodney Stark, "Policy and the Pros: An Organizational Analysis of a Metropolitan Newspaper," *Berkeley Journal of Sociology,* 1962, pp. 11-32; and William E. Porter, "Professionalism of the Press," ANPA Paper at the Reston Conference, in *Education for Newspaper Journalists in the Seventies and Beyond,* 1973.

[24]John W. C. Johnstone, Edward J. Slawski, and William W. Bowman, *The News People: A Sociological Portrait of American Journalists and their Work* (Urbana: University of Illinois Press, 1976), p. 4.

[25]John W. C. Johnstone, Edward J. Slawski and William W. Bowman, "The Professional Values of

American Newsmen,'' *Public Opinion Quarterly,* Winter 1972-73, p. 527.

[26]Johnstone, Slawski, and Bowman, *The News People*, p. 182.

[27]"Tearing Down the Paper Curtain,'' special section, compilation of series on the news media, entitled, "The News Machines,'' Aug. 25-Sept. 6, 1975, *see* "Surveyed Reporters Reveal Liberal Political Bent,'' *Minneapolis Star,* p. 12 reprint of series. The survey mentioned was conducted by Prof. Arnold Ismach and the author, both of the University of Minnesota, and the series article was written by Peter Ackerberg.

[28]Arnold H. Ismach and Everette E. Dennis, "A Profile of Newspaper and Television Reporters in a Metropolitan Setting,'' *Journalism Quarterly* (in press).

[29]Chris Argyris, *Behind the Front Page, Organizational Self-Renewal in a Metropolitan Newspaper* (San Francisco: Jossey-Bass, 1974), p. 47.

[30]Ibid., pp. 50-52.

[31]Ibid., pp. 268.

[32]David M. Rubin, " 'Behind the Front Page,' '' (MORE), Nov. 1974, p. 23.

[33]William E. Porter, "Journalism,'' *International Encyclopedia of the Social Sciences,* vol. 8, (New York: Macmillan and the Free Press, 1968).

[34]Leon V. Sigal, *Reporters and Officials, The Organization and Politics of Newsmaking* (Lexington, Mass.: D.C. Heath, 1973), quotation from back cover, taken from *Columbia Journalism Review.*

[35]Ibid., p. 5.

[36]Ibid., p. 195.

[37]Delmer D. Dunn, *Public Officials and the Press* (Reading, Mass.: Addison-Wesley Publishing Co., 1969), p. 30.

[38]Charles W. Wiggins and J. Paul Yarbrough, "Reporters and the Legislative System: A Study of Perceptions and Performance,'' (Paper delivered at annual meeting of Midwest Political Science Assn., May 3-5, Chicago, Ill., 1973, p. 1).

[39]David L. Grey, "Decision-Making By a Reporter Under Deadline Pressure,'' *Journalism Quarterly,* 43, pp. 426-28, 1966.

[40]Chester A. Newland, "Press Coverage of the United States Supreme Court,'' 17, *Western Political Quarterly,* p. 15, 1964.

[41]Seth Goldschlager, "The Law and the News Media, A Study of the Ways in Which the News Media Transmit Information About Legal Process With Particular Emphasis on the Reporting of the U.S. Supreme Court Actions and the Concomitant Images of the Legal Process Thereby Communicated,'' (thesis, Yale Law School, 1971), p. 12.

[42]Everette E. Dennis, "Another Look at Press Coverage of the Supreme Court,'' 20, *Villanova Law Review 765 at 797 (1975).*

Part 3

Media Criticism and Analysis

"When we hear news we should wait for the sacrament of confirmation."

—*Voltaire*

Chapter
8

Instruments For
Media Criticism

It was an unusual scene. On a blustery Saturday in March 1974, 400 "working journalists" filed into a small auditorium on the campus of the University of Minnesota in Minneapolis. Inside, the room was crowded beyond capacity as dozens of persons crouched on the floor and pressed against the walls. They had come voluntarily at 8:30 a.m. on their day off and were willing to endure some temporary discomfort to attend the first Midwest Working Journalists' Forum. They had come to criticize, analyze, and monitor media.

The lively meeting, a Midwestern version of the better known A. J. Liebling Counter-Convention, was the culmination of two years of activity by the *Twin Cities Journalism Review*. And, as one young reporter attending the forum put it, "If TCJR hasn't done anything else, it has brought us together." To some the very existence of the meeting was an indication of how deeply the media criticism movement of the late 1960s and early 1970s had cut. "Anytime 400 people come out on a Saturday morning, you've got something going on," one participant said. At the forum reporters, copy editors, radio-television personnel as well as public relations people and students, many of whom had never met before, were discussing and debating news policies, practices, and other issues.

While TCJR did bring together newspeople with common concerns (both in meetings and on its pages) it did much more. In the world of

journalism reviews where survival is no small accomplishment, TCJR appeared at regular two-month intervals since February, 1972 and is still being published as this book is being written. Boldly, the little journal has taken on sports coverage, women's pages, specialized coverage of everything from corrections to public power. It has aired newsroom grievances, questioned media hiring practices, and chided newspapers and broadcast stations for lethargy. At the same time, it provided an outlet for the *Review's* critics, thus encouraging a continuing discussion and debate about journalism.

What was unusual about the March 1974 forum (and the several that have followed it) was that reporters and other media people were meeting at all. For years there was a traditional taboo against reporters openly criticizing the management of their news organizations. Wags used to say, "you take the King's shilling, you fight the King's war." But all that had begun to wear thin by the winter of 1969-70. The birth of the *Chicago Journalism Review* the previous year had given rise to discussions of "reporter power" in cities across America.[1] In Minneapolis and St. Paul, the first stirrings of media-criticism by reporters came during the 1969-70 *Minneapolis Tribune* revolt. As Molly Ivins, one of the revolt's leaders, put it:

I guess it all started with the bitching. Newsmen are notorious bitchers; it is with some a passion, with others an art. For many years bitching headquarters for *Star* and *Trib* staffers had been the

"Little Wagon," a watering spot beloved largely for its proximity to the paper and its martinis. Sometime during 1969, without anyone much noticing at first, the bitching took on new dimensions. It was less frequently spiked with laughter, less given to wry anecdote and increasingly bitter.[2]

The reporters said that the *Tribune,* flagship paper of the Cowles publishing empire which had once been on everybody's "best ten papers" list, was slipping. As Ivins and others have asserted, a paper known for individualism and a reportorial star system was becoming increasingly dehumanized. Its symptoms were a rapid staff turnover and increasingly dull copy. The paper "is boring," said Ivins. "It is boring, dear reader, because the ever-vigilant pencils of copy editors are busily protecting you from anything that smacks of subjectivity."[3] Ivins accused the editors of the *Tribune* of striking out all "lightness, wit, satire, and fun [as well as] all efforts to portray human emotion, human drama and human vulgarity."[4]

The revolt, wrote former *Tribune* reporter Jack Miller who left the paper to found an alternative journal, "was an attempt by a group of workers to gain some control over what they were doing."[5] The disgruntled *Tribune* staffers (a small segment of the staff, calling themselves the Association of Tribune Journalists) met regularly to discuss improving their lot—and the paper's quality. A number of reporters involved, including Ivins, would eventually leave the paper feeling they had contributed something to a subsequent management shakeup, which brought a new editor and promises of better times. As she left town, Ivins could not resist the temptation to take a parting shot at her old employer, writing in a local magazine, "I worked for the *Minneapolis Tribune* for three

years. No, the paper is not hell, just a stone wall drag."[6]

About the same time, down the Mississippi River in St. Paul, staffers of the *Pioneer Press* and *Dispatch,* newspapers owned by the Ridder group, watched the Minneapolis situation with more than passing interest. Reportorial stirrings in St. Paul did not take the form of a revolt, but, said one reporter, "There was a much greater sense of frustration." Salaries on the St. Paul papers, negotiated in a separate Newspaper Guild contract, were lower than those in Minneapolis, and the papers were "mediocre" by comparison. Ironically, though, it was the latter problem—the quality of the papers—that caused a young and aggressive staff to butt heads with management. A group of reporters, copy editors, and others from middle-management, began meeting to discuss ways to increase their own involvement in improving the papers. These grievance meetings in the summer of 1970 were held under the auspices of the Twin Cities Newspaper Guild. Perhaps because the Guild was used for economic bargaining, the meetings often took on the spirit and manner of contract negotiations. "We were never able to make management understand that our real concerns were a better newspaper product," said Carol Lacey, a *Pioneer Press* reporter. Eventually, the group gave way to another, and yet another, which for more than two years looked for outlets for their frustrations. They investigated the possibility of a press council, only to be preempted by a publisher's organization that was instrumental in founding the Minnesota Press Council. Late night gab-fests and planning meetings led to a decision to establish a journalism review. By that time, the previously-mentioned *Chicago Journalism Review* was already more than three years old and reviews were cropping up in a number of other cities.

NEW THRUST FOR
MEDIA CRITICISM

The preceeding example of the *Twin Cities Journalism Review* is reflective of the climate of media criticism at the beginning of the 1970s and profiles one metropolitan area's response. There is nothing particularly unusual about this since it was happening in other areas during an especially visible period for media critics and criticism. This chapter comments briefly on scholarly treatment of some of the major instruments for media criticism: the already-mentioned journalism reviews, press councils, ombudsmen, in-house critics, worker participation committees, and schools of journalism. Some of these activities have links with the scholarly literature we have surveyed in earlier chapters, some do not. But all are concerned with both internal and external problems of the press.

Although many social scientific studies of the press have been concerned with issues of press performance, they rarely form the basis for media criticism. In this chapter, the scholarly accounts to which we look are more often the work of legal scholars, historians, and literary critics. Their methods are somewhat different than those of other scholars whom we have relied upon to this point. The legal scholar, for example, especially if he uses traditional methods of legal scholarship, posits a notion and then seeks out documentary evidence to support it. His pursuit of truth assumes that a later article by a legal scholar might come along and argue with the original hypothesis and with the evidence assembled. Thus, the legal scholar's method is adversarial. (There are also be-

haviorally oriented legal scholars who look for empirical evidence.)[7] By contrast, the historian immerses himself in all the evidence available or starts with a general question and seeks out the most likely sources in an orderly fashion, sifting and sorting all the relevant evidence. The historian reconstructs the past from fragments and in the context of media criticism often compares and contrasts between and among several periods or developments.[8] Of course some historians are also using quantitative data today. The communication scholar, who uses the methods of literary criticism, evaluates media performance against some predetermined standards.

Obviously these varied methods of analysis yield different kinds of data that can be generalized with greater or lesser certainty depending on the depth and scope of evidence. The different instruments of media criticism, whether press councils, ombudsmen, journalism reviews, or articles in popular magazines represent varying approaches to social responsibility of the press. And all have come into being during an extraordinary time for media criticism. In other chapters we have traced the growing public and scholarly awareness of the press and its role in society. Since the mid-1960s, mass communication has quite often been on the public agenda. The instruments of media criticism are for the most part designed to make the press more responsible to the public. Recognizing the growing importance of media and its impact on our daily lives, persons both within and outside the press have sought to reduce their sense of powerlessness. This has been especially important as a larger and larger share of the communications industry is concentrated in a few hands.

Reporters feeling a lack of involvement with

the decision-making apparatus above them have formed worker participation committees, roughly modeled on the example of the great French newspaper, *Le Monde*. Readers and viewers wanting access to the press, a personal voice connected with the corporate bigness of the media, have found a number of avenues for expression. Some have looked to media ombudsmen and reader's representatives to adjudicate their problems. Others have joined or initiated citizen committees to challenge broadcast licenses through the Federal Communications Commission procedures. Still others concerned about the paucity of content with regard to a certain group or subject have sought relief through special interest groups. Thus, there are groups that decry violent content in children's television programming, groups that seek more equitable coverage of Blacks, Chicanos and Native Americans, not to mention the many individuals who seek resolution to particular problems they have with the press.

Even though there has been media criticism since the nineteenth century, there has never before been such a multiplicity of channels for it. As in other chapters, we are not attempting a complete inventory here of what is, but rather we offer commentary on scholarly assessment of the instruments for media criticism. Generally, there has been some fragmented link between these instruments and the notion of social responsibility theory, though many of today's media critics may not recognize it by name.

A SOCIALLY RESPONSIBLE PRESS

For years books on the media in America have made yawning mention of the Commission on Freedom of the Press, also called the Hutchins Commission. The mention was somewhat per-

functory because the Hutchins Commission, a blue-ribbon group of scholars, thinkers, and activists, seemed unconnected with the social reality. The Commission's 1947 report made noble pronouncements about the press and suggested how it might be improved. Then they disbanded. Of course, the Commission and its findings, obscure by any account, were remembered in journalism schools and in books on the media, but their impact seemed small indeed. Remembered mainly for its specific recommendations for the public, government, and the press, much less was said about the intellectual impact of the Commission. Much of that impact would not be seen until years later. Indeed, a 1967 article reviewing the Commission's recommendations after twenty years could report only mixed success.[9] As late as 1967, many of the Commission's findings and recommendations still seemed ivory-towerish. The Commission wanted the press to improve itself, to become more accountable and thus to remain free. Some commission members worried that the forces of totalitarianism might swallow up a free press unless it was at the same time responsible. The press, the Commission reasoned, must be both free and responsible.

Largely forgotten by those who look back on the Commission's work are the several scholarly works and position papers that the group initiated. Some were social scientific assessments of media problems and issues, others were philosophical treatises. Among them was one of the most powerful and intellectually stimulating books ever written about the American news media: William Ernest Hocking's *Freedom of the Press*. Hocking, an internationally acclaimed philosopher aware of the technological and economic changes in the press, declared that the work of the press should be clothed with a public interest. At the same time, he warned that:

> protection of the freedom of the issuer is no longer sufficient to protect automatically either the consumer or the community. The general policy of laissez faire in this field must be reconsidered.[10]

With careful logic and powerful persuasion, Hocking took on the idea of a libertarian press operating freely in the marketplace of ideas without any protections or restraints. Modern times, he reasoned, had caught up with Milton's noble admonition from *Aeropagitica* that had truth winning over falsehood in an open marketplace. While the Commission's recommendations were by no means a direct operationalization of Hocking's views, his basic notions about social responsibility were reflected there. What did the Commission propose be done? Three arenas for action were identified:

Recommendations for the Government

1. ...that constitutional guarantees of the freedom of the press be recognized as including the radio and motion pictures.
2. ...that government facilitate new ventures in the communications industry, that it foster the introduction of new techniques, that it maintain competition among large units through the antitrust laws, but that those laws be sparingly used to break up such units, and that, where concentration is necessary in communications, the government endeavor to see to it that the public gets the benefit of such concentration.
3. ...as an alternative to the present remedy for libel, we recommend legislation by which the injured party might obtain a retraction or a restatement of the facts by the offender or an opportunity to reply.
4. ...the repeal of legislation prohibiting expressions in favor of revolutionary changes in our institutions where there is no clear and present danger that violence will result from the expressions.

5. ...that the government, through the media of mass communication, inform the public of the facts with respect to its policies and of the purposes underlying those policies and that, to the extent that private agencies of mass communication are unable or unwilling to supply such media to the government, the government may itself employ media of its own.

Recommendations for the Press

1. ...that the agencies of mass communication accept the responsibilities of common carriers of information and discussion.
2. ...that the agencies of mass communication assume the responsibility of financing new, experimental activities in their fields.
3. ...that the members of the press engage in vigorous mutual cirticism.
4. ...that the press use every means that can be devised to increase the competence, independence, and effectiveness of its staff.
5. ...that the radio industry take control of its programs and treat advertising as it is treated in the best newspapers.

Recommendations for the Public

1. ...that nonprofit institutions help supply variety, quantity, and quality of press service required by the American people.
2. ...the creation of academic-professional centers of advanced study, research, and publication in the field of communications. We recommend further that existing schools of journalism exploit the total resources of their universities to the end that their students may obtain the broadest and most liberal training.
3. ...the establishment of a new and independent agency to appraise and report annually upon the performance of the press.[11]

In calling for "a truthful, comprehensive, and intelligent account of the day's events in a context that gives them meaning," the Commission also sought:

—a forum for the exchange of comment and criticism;

—a representative picture of the constituent groups in society;

—the presentation and clarification of the goals and values of society, and

—full access to the day's intelligence.

While seemingly innocuous on the surface, the standards set down by the Commission were high and represented a sharp break with traditional practices. For example, the notion of a "representative picture" of the constituent groups of society has been a battleground for most of the attacks by special groups seeking better coverage in the press. This is a conflict that still rages, though the groups and interests may change.

Perhaps even more important than the idealistic nature of the recommendations were the way that they departed profoundly from the libertarian theory of the press. Theodore Peterson explains:

1. The negative freedom of libertarian theory is inadequate to modern society. (The view of the press to gain free access to information reflects this view.)
2. Freedom carries with it responsibility. (The various media codes of performance reflect this view.)
3. Man is not a wholly rational creature; he is not so much irrational as lethargic, and his reluctance to use his reason makes him ready prey for special pleaders. (The various codes except the Canons [of journalism of the American Society of Newspaper Editors] reflect this view. And so does the great bulk of advertising that all of the media carry.)[12]

Peterson eloquently articulated a theory of social responsibility building on Hocking's work in the important 1956 book, *Four Theories of the Press,* coauthored with Fred Siebert and Wilbur Schramm. The media, Peterson said, must assume the obligation of social responsibility, and if they do not someone else, whether forces of the public and private sector must see to it that they do. What the social responsibility theory did was recognize the existing state of the press and propose solutions for improvement. The old libertarian model of a free marketplace simply didn't work. In a society where the ability to publish a newspaper or develop a telecast does not belong to every citizen, other means of access must be devised.

A number of scholars have extended the Peterson position, elaborating, expanding, and developing it along different lines. Among them are: Jerome Barron's *Freedom of the Press for Whom?,* which proposes a theory of access to the press for the citizenry; Benno C. Schmidt's *Freedom of the Press vs. Public Access,* which treats the dual strains of access and responsibility without compromising freedom. Finally, John Merrill's *The Imperative of Freedom* proposes a philosophy of journalistic autonomy.

PRESS COUNCILS

With the Hutchins Commission's specific recommendation for a media council (public recommendation, No. 3), one might have anticipated more rapid implementation of such a notion. But it was not to be. Leading communication scholars like J. Edward Gerald and Donald Brown provided a scholarly base and argued for such bodies, especially in light of the highly-successful British Press Council, but it was not until the late 1960s, that the strains of the press council movement saw a transition from knowledge to action. With the media under attack by government and a general recognition that there was little public support for the press as an institution, media entrepreneurs were more receptive to the press council idea. There had been local media councils in the United States before the late 1960s, usually the creation of a single publisher, but they had no wide currency or support.

The happy coincidence of scholarly interest, backed by dollars led to the development of local press councils after 1967. In that year Ben Bagdikian, a respected newspaperman and critic, became president of the Mellett Fund for a Free and Responsible Press, a small foundation that had only $40,000 to carry out the donor's bequest to "encourage responsible press performance without infringing on First Amendment freedoms,"[13] writes William L. Rivers. Bagdikian looked for a worthy project for the available funds and he:

> suggested that the money be used to support university researchers in making press council experiments. The result was that six councils were established. Four of them were newspaper councils (one in California, one in Oregon, and two in Illinois). Another council was established in Seattle and still another in St. Louis, involving broadcasters as well as publishers. The Seattle and St. Louis councils brought the newsmen together with spokesmen for the black community in each city.[14]

The results of some of these experiments are chronicled in a doctoral dissertation by William Blankenberg and in a book by Rivers and three co-authors, *Backtalk, Press Councils in America*. (The Seattle Council is not included.) The concept of these and other subsequent press councils was to provide a channel for citizen and group complaints against the press outside of the legal system. Serious minded citizens working with media personnel heard the complaints and suggestions and tried to seek equitable resolutions. Later a press council was set up in Honolulu after a local dispute between news personnel and the mayor. Quieter forces were at work when the Minnesota Press Council got

underway in 1971. Some of those forces are mentioned at the outset of this chapter. The Minnesota Council, made up of a blue-ribbon panel of the public and media members, would produce a number of important determinations and also be the stimulus for research on press councils. It was the first statewide press council.

In 1971, another foundation entered the picture. The Twentieth Century Fund of New York, concerned about attacks on the news media and the lack of public access, formed a task force to study the feasibility of a national news council. The task force made a positive recommendation and the Council was set up in 1973. A description of the work of the task force and its recommendations is found in a useful report, *A Free and Responsive Press*, published by the Twentieth Century Fund Task Force. The report has a detailed description of some of the local and state press councils as well.

The National News Council came into being in August 1973 with the avowed purpose of serving "the public interest in preserving freedom of communication and advancing fair reporting of news."[15] In spite of major opposition from the *New York Times*, which saw the council as an intrusion to freedom of the press, the Council acted on fifty-nine complaints during its first two years of operations. A summary of those complaints is found in another useful publication, *In The Public Interest, A Report of the National News Council, 1973-75*. Similarly, the Minnesota Press Council has published a compilation, *Determinations by the Council*, covering the first three years of its operation. How well did the councils fair? The assessments are mixed. Stanley H. Fuld, chairman of the national council, expressed a sense of optimism in his report and went on to say,

> For two years the Council's members, advisers and staff have been examining with concern and with care complaints about the accuracy and fairness, on the part of national news organizations, of news read, seen, or heard by the American people. It has initiated studies, and has issued reports, concerning problems involved in the maintenance of a free flow of information in a nation built on a foundation of freedom.[16]

If Justice Fuld seemed somewhat satisfied, press critic David Rubin was not. Writing in (MORE), Rubin chided the council and decried its weakness and lack of activity. Measured against an ideal, the council may have fallen short, but to some its very existence was cause for rejoicing. Rubin, however, sets a higher standard and finds the National Media Council in a terrible dilemma:

> The truth is, that the press and public in the United States are not ready for a press council and one cannot survive if it gets too tough with the media, yet it won't survive if it doesn't.[17]

Facing opposition from the *New York Times,* having trouble raising money and getting major figures to serve on it, the council obviously may be in some difficulty.

Fred J. Johnson in two studies of the Minnesota Press Council found more cause for optimism. In one of its determinations, the Minnesota council sharply criticized publishers of weekly newspapers for printing a press release without identifying its source. Johnson administered a questionnaire to the twenty-six publishers who were criticized. His purpose: to find out how the publishers felt about the council's decision and whether they had changed their policies for handling press releases. A strong majority responded that they would try to avoid the practice of not identifying press releases in the future and Johnson concluded that "the sur-

vey data strongly indicate that the Press Council in this situation has functioned effectively in terms of improving journalistic standards."[18]

In another study, Johnson sought to learn how citizens who had taken complaints to the council felt about the council's work. The majority of respondents approved of press councils in general and of the Minnesota Council in particular. Even citizens who had lost their complaints expressed confidence in the fairness and equity of the council. Indeed, Johnson found that the respondents to his survey had more confidence in the Council than they did in the press generally.[19]

One scholar who observed press councils in the Mellett Fund experiments commented that councils have three important effects:

1. A council tends to lead news executives to a greater awareness of the need for responsible press performance.
2. A council serves a valuable public relations function. It enables news executives to explain newspaper policy and practice to their audiences and at the same time allows citizens to make their needs known.
3. The presence of a council increases the esteem and understanding of the news media in the eyes of council members and other citizens.[20]

Generalizing about press councils is impossible. Some were tiny local groups in small communities where there was strong media support, others were metropolitan-wide or statewide in their concerns. And, of course, the National News Council had nationally oriented media as its charge. Much more research on press councils is needed and it might be useful to compare the fledgling American councils with well-established councils in other nations around the world. As French media critic Claude-Jean Bertrand has observed, "virtually every developed nation in the world—and some that are not—have press councils."[21] The literature about press council performance is sparse but growing and promises to be an intriguing arena for investigation.

JOURNALISM REVIEWS

If the literature of press councils is limited, scholarly discussion of journalism reviews is even more lacking. The reason: almost as soon as journalism reviews began with a bang in Chicago in 1968, they started to die. The movement, which once claimed between fifteen and twenty reviews, saw a sharp decline in the mid-1970s. By 1977 only a few of the stronger reviews remained. As we mentioned earlier in this chapter, among journalism reviews survival was no small accomplishment.

Treatment of the reviews by scholars has been mostly limited to historical and critical commentary. As the reviews began publication, their birth was often chronicled by the well-established academic publication, *Columbia Journalism Review,* which provided considerable support and encouragement. (The journalism reviews as we are considering them here were mostly the publications of working journalists commenting on media performance in their cities or states. Thus the traditional trade publications and earlier academic endeavors are not included here.)

James Aronson in his perceptive and highly critical book, *Deadline for the Media,* traced the development of journalism reviews in the context of media criticism, generally. With mention of reviews in Chicago, Denver, St. Louis, Southern California, Hawaii and several other locations, Aronson observed:

> It may be that the reviews will not become permanent because some of their organizers actually regard them as temporary—and this in itself sets limits to their effectiveness. With few exceptions,

the reviews are reformist, not radical. All of those involved see with varying degrees of clarity the faults and evils of the media; but for most of them the task, as they see it, is to force changes within the media to make them more honest and serviceable, and therefore less degrading, places to work. To be sure, they probably see themselves as rebels, but rebels within the cause—the cause being the establishment of journalism itself.[22]

The author and William L. Rivers studied journalism reviews in the context of "dissatisfaction with existing standards and styles" in the press in *Other Voices: The New Journalism in America.* Here the approach was historical with capsule histories of six major journalism reviews and an indication of their content. We concluded in this 1974 account:

> Much of the future of the journalism reviews is tied directly to adaptation. Will the executives listen to their unhappy reporters and deskmen? Many executives are, though grudgingly, and it may be that relatively few reviews will continue. Still, it is possible that those who devote themselves to more than intramural complaining, taking up broader questions, will gain readers because of the widening public interest in the processes of mass communication.[23]

At this writing there is no definitive study tracing the rise and fall of the journalism reviews, although the previously mentioned Bertrand was hard at work on one. However, several trends and conditions can be observed. First, the journalism review movement blossomed at about the time that an economic recession hit American business. Newspapers (less so broadcast stations) tightened their belts, spent less on the editorial product. With fewer jobs and a substantial pool of journalistic man (and woman) power, the strident voices of the early journalism reviews were muted. And, concurrently, the American Newspaper Guild expressed interest in worker participation committees that went a long way toward answering some of the complaints of reporters who saw the reviews as a vehicle for internal improvement.

Secondly, it can be said that the journalism review was a passing phase in media criticism. Many critics have not been silenced but are finding broader markets for their commentary. General and specialized magazines are publishing larger and larger quantities of media criticism and analysis. Even newspapers are running columns of media criticism. Especially active in media criticism have been new weeklies and other alternative and advocacy publications. Publications like the *Village Voice* have a regular media critic. Magazines like *Harper's, The Atlantic, New York,* and others publish a good deal of media criticism in the course of a year.

Thirdly, the structure and operational style of many journalism reviews doomed them to failure. They were the product of parttime writers and editors who had other obligations that often seemed more pressing. They had limited funding and an editorial content unlikely to win favor with many advertisers. Staffs were unstable and in few instances were there forces that would perpetuate the publication. The publications required a certain amount of passion and a considerable amount of energy for sustained operations. In few instances were there persons willing to assume this on a permanent basis with so little reward and remuneration.

Finally, of those that did survive, there was some built-in continuity. *The Twin Cities Journalism Review,* for example, was governed by a board and staff of editors who changed places each year. There was always some continuity in personnel, but as long as editorial chores were shifted around to several different persons, making no long-term demands on any of them,

success was assured. On the economic front, TCJR found ready funding in its annual conferences and managed to keep its expenses down. Other reviews were the products of journalism students or journalism schools. Here institutional stability played a role in keeping the journalism review alive. Others, like New York's flashy (*MORE*) were private businesses from the start and sought a larger newsstand sale.

It may be that study of media reviews in the future will conclude that they were not an end in themselves, but a stimulus for other developments in media criticism. However, this does not discount their importance as vehicles for expression, mostly by journalists, which is likely to be regarded as a significant development in the history of American journalism, or what James Aronson has called, "the revolt of the slaves."

WORKER PARTICIPATION COMMITTEES

The journalism reviews were one vehicle for the "reporter power" movement that took root in the late 1960s and early 1970s. If the journalism reviews were "a sign of growing professionalism—a willingness to confront shortcomings in media performance,"[24] it was also a forum for the discussion of newspaper (and broadcast) management. In fact one journalism review that fizzled channeled itself into management concerns exclusively and the reporters decided that working within the organization itself had more utility. This happened at the *Kansas City Star* where a shortlived William Rockhill Nelson Society *Newsletter* chose the other internal route.[25] Concurrent with the "reporter power" movement that was mostly talk came interest in worker participation in management. Worker participation, which grows out of labor unions in industrial democracies, is also called industrial democracy and involves worker representation on boards of directors and shared decision making in the appointment of supervisers, and so forth. As John Roach wrote in *Worker Participation: New Voices in Management:* "worker participation emerges in any given situation as a blend of overlapping socio-political, economic and labor-management relationships."[26]

A notable success in worker participation in the communications industry had occurred in Paris at *Le Monde*. At the prestigious French newspaper working journalists exercise editorial control of the paper through a program of shared management. In the words of a *Le Monde* editor, the journalist involvement in the management of the paper ended "magisterial journalism where editorial arrangements are determined by fiat."[27] The result said Jean Schwoebel was the elevation of journalist's status and a marked improvement in the newspaper. As a result of worker participation, Schwoebel said, *Le Monde* became "efficient, prestigious and exceedingly profitable."[28]

Worker participation committees in various forms have been established in the United States at the *Kansas Star and Times, Milwaukee Journal and Sentinel, Denver Post, Providence Journal and Bulletin,* and *Minneapolis Star and Tribune*. What do the workers want? Edwin Diamond, writing in *Columbia Journalism Review,* answers, "the new benefits that journalists have begun to seek go far beyond the usual guild bargaining points of wages and hours. The new grievances involve, first of all, moral—almost theological concerns."[29]

The worker participation committee at the *Minneapolis Star and Tribune* is especially significant according to John Carmichael, executive secretary of the Twin Cities Newspaper Guild, who explains that his is the only Guild local that has "worker participation" written into its contract. Ola Shobowale in a study of the Minneapolis example points up some of its features:

> In effect, the appointment of newsroom supervisors—on a joint Guild-Management consultative basis—is a tribute to a double coincidence of needs of the Guild and staffers. On the one hand, the demand of newsroom staffers was to have an effective voice in shaping the "product"—possibly through editorial control of the newsroom. The appointments of key newsroom supervisors through a Guild-Management consultation appears to be a step in that direction. On the other hand, the Guild might have gained an extra chip—a much needed one at a time in its bargaining unit through the inclusion of newsroom supervisors amongst its ranks.[30]

Shobowale reported that there were flaws in the Minneapolis experiment, but that it had won support of both union and management spokesmen. Studies of participatory efforts in other cities will lead to a better understanding of this new vehicle for internal press criticism and discussion.

OMBUDSMEN

Americans borrowed the press council idea mainly from Britain (although other countries had them) and the ombudsman idea from Sweden, where ombudsmen have been expediters and problem solvers in the government for sometime. In 1969, as Sweden reorganized its press council it established the office of General Public's Press Ombudsman "to serve as a commissioner of grievances and to prosecute violations of press ethics."[31]

The idea attracted some attention in the United States but with typically American adaptations. In the U.S., the ombudsman was established as a position in the private sector on individual newspapers. Actually, the first American newspaper ombudsman predated the Swedish press council reorganization, though the concept was thoroughly Swedish. In 1967, the *Louisville Courier-Journal* appointed an ombudsman as a vehicle for reader complaints. The *Washington Post* followed shortly thereon. Other newspapers following on an old example from American journalism (the *New York World* did it in 1913) established Bureaus of Accuracy and Fair Play to deal with reader inquiries and complaints. Such papers as the *Minneapolis Star and Tribune* and the *St. Petersburg Times* have such operations.

How widespread is the ombudsman idea? In a 1973 study for the American Newspaper Publishers Association Research Center, Keith P. Sanders tried to determine what systems of accountability to readers and news sources were being employed by daily newspapers in the United States.

In a sample that included 200 newspapers (and 135 responses) spanning nine geographic regions of the country, Sanders found:

> Most of the daily newspapers in the United States are doing something to be accountable to their readers. Seventy newspapers, or about 52% of those studied, have a fairly formal system developed. Another 34 have fairly informal procedures of dealing with the matter of accountability. Only 31 (23%) of the 135 editors responding said they had no system of accountability.[32]

Breakdowns from the Sanders figures are seen in Table 8.1. At the time of the study only twelve newspapers had ombudsmen, but sev-

TABLE 8.1
ACCOUNTABILITY SYSTEMS
CATEGORIZED BY NEWSPAPER CIRCULATION

Circulation:	100,000+ N=38	50,000-99,999 N=30	20,000-49,999 N=39	Up to 20,000 N=28	Total N=135
System:					
Ombudsman	8(21%)	2 (7%)	1 (3%)	1 (4%)	12 (9%)
Press Council	0	0	1 (3%)	3(11%)	4 (3%)
Advisory Board	3 (8%)	1 (3%)	4(10%)	4(14%)	12 (9%)
Accuracy Forms Sent to Sources	7(18%)	5(17%)	3 (8%)	3(11%)	18(13%)
Accuracy Forms Published in Paper	3 (8%)	1 (3%)	0	1 (4%)	5 (4%)
Standing Head for corrections	9(24%)	3(10%)	2 (5%)	3(11%)	17(13%)
"Other" System	11(29%)	13(40%)	25(64%)	16(56%)	65(48%)
No Formal System	7(18%)	6(20%)	15(38%)	3(11%)	31(23%)

Several newspapers have more than one system of accountability. Percentages are based on the number of newspapers responding within the circulation category. For example, eight newspapers of the 38, or 21 per cent, responding in the largest circulation category indicate the use of an ombudsman program.

Source: *News Research for Better Newspapers,* Vol. 7, edited by Galen Rarick, ANPA Foundation, 1975.

eral others were planning to initiate such a program. Sanders found that "those who have implemented some kind of accountability system are generally pleased with the results although they see the need for improvements."[33]

A 1976 study carried out by the Associated Press Managing Editors' Reader Relations Committee found some slight gains over Sander's 1973 figures, but a much expanded concept of the ombudsman. While only fifteen papers (out of 105 surveyed) said they had a fulltime person working in an ombudsman capacity, thirty-five others said they had found ways to carry out much of this function by use of regular staff. The ombudsman's task was both external (handling reader problem) and internal (working with staff on improvement of the product.) Management reaction to the ombudsman—"mostly excellent," says a report by Thomas W. Jobson of the *Ashbury Park* (N.J.) *Press,* who summarized the APME findings:

> The reaction of the public has also been good in most cases. Staff reaction is another thing; it was reported excellent on three papers whereas on the others it was listed as fair to good. This bears out what many in the profession know about reporters and editors involved in production—some of them are sensitive souls, adverse to criticism, all too often reluctant to admit mistakes. In all instances the press critic or ombudsman reported that management has been supportive of his work. One put it this way, "There is not agreement with all my views, but I am free to express them."[34]

As the study suggests, ombudsmen not only handle internal complaints and take reader's suggestions, but quite often write regular columns that give public exposure to their work. A column that has been syndicated nationally from this group is Charles Seib's from the *Washington Post.*

Not all the ombudsman experiences have been quite as pleasant as those reported in the APME survey. A celebrated resignation was that of Ben Bagdikian who served as the *Washington Post* ombudsman for a year. There was "disagreement with other members of management on the role and function of the in-house obudsman. Bagdikian found that handling reader complaints interfered with the function of general critic,"[35] reports Lee Brown in a useful survey of press criticism, *The Reluctant Reformation: On Criticizing the Press in America.* Bagdikian's complaints amounted to a prescription for the ombudsman position:

1. That the *Post's* press critic be hired for a short-term, renewable contract.
2. That the critic not be burdened with handling reader complaints.
3. That the critic work outside the newsroom so as to avoid the appearance of undercutting operating editors.
4. That assessments of the work of staff members be shown to those involved, with a right of reply offered.
5. That the critic have space guaranteed in the paper, so as to avoid the charge that the paper prints only what it agrees with.
6. That the critic be a person whose standards are in fundamental agreement with the newspaper's traditions.[36]

When one thinks about these complaints in the context of our discussion of organizational problems within the press (presented in an earlier chapter), the need for research on criticism as it fits into the journalistic organization is evident. The ombudsman role is new enough that such research has not yet appeared.

SCHOOLS OF JOURNALISM

It is particularly difficult to sort out the media criticism work of schools and departments of journalism for much of it is subtle, presented in the context of teaching with little fanfare. And much of what has been discussed in this chapter already has had a journalism education link. Several journalism reviews have had frequent contact with journalism schools and some have actually been founded by them. The same is true with press councils. The community press council experiments were done in cooperation with educators, indeed, they would have not existed at all if it had not been for the organizational and administrative efforts of the educators. In other instances, the intellectual leadership of an authority on press councils helped get a statewide council started. And interestingly enough, the same man's former Ph.D. student started a major metropolitan press council.

Additionally, there are courses on press ethics in many schools, and of course, journalism educators are the main source of books on and about journalism. Many of these books are press criticism. There is a considerable amount of literature by journalism educators exhorting each other to provide more criticism of the press, but it is doubted that this was very effectively carried out. The schools are also hiring halls for the media, and journalism administrators have as one of their functions the maintenance of good relations with the state press. Ben Bagdikian once suggested a reciprocal agreement among the schools of journalism that would have schools in Iowa criticizing the press of Kansas and visa versa. This, he reasoned, would cut down on any retaliation the legislatures of the two states might direct toward the schools.[37]

In spite of timidity, in recent years some ambitious efforts by schools of journalism have provided solid criticism of the media. William L. Rivers and David Rubin of Stanford produced a book-length critical analysis: *A Region's Press: Newspapers in the San Francisco Bay Area,* and several educators were involved in newsman Loren Ghiglione's *New England Daily Newspaper Survey,* another ambitious project.

In a 1974 survey, Herbert Strentz and several coauthors examined criticism of the news media in journalism education. Their study, a detailed summary of activity, concluded thusly:

> The self-protective syndrome, in vogue for so many years, has given way to a fuller understanding of what press responsibility and professionalism imply. In the absence of a public-based media lobby and in the interest of preventing government intervention, journalism educators are fashioning a role as intermediaries between the media and their publics and the media and government. The role, so far, is largely undefined but beginning to take shape.[38]

Schools of journalism are, of course, centers for various conferences and meetings attended by media personnel. Similarly, they are sponsors and stimuli for various professional groups, including student and professional chapters of the Society of Professional Journalists (Sigma Delta Chi) and Women in Communications (formerly Theta Sigma Phi). While acknowledging that journalism education has been somewhat slow to involve itself fully in media criticism, David Anderson and Loren Ghiglione write about its potential:

> Journalism schools' cooperative efforts with the press and its organizations may have greater potential for reforming newspapers than more glamorous forms of media criticism.[39]

SUMMARY AND CONCLUSION

In this chapter our attention has turned to the instruments and channels for media criticism in

America. After a brief case study of a journalism review, we examine the factors that have led to a new thrust for media criticism since the late 1960s. Consideration is also given to philosophical concerns about a responsible press that were stimulated by the Hutchins Commission Report. Finally, we examine the instruments of media criticism themselves, including press councils, journalism reviews, worker participation committees, ombudsmen, and schools of journalism.

Any cataloging of the various instruments of media criticism and their current status suggests a surge of activity unparalleled in earlier times. There is simply more of it and in different forms. Many ideas and proposals that have been in evidence for years are finally being implemented. Certainly this is true with press councils, although journalism reviews were an unexpected bonus for media critics and the public. Media criticism, regardless of the form it takes or the instruments it uses, is greater today than ever before. But all this may be deceptive because the form may change and may make subtle inroads into unexpected quarters. This is already happening in the general circulation and specialized magazines. Thus researchers who want to study the effects of such criticism may have to cast a wider eye to make certain they find it all. A growing number of academic studies, especially doctoral dissertations and master theses, are expanding the literature of media criticism, but much more needs to be done before it will be possible to have a full understanding and view of its range and scope.

A word of caution: as dramatic as new developments in media criticism have been (journalism reviews, press councils and ombudsmen, for example) where none existed a few years ago, it must be remembered that these instruments affect only a small part of the American press. They are imperfect instruments in their earliest stages of development, and it must be remembered that most Americans have never heard of any of them. This does not undermine their importance and potential impact however.

Notes

[1] For a fuller discussion of the TCJR example and its context *see,* Everette E. Dennis, ''Monitoring Media in the Land of Sky Blue Waters: The Twin Cities Journalism Review,'' *Grassroots Editor,* Sept.-Oct. 1974, p. 16.

[2] Molly Ivins, ''The Minneapolis Tribune is a Stone Wall Drag,'' *Twin Citian,* Aug. 1970, p. 14.

[3] Ibid., p. 18.

[4] Ibid.

[5] Jack Miller, ''1969-70 Trib Revolt: It Wasn't Much Fun While It Lasted,'' *Twin Cities Journalism Review,* July 1972, p. 19.

[6] Ivins, ''the Minneapolis Tribune is a Stone Wall Drag.''

[7] Donald M. Gillmor and Everette E. Dennis, ''Legal Research and Judicial Communication,'' in *Political Communication, Issues and Strategies for Research,* ed. Steven H. Chaffee (Beverly Hills: Sage Publications, 1975), pp. 283-306.

[8] *See* generally, John D. Stevens, ''Some Decision Points in the Historical Research Process,'' in *Studies in Journalism and Communications, Decision Points in Mass Communications Research: Survey, Content Analysis, Historical and Experimental Methods,* ed. Donald L. Shaw (Chapel Hill, N.C.: School of Journalism, University of North Carolina): *see also* Stevens, ''Historical Research on Political Communication,'' in Chaffee, *Political Communication.*

[9] ''Hutchins Report, A Twenty Year View,'' *Columbia Journalism Review,* Summer 1967, special issue.

[10] William Ernest Hocking, *Freedom of the Press: A Framework of Principle* (Chicago: University of Chicago Press, 1947), p. 164.

[11] *See* generally, Commission on Freedom of the Press, *A Free and Responsible Press* (Chicago: University of Chicago Press, 1947).

[12] Theodore Peterson, ''Social Responsibility— Theory and Practice,'' in *The Responsibility of the Press,* ed. Gerald Gross (New York: Simon & Schuster, 1966), p. 44.

[13] William L. Rivers, William B. Blankenburg, Kenneth Starck, and Earl Reeves, *Backtalk: Press Councils in America* (San Francisco: Canfield Press, 1972), p. 14.

[14] Ibid.

[15] The National News Council, *In the Public Interest, A Report by the National News Council, 1973-75,* p. 1.

[16] Ibid.

[17] David Rubin, ''Who's Afraid of the NNC?,'' (MORE), March 1976, p. 8.

[18] Frederic J. Johnson, ''The Minnesota Press Council: How is it Working?,'' (master's paper, University of Minnesota, Winter 1976), p. 27.

[19] Frederic J. Johnson, ''The Minnesota Press Council: A Study of Its Effectiveness,'' (master's paper, University of Minnesota, Spring 1976).

[20] Donald Brignolo, quoted in Rivers, *Backtalk,* pp. 115-16.

[21] Comments at Minnesota Press Council, Sept. 8, 1976.

[22] James Aronson, *Deadline for the Media, Today's Challenges to Press TV and Radio* (Indianapolis: Bobbs-Merrill, 1972) p. 111.

[23] Everette E. Dennis and William L. Rivers, *Other Voices: The New Journalism in America* (San Francisco: Canfield Press, 1974), p. 206.

[24] Marty Coren, ''The Perils of Publishing Journalism Reviews,'' *Columbia Journalism Review,* Nov.-Dec. 1972, p. 43.

[25] Rivers, et al, *Backtalk,* pp. 94-95.

[26] John M. Roach, *Worker Participation: New Voices in Management* (New York: The Conference Board, 1973), p. 35.

[27] Jean Schwoebel, ''The Miracle Le Monde Wrought,'' *Columbia Journalism Review,* Summer 1970, p. 13.

[28] Ibid.

[29] Edwin Diamond, ''Reporter Power Takes Root,'' *Columbia Journalism Review,* Summer 1970, p. 13.

[30] Ola Shobowale, ''Worker Participation in

Newspaper Management, Journalists' Quest for Professionalism,'' (Paper, University of Minnesota, School of Journalism and Mass Communication, Winter 1976), pp. 27-28.

[31] Lee Brown, *The Reluctant Reformation, On Criticizing the Press in America* (New York: David McKay, 1974), p. 87.

[32] Keith P. Sanders, ''What Are Daily Newspapers Doing to Be Responsive to Readers' Criticisms?, A Survey of U.S. Daily Newspaper Accountability Systems,'' in *News Research for Better Newspapers,* ed. Galen Rarick ANPA Foundation (Washington, D.C., 1975), p. 167.

[33] Ibid.

[34] Thomas W. Jobson, summary of Associated Press Managing Editors report, unpublished notes presented at Washington Journalism Center program on media criticism, 1976.

[35] Schwoebel, ''Reporter Power,'' p. 52.

[36] Supra. Schwoebel, ''Reporter Power,'' pp. 52-53.

[37] Ben H. Bagdikian, ''The Hutchins Commission Revisited,'' (Panel discussion at Association for Education in Journalism meeting, Lawrence, Kansas, 1968).

[38] Herbert Strentz, Kenneth Starck, David L. Anderson and Loren Ghiglione, ''The Critical Factor: Criticism of the News Media in Journalism Education,'' *Journalism Monographs,* Feb. 1974, p. 22.

[39] Ibid., p. 32.

"A great newspaper is a public service institution. It occupies a position in public life fully as important as the school system or the church or the organs of government. It is entitled to criticism and subject to criticism as they are. The value of such criticism is directly proportionate to the steadiness with which the ultimate end of a better news system is clearly and dispassionately kept in mind."
—Walter Lippmann and Charles Merz
in The New Republic *(1920)*

Chapter 9

The Media Critics

There was considerable satisfaction for James Aronson that spring day in 1975 when he left his handsome reconverted rowhouse in New York's East Village for the trip uptown to the Columbia University School of Journalism. Honored with one of Columbia's prestigious alumni awards, Aronson could smile knowingly and recall a time when establishment journalism in America regarded him more as a pariah than an honored critic.

A radical journalist who survived McCarthyism and the Cold War, Aronson later directed his considerable energies and critical powers to a continuing and caustic examination of the news media. Once an employee of the *New York Times,* Aronson had years before forsaken conventional journalism to edit the radical *National Guardian.* His paper's primary obligation, he said, was to "fix its attention not on the merits or demerits of revolution abroad but on the enemy of revolution at home."[1] Among his targets: the monopoly press, which he saw as tied closer to the raw interests of capitalism than to any concept of the public interest. As Aronson wrote in his book *Packaging the News:*

> For these proprietors, newspapers are no longer entities in themselves, with individual character, courage, and a dedication to the public service, but simply properties to be listed among their holdings along with real estate, fertilizer, electronics, and aerospace rocketry. . . . The economic centralization of newspapers, along with the rest of industry, is a disastrous departure from what

was once known in town hall forums as the free exchange of ideas in the marketplace of public opinion.[2]

Not only is the press the creature of big business, said Aronson, but it is also a voluntary arm of the government. In a 1970 book, *The Press and the Cold War,* he accused the U.S. press of being a propagandist for Washington foreign policy.

In an era when criticism was muted, Aronson's indictments of the press were heard mostly in the leftist press, but by 1970 the climate of criticism was such that the former alternative editor's well-documented and passionate commentary got wider exposure. He began editing a civil liberties journal, *Rights,* had a regular column in the *Antioch Review,* and published three books of press criticism in rapid succession. In addition, he began teaching at the experimental New School for Social Research and was appointed to the faculty at Hunter College. The Columbia award in 1975 not only provided personal recognition for Aronson, but it also signified a new respectability for press criticism.

And, press criticism has not always been respectable. In 1919 when Upton Sinclair wrote his book *The Brass Check* about a cowardly and servile press he had to publish it himself. Indeed, press criticism had always been more the exception than the rule. Much of the media criticism of earlier years had been done in the context of competition. The newspaper wars in

New York during the nineteenth century, for example, stirred many columns of continuous coverage of media and media problems. In a more humorous vein, the leading comic weeklies of the 1880s and 1890s, *Puck* and *Judge,* often depicted the top editors and publishers of the day in ridiculous situations. At times, the battles between and among media and media folk were much more savage than they are today.

Not more than a few blocks from where James Aronson writes today, *The Masses,* a socialist magazine, led a feisty battle during the second decade of the twentieth century. One of *The Masses'* targets was the Associated Press. Denouncing AP's coverage of a celebrated coal strike in West Virginia in 1913, the magazine charged that AP had withheld and distorted the news. Max Eastman, the magazine's editor called the AP "the worst monopoly," and wrote that:

> So long as the substance of current history continues to be held in cold storage, adulterated, colored with poisonous intentions, and sold to the highest bidder to suit his private purpose, there is small hope that even the free and the intelligent will take the side of justice in the struggle that is before us.[3]

Along with Eastman's stinging article was a cartoon by Art Young that showed a man personifying the Associated Press kneeling over a reservoir in which the water was labelled, "the news." Into the water the AP poured the dark contents of bottles labelled, "lies, suppressed facts, prejudice, slander and hatred of labor organization." The AP, smarting from the scathing criticism, asked the government for an indictment against *The Masses* on charges of criminal libel. A grand jury obliged, but indictments were dropped about a year later and the defendants' bail was returned. As the legal maneuvering dragged on, a rally for Eastman and Young drew 2,500 people to the Cooper Union where prominent lawyers, clergymen and labor leaders spoke in their support. Among the speakers that night was Lincoln Steffens, the muckraking journalist.

The AP's harsh response to their criticism did not deter the editors of *The Masses* who continued to take on the press during the life of the magazine (1911-1918).

PERSPECTIVES ON PRESS CRITICISM

While much of the early press criticism was really a kind of "situation ethics" response to a particular news event or treatment, some was more far-reaching. For example, the press lords and the general pattern of the economics of the press was much criticized. Oswald Garrison Villard, the respected editor of *The Nation,* expressed deep concerns about the economic concentration of the press:

> Undoubtedly the newspaper chain is as much a response to an economic urge or tide as the recent grouping of railroads and the development of chain cigar or food stores. It is in the air; it is part of the transformation of almost every business which is going on under our eyes, and if it had not been Scripps, Gannett, or Copley, it would have been someone else. The economic drift is what counts—the nation-wide combinations to decrease competition, to restrain trade, and to deal in larger and larger units. There was at bottom no reason to expect that the newspaper business would be spared the economic forces which are remodeling our industrial life and making the relationship of government to the staggering combinations of capital the paramount issue of the day.[4]

Others who attacked the press lords in addition to Villard, who wrote *Some Newspapers and Newspaper-Men* (1923), were George Seldes

(*Lords of the Press,* 1938), Harold L. Ickes (*America's House of Lords,* 1939), Ferdinand Lundberg (*Imperial Hearst,* 1936), and Will Irwin, *Propaganda and the News* (1936). Still, press criticism was spotty and had little continuity.

THE WAYWARD PRESSMAN

There was one exception, though, and that was the *New Yorker* magazine. From its inception in 1925 the magazine carried a column of press criticism. Under headings like "Behind the News" and "The Current Press," the magazine ran articles about the press until 1927 when it adopted the catchy title "The Wayward Pressman." From 1927 until 1939, the column was written by the witty and brilliant writer Robert Benchley, though this was by no means Benchley's best work. The column was discontinued until 1945 when the magazine hired a man who would provide thoughtful and sustained criticism from then until his death in 1963. Even today, A. J. Liebling seems like the consumate press critic. A veteran newspaperman who had done graduate work at Columbia University School of Journalism, which he said "had all the intellectual status of a training school for future employees of the A & P,"[5] Liebling wrote thoughtfully-witty columns about press performance.

Although most of his criticism was concerned with the specific problems of newspapers and wire services in New York City, there were general themes that ran through his work. Liebling hated the increasing uniformity of the press, the sameness of content. Wire services and syndicated copy were giving the press a dulling sameness, he charged. Similarly he disliked monopoly operations, the growing con-

centration of media in a few hands as well as the conservative business impulses of the press that made it pro-Republican and anti-Labor. He saw a need for diversity of views in the press and he was discouraged by what he regarded as diminishing access. As Edmund Midura has written in a study of Liebling and his work, "The press was a public utility in Liebling's eyes and he was bothered that the life or death of a paper could be decided by the advertising office of a New York department store. He detected a mistrust of the press in the American people."[6]

There was nothing systematic about Liebling's approach to press criticism, says Midura, but was instead "good case histories to support and illustrate his charges of journalistic malpractice. . . ."[7]

Often Liebling's work could be described as situational ethics. A skilled writer, his articles attracted attention well beyond the audience of *The New Yorker.* Two books of his collected criticism, *The Press* and *The Wayward Pressman* sold well. Midura says it is difficult to assess whether Liebling had any influence on stimulating a climate for press criticism in the latter part of the 1960s, but it is clear that he was a critic whose work had continuity, especially in a period when there was little criticism. And Liebling is remembered: he is still widely-quoted, and an award, a lecture series, and an annual conference all bear his name. To be sure he set a high standard for criticism and provided an example at a time when few were available.

ACADEMIC INTEREST IN CRITICISM

When one considers the range of media in America, the thousands of subjects they consider, the multiplicity of issues ranging from style to ethics and economic concentration, the task of the press critic becomes formidable. Press criticism "should not be taken to mean petty fault-finding—criticism of the carping, captious, censorious, caviling type,"[8] Jay Jensen wrote in a 1960 essay. It should, instead, involve judgment with knowledge and propriety. In order to be "valid and fruitful," criticism should be conducted:

(1) in an "objective manner";
(2) with due regard for the influence of political, social and cultural forces in their historical development; and
(3) with due regard for the contextual relationships of the media with their environment—with the demands, the values the aspirations and life interests of the society in which they exist.[9]

To Jensen fragmented criticism that does not take into account the institutional context of the media has little value. Journalism and the journalist live in an institutional order, they are part of a social system, and criticism that does not recognize this is unrealistic at best. Critical commentary conducted in a thorough, well-documented, systematic manner that recognizes the nature of press operations could lead to social change, Jensen and others have posited.

To James Carey, writing in 1976, criticism of the press, like that of all institutions, "must be based upon precise observation, clear procedure, unemotional language, subject to the cooperative correction of others, and occurring in the public forum where all affected by the institution can at least observe and comment on the critical process."[10] Carey sees three strains of media criticism:

First, . . .criticism by standards of public or social responsibility. . . . It involves the discussion of freedom, rights and objectivity.

A second critical tradition to connect the public with the media is that proposed by social scientists and might be called scientific criticism. Here the standards for judging the press are not abstract rights, or codes of press performances or press council evaluations of responsibility—all things on which social scientists are rather quiet—but standards derived from scientific studies of the impact of media upon audiences.

A third tradition of criticism can be termed cultural criticism and is defined, first of all, by what it excludes. . . . By cultural criticism I mean an ongoing process of exchange, of debate between the press and its audience and, in particular, those among the audience most qualified by reason of motive and capacity to enter the critical arena. . . .[11]

Carey's typology is particularly useful in making sense out of the wide ranging activity that passes for media criticism. In the first category of critics concerned with social responsibility one would find Walter Lippmann, William Ernest Hocking, John Merrill, John Hulteng, and others. This strain of criticism is tied closely to a libertarian view of the First Amendment and sets moral standards for performance. Freedom and responsibility go hand-in-hand. By no means is this strain of criticism confined to the left of the political spectrum. Former Vice-President Spiro Agnew, Russell Kirk, and William F. Buckley, Jr. as well as publications like the *National Review* and *The Alternative* are in this tradition.

On the left, James Aronson, Thomas Powers of *Commonweal,* Charles Seib of the *Washington Post,* and publications like the *New Republic* and *Commentary* lean toward a social responsibility model. But, then, so do less ideological and more neutral organs of media criticism like (MORE), the New York media review, and *Columbia Journalism Review,* an establishment voice if ever there was one.

Scientific criticism is practiced by those who offer empirical evidence to support their assessment of the press. The work of the various governmental commissions discussed in Chapter 2, for example, was social scientific and examined the press in that context. Radical, feminist, and various interest-group critiques might also use social science methods in content analyzing a particular newspaper and decrying its lack of treatment of the group or cause.

Much of the examination of the New Journalism in the 1960s and the attacks on the so-called objective form in journalism fell into the category of cultural criticism. Clearly it was closer to literary criticism than to the usual pronouncements by social responsibility critics.

If Jensen and Carey have provided standards for media criticism, a good many other academics, especially from journalism education, have led the way with forceful criticism of media and media institutions. John Merrill, for example, has been involved in the search for an appropriate journalistic philosophy. William L. Rivers has concerned himself mostly with the mass media and government articulating an adversarial relationship and studying its nature and consequences. J. Edward Gerald was more concerned with the internal dynamics of the press, examining economic variables and professional values. If Gerald's criticism was understated, Robert Cirino's was not. Cirino, believing the media to be manipulated and manipulator offered a strongly worded study of mass media use of bias and distortion.[12]

QUASI-ACADEMIC CRITICS

A number of commentators are performing a scholarly job on media criticism in the conventional press. Three whose work is particularly noteworthy are Ben Bagdikian, Edward Jay Epstein, and Paul Weaver. Bagdikian, a former ombudsman of the *Washington Post* and veteran newspaperman, writes about management issues, economic problems of the press, and obstructions to First Amendment freedom. His earlier writings were somewhat polemical, though always based on real experiences and situations. In recent years, however, he has demonstrated solid scholarship in his commentaries. In addition, he led the Rand Corporation's inquiry into the future of the media, which resulted in Bagdikian's forward-looking book, *The Information Machines*. His critical analysis of press-government relations during the late 1960s and early 1970s, *The Efete Conspiracy* was similarly well-documented, though it clearly had a liberal press bias. Bagdikian's work appears regularly in *Columbia Journalism Review* and is usually somewhat impressionistic. At the same time, the former newsman's solid managerial analyses have been included in books on communication research.

Edward Jay Epstein, a man many years Bagdikian's junior, was trained as a political scientist at Harvard. He chose, however, not to use his Ph.D. as a teaching credential, preferring a career as a professional writer doing commentaries on the press. Epstein's *News From Nowhere*, a scholarly study of network news, is replete with statistical data and information from his personal interviews and observations. However, the writings he collected in a book entitled, *Between Fact and Fiction, The Problem of Journalism,* were a mixture of heuristic study, investigative reporting, and essay-writing.

Similarly, Paul Weaver, also a Harvard-trained Ph.D. in political science, has worked both sides of the fence. His doctoral dissertation, an analysis of a metropolitan paper, followed the formal rules of scholarship. Yet his essays and commentaries in *Fortune* and *The Public Interest* are insightful cultural studies. Weaver, like Epstein, chooses to work outside of the academy.

THE EDITOR AS CRITIC

For years a mainstay of media criticism has been from news executives in the field. Publications like the *Bulletin* of the American Society of Newspaper Editors, studies and commentaries by the various committees of the Associated Press Managing Editors Association and the Radio and Television News Directors Association have provided a stream of commentary and criticism. Similarly, publications like *The Masthead,* organ of the National Conference of Editorial Writers, and *The Quill,* magazine of the Society of Professional Journalists, have contained critical material. These publications were once much more timid than they have been since the early 1970s.

Another type of critic within the journalistic family is the distinguished retired editor. Men like Harry Ashmore and Herbert Brucker are among those who have switched from editor to critic with grace. The Center for the Study of Democratic Institutions and its well-edited *Center Magazine* has provided a forum for such persons. Some prominent media figures less advanced in age have found similar institutional support at the Woodrow Wilson Center for Scholars. Sander Vanocur and George Reedy, for example, both wrote books while at the Wilson Center. The tendency of criticism from the senior editors of the field has been broad-gauged and has generally avoided personal reflections based on a single newspaper.

Although sometimes criticized for its excessive cronyism, the Aspen Institute's program on communication and society has been another stimulus for critical commentary about the media. Through summer conferences where invited participants help produce "instant books" of conference proceedings, useful analysis of media and government, cable television, and other subjects has been forthcoming. Aspen in cooperation with Praeger Publishers has also published an expanding bookshelf of studies on media and society subjects. Occasionally, the program supports a journalist-critic who is producing a critical work about the media. For example, Lou Cannon of the *Washington Post* spent time at Aspen while writing his book on journalists in America.

To what extent are editor-writers (young, old or midcareer) effective commentators on the press? Can they be discerning critics of institutions of which they are a part and to which many of them will return. Some, like Ben Bagdikian produce solid works of scholarship. Others, like Harry Ashmore provide useful philosophical insights. Still others produce carping memoirs to prove the "rightness" of their position. To be sure the criticism is uneven. A collection from the New York review (MORE), for example, called *Stop The Presses* was entertaining while narrow, strongly biased against change and patently antiintellectual. But these apparent shortcomings may not render such work useless. Indeed, there is such a rich mixture of media criticism that the "bitching" of individual journalists about problems of short duration can also have a place in this diverse field.

TRENDS IN CRITICISM

When A. J. Liebling was doing his work in the 1940s and 1950s being a press critic was a lonely and isolated existence. Today, when Alexander Cockburn writes his terse commentaries on the press in *The Village Voice* he is one of dozens of critics in the United States who write for newspapers and magazines, work in universities, run journalism reviews or produce book-length, nonfiction studies of the press. There is a growing need and demand for press criticism in conventional and alternative media because editors perceive the public as being inherently interested in the internal operations of the press which, in turn, have an influence and impact on their lives.

During the 1976 presidential campaign, researcher Michael Robinson mused that there were almost as many journalists watching the people who were covering the candidates as there were journalists covering the candidates themselves. The success of books by Timothy Crouse (*Boys on the Bus*) and James Perry (*Us and Them: How the Press Covered the 1972 Election*) spurred a wide range of journalistic enterprise in covering the 1976 election.

Most commentators agree that there was a greater amount of press criticism in America by the mid-1970s than there had ever been before. But no one was quite sure why this was so. Some suggested that it was a part of the increasingly combative posture of the American press since the Johnson administration. The 1960s seem to have been a formative time when the press was less and less concerned about playing a consensus function in society. If the press had been a lacky of the State Department in propagandizing for foreign policy during much of

American history, this was not to be in the 1960s when the political consensus burst apart at the seams. By no means was the press universally antigovernment, but many major press institutions were bluntly critical.

The growing gulf between the Presidency and the press that began in the Johnson administration and widened during the Nixon administration was also a factor. With the attacks of Spiro Agnew on the press in 1969 and the continued call of the Nixon administration to a ''silent majority,'' there was strong evidence that the press was not widely trusted or respected by the general public. Like other American institutions, the press faced a crisis of confidence.

The desire to win public support and confidence, to be understood, was doubtless a strong influence in the willingness of the press to respond to criticism, even to invite it. Later successes in the press, especially the triumph of reporters Woodward and Bernstein in the Watergate affair, stimulated public curiosity about the press itself. There were, of course, many other factors that had an impact on the growth of media criticism, not the least of which was the turmoil within the press itself. Various internal and external pressures stimulated media criticism. The previous chapter discusses some of the instruments of criticism that arose.

SUMMARY AND CONCLUSIONS

This chapter has treated some of the major press critics and has inventoried their concerns. Historical references put the long legacy of media criticism into a modern perspective. The seminal media criticism of A. J. Liebling is presented as a prelude to academic criticism of the press, quasi-academic critics, editors as critics and other journalists who through books and articles provide day-to-day criticism and analysis.

If media criticism had begun with wacking broadsides in its earlier days, it had become much more specialized with more discrete targets by the mid and late 1970s. Critics with quite varied backgrounds were engaging in diverse criticism of the press. And while there had been some bizarre forms of criticism, for example, the kidnapping of heiress Patricia Hearst and *Atlanta Constitution* editor Reg Murphy, most of the criticism identified grievances against the press and suggested constructive pathways for improvement. Some critics represented special interests and sought an advocate's advantage for their causes; others spoke of helping the public get access to the press; still others wanted to take on government and governmental institutions like the FBI and CIA, which they saw infringing First Amendment rights in a variety of ways. One phrase in the litany of the critics that echoed through much of their commentary was "the public interest." All seemed to agree that the press should serve the public interest (which they usually saw as synonymous with their cause or pleading). All of the critics James Carey identified, those using a social responsibility model, those adhering to the methods of social science as well as the cultural critics probably could all agree on the desirability of a press that was governed by and attune to the "public interest." Of course, they would doubtless find little agreement about how "the public interest" was defined or who should determine just what it might be. The next chapter explores the dimensions of this most intriguing of concepts that endures as an issue in media criticism, analysis, and scholarship.

As for media critics and criticism, the research evaluating their efforts is still sparse. There are few codifications of what they are saying, to whom they are speaking and what, if any, affect they are having. These concerns should be the basis for many studies in the next few years.

Notes

[1] James Aronson, "A Radical Journalist in the 1950s, Conclusion," *Nieman Reports,* Summer 1975, p. 21.

[2] James Aronson, *Packing The News, A Critical Survey of Press, Radio, TV* (New York: International Publishers, 1971), pp. 15-16.

[3] Quoted in Art Young, *Art Young His Life and Times* (New York: Sheridan House, 1939).

[4] Oswald Garrison Villard, "The Press Today: The Chain Daily," *The Nation,* May 21, 1930, p. 596.

[5] A. J. Liebling, *The Wayward Pressman* (Garden City, N.J.: Doubleday, 1947), p. 28.

[6] Edmund M. Midura, "A. J. Liebling: The Wayward Pressman as Critic," *Journalism Monographs,* No. 33, April 1974, p. 13.

[7] Ibid., p. 22.

[8] Jay Jensen, "A Method and a Perspective for Criticism of the Mass Media," *Journalism Quarterly,* Spring 1960, p. 262.

[9] Ibid., p. 263.

[10] James Carey, "But Who Will Criticize the Critics?," *Journalism Studies Review,* Cardiff, Wales: University College, June 1976), p. 7.

[11] Ibid., pp. 9-10.

"A newspaper must avoid both impropriety and the appearance of impropriety, as well as any conflict of interest or the appearance thereof. Promotion of any interest contrary to the general welfare, for whatever reason, is not compatible with honest journalism. Newspaper people should accept nothing, nor pursue any activity, that might compromise or seem to compromise their integrity. They should be free from all obligations except that of fidelity to the public interest."

—Article III, Statement of Principles, American Society of Newspaper Editors (1975)

Chapter 10

The Press and the Public Interest

It is unnecessary, the Senator's assistant said, to mention one's religious affiliation when writing about the abortion issue. William F. Gavin, a special assistant to then Senator James L. Buckley of New York, was disturbed by the *New York Times* coverage of the volatile abortion issue. The paper, he said, was trying to prejudice its readers against the issue by specifically pointing out Roman Catholic affiliation to the exclusion of all others.

What to do about it? In earlier times Gavin might have simply grumbled about the coverage or perhaps written a letter to the newspaper. But when the issue arose in 1974, Gavin turned to the National News Council and asked that the problem be resolved.

So the Council took up Gavin's complaint, looked at a series of articles he supplied, sought (without success) the cooperation of the newspaper, which has opposed the Council since its inception, and finally wrote an opinion.

Council members present that day in October, 1974 who would vote on the issue included such diverse persons as Judge Stanley H. Fuld, formerly chief judge of the New York State Court of Appeals, William Rusher, publisher of the conservative *National Review,* Irving Dilliard, former editorial page editor of the *St. Louis Post Dispatch* and an articulate media critic, as well as Molly Ivins, then co-editor of the liberal *Texas Observer.* (You'll recall that we met Ms. Ivins earlier in the discussion of journalism reviews.)

When the Council voted it demonstrated how difficult it is to sort out "the public interest" in an issue of this or any nature. Ivins was asked to write the opinion. Five members concurred with her finding. William Rusher wrote a dissent. Two members joined him. And two members abstained from voting at all.

While finding the issues complex and worthy of further examination, the Council majority found the complaint unwarranted. As they put it:

> While Mr. Gavin is justifiably concerned about the misconception that the antiabortion movement comprises only Roman Catholics, it is not clear that the *Times* is contributing to that misconception in these articles. None of the instances of religious identification is gratuitous. In those cases in which religious convictions play a major role in secular decision-making, the religious affiliation of those involved is a legitimate news item. . . .[1]

The majority saw the religious identification as relevant, the minority did not. As the dissenting opinion put it:

> We . . . believe that a publication leaves itself open to criticism when it mentions an individual's Catholicism, unless there is special relevance to that fact and unless it also mentions equally relevant religious or ethical beliefs of others mentioned in the same article.[2]

At the National News Council the members examine the facts of a case, apply their own logic, and reach a conclusion. They say their purpose is "to serve the public interest," but arriving at it sometimes proves difficult as the previous example indicates.

At the heart of this and many other press council determinations is the resolution of a thorny problem: whether the interest of the press as the *issuer* of information is necessarily the same as that of the public as the *consumer* of the information.

What we see played out in the press council cases is a conflict of interests between the individual and the mass media. Most often attempts to resolve this conflict invoke the concept of *the public interest*. Just what is the public interest and how does it help in our understanding of the relationship between the media and society? Although it is a truism to say that the press should serve the public interest, indeed that it should operate in the public interest, in every chapter of this book, the public interest has never been outside our line of vision. In Part I the impact, influence, and effect of the media on society was measured by researchers on the basis of hard evidence. This generated needed knowledge so that the researchers and other concerned individuals in society could resolve questions of importance about media. Always the answers to these questions were resolved in favor of policies and strategies that would serve the public good. Of course just what that public good was to be was not always so easily determined. Similarly, in Part II of this book, students of the internal dynamics of the press were concerned not only with what was happening inside the media, but also with the consequences of that action. And the question was raised often: does the work that goes on in manufacturing the message serve the public interest? Are the right decisions being made for the right reasons? We study journalists in part because we want to know about their attitudes and professional standards in order to evaluate their work and its impact. In Part III the larger macrocosmic concerns of Part I and the magnified microscopic concerns of Part II came together as we looked at studies and commentaries that touch on media criticism, performance and analysis. Again, judgments were made by the critics on the basis of the press's ability to serve the public interest, to respond to its constituencies in the larger society.

This chapter brings together many of the problems raised in earlier chapters by examining the concept of the press and the public interest in some detail. And this review of the public interest as it has been interpreted by the world of scholarship leads us to a model for the mass media in America as they confront matters of public interest.

THE ISSUER AND THE CONSUMER

"There are two distinct interests," wrote philosopher William Ernest Hocking, "only one of them needs . . .protection; to protect the issuer is to protect the consumer." Freedom of the press, Hocking suggested, "has always been a matter of public as well as individual importance. Inseparable from the right of the press to be free has been the right of the people to have to have a free press."[3]

Examining the public interest concept in terms of the motivation for legislative attacks on executive secrecy, political scientist Francis E. Rourke noted that the strongest efforts had come from the press and the scientific community. This, he said, "reflects the wide variety of interests [but] each . . .can also point to a clear public interest in the success of its special efforts."[4] Rourke explained further:

The public has an obvious stake in the effective performance of the legislative task, as it does in the availability of information in the hands of executive officials to the media of communication upon which the people depend for knowledge concerning the affairs of government. And the public has no less an interest in keeping open the channels of communications upon which the economic progress of society may be said to depend.[5]

Rourke's belief that the public has a deep interest in the free flow of information, and thereby in a free press, is frequently echoed by students of government and the press as well as journalists and judges. That is what Mr. Justice Brennan had in mind in the landmark case of *New York Times v. Sullivan* (which made it difficult for public officials to win damages in libel suits) when he enunciated a profound national commitment to the principle of debate on public issues that he said should be ''uninhibited, robust, wide open.''[6] This view brought an exasperated response from Jerome A. Barron, law professor and authority on public access to the news media. Fumed Barron: ''newspaper publishers' interests and the public interest are held to be identical'' and the result of the *Times* decision was ''romantic and lopsidedly pro-publisher.''[7]

Clearly, Barron and others believe that the *consumer* of communication should have some voice in determining what freedom of the press is all about. In Barron's view this would serve the public interest. Such a position is sharply at odds with the previously-mentioned 1947 Commission on Freedom of the press which stated [that] ''the work of the press always involves the interest of the consumer; but as long as the consumer is free his interest is protected in the protection of the freedom of the issuer.''[8]

SEARCH FOR DEFINITION

Few concepts have attracted as much scholarly probing as the public interest. ''It is probable that as much mischief has been perpetrated upon the human race in the name of 'the public interest' as in the name of anything else,''[9] wrote sociologists Daniel Bell and Irving Kristol in introducing a new journal, *The Public Interest,* in 1965. Although the concept traces its origins to the writings of Plato and Aristotle and has provided the substance for many books, papers and scholarly presentations, the public interest is little more than ''a conceptual muddle,'' says political scientist Frank Sorauf, who wrote: ''Clearly, no scholarly consensus exists on the public interest, nor does agreement appear to be in the offing.''[10]

In part the disillusionment with the concept springs from the vague and confused meanings that have been attached to it. The term ''the public interest'' seems to belong to that class of euphemisms that includes the public welfare, the common good, and the national interest. In part, the problem with the concept is its idealistic and pristine nature that was demonstrated in Walter Lippmann's comment that ''the public interest may be presumed to be what men would choose if they saw clearly, thought rationally, acted disinterestedly and benevolently.''[11] The British writer Robert Skidelsky, however, sees the term as a dying metaphor because one man's metaphor is always another man's reality.[12]

The despair of the critics not withstanding, the term is not to be escaped. It is pervasive in the literature of the First Amendment and serves as a guiding principle for the courts and the public philosophers. The public interest ''is the central concept of a civilized policy (and) its genius lies not in its clarity but in its perverse and persistent moral intrusion upon the internal and external discourse of rulers and ruled alike,''[13] wrote political scientist Samuel Bailey.

Some of the definitional vagueness of the public interest is eased by considering the amalgam of individual, parochial interests that make up the public interest. A lively debate between two economists, Anthony Downs and Gerhard Colm, has done much to enlarge understanding of this aspect of public interest doctrine. In his "Economic Theory of Political Action in a Democracy,"[14] Down suggests that there exist only individual self-interests. It is, he says, the demands of the individual that influence the political system of a democracy because "the government is interested (in each adult citizen's) vote, not his welfare."[15] Within the framework of his theory Downs finds that the public interest has utility; specifically it has three functions:

> First, it serves as a device by which individual citizens can judge government actions and communicate their judgments to one another.

> Second, since the concept implies that there is one common good for all members of society, transcending the good of any one member, appeals to the public interest can be used to coopt or to placate persons who are required by government policy to act against their own immediate interests.

> Third, the concept serves as a guide to and a check on public officials who are faced with decisions regarding public policy but who have no unequivocal instructions from the electorate or their superiors regarding what action to take.[16]

This approach to the public interest brought a sharp response from Gerhard Colm who compared Downs to "the hedonistic and utilitarian philosophers of an earlier epoch who sophistically made allowance for social values."[17] He further charged that Downs had "permit[ted] the public interest a kind of incognito entrance through the back door."[18]

The public interest concept, he asserted, is needed because:

First, policy is concerned not only with the welfare of the present but also with that of "our posterity," as the United States Constitution calls it. . . .

Second, the tremendous importance of functions related to the United States position in the world makes it especially artificial and labored to interpret all international and defense activities as designated to meet individuals' self-interest in national security and prestige. . . .

Third, the satisfaction of many self-interests has indirect beneficial effects for society as a whole.

Fourth, in a democracy many specific interests are shared by only a minority of the voters (such as the interests of farmers in adequate prices of farm supports).[19]

This leads Colm to a discussion of four analytical perspectives including: the meta-sociological, where there is a unitary value system and one clear, self-evident public interest; the sociological, where public interest is determined by social articulations—the expressions of individuals and groups; the legal, where government restricts personal or corporate activity for the public interest; and the economic, wherein the forces of the marketplace determine the public interest. But, public interest and individual interests are *not* mutually exclusive, Colm argues:

> Producers and actors who present a play and the people who come to see it are all motivated by self-interest, be it the desire to earn money or to gain fame or to be entertained. Nevertheless, the varying self-interests of all of them will not be satisfied for long unless the producers and the players and the audience find a common ground under the spell of the play as a work of art. To satisfy self-interests, those concerned with a play and those concerned with conduct of government must in some respect transcend their self interests.[20]

Those who attach value judgments to

Downs' ideas about individual interests, have suggested a "trickle-down" theory of the public interest. "a 'trickle-down' policy, of course, is one that concentrates its direct benefits on relatively affluent groups, counting on the second, third, and fourth-order effects to help the less fortunate,"[21] writes economist Alan Altshuler. He sees the "trickle-down" explanation as potentially useful in refining and examining the public interest.

Even though a political scientist's 1960 observation that "there is no public interest theory worthy of the name,"[22] remains valid today, there have been some notable attempts in recent years to explicate the concept more fully. One of the best efforts is a brilliant treatise by political scientist Virginia Held, *The Public Interest and Individual Interests*.[23] Before defining the concept in her own terms, she synthesized the literature of the public interest and proposed three classifications: (1) preponderance theories, (2) the public interest as common interest, and (3) unitary conceptions.

The preponderance theories are based on the assumption that if the public interest has any meaning at all it "cannot be in conflict with a preponderance or sum of individual interests, although this preponderance may be thought to be constituted and to be calculable in very different ways."[24]

The preponderance theories are traced to the writings of Hobbes, who believed in a preponderance of force; Hume, an exponent of preponderance of opinion; and Bentham, who advanced the idea of superior sum of individual interests. A contemporary application of preponderance theory is the relationship between the Federal Communications Commission and the networks' programming on television, a kind of lowest common denominator guided by

ratings, designed to give the public what it says it wants.

In examining the public interest as a common interest, Ms. Held says, "the equation of the public interest with those interests which all members of a polity have in *common*,"[25] forms the core of this idea. This concept is in agreement with preponderance theories in not ruling out the possibility of justifiable conflicts of individual interest, but it defines the public interest in terms of unanimity and compatibility. Common interest theory finds support in the writings of Rousseau who spoke of the common good and the general will. A modern application of this common interest theory would be shared interest and mutual trust. The unitary idea is based on universal moral precepts and hence,

> individual interests cannot justifiably conflict with the public interest or with each other. Only a universal moral order can confer validity, or justifiability, and the same universal order which renders a judgment that a given action or state is right or good cannot also render a judgment that the same action or state is wrong or evil.[26]

The formulation advanced by Ms. Held is an attempt to outline a norm for public interest that would function within the political and legal systems and would be governed by authoritative rules of conduct. She asserts that

> the polity may be understood as a system which validates public interest claims . . .[and] . . .that only the political system provides an effective decision method which could be associated with the term *public* for claims of what is or is not in the public interest. Any such decision method, or network of methods for a given society is constitutive of a political system.[27]

This system suggests that "no judgment concerning the public interest can be valid outside the political system whose decision procedures validate claims about it, although judgments concerning . . .the public interest, and the political system can itself be judged in moral terms.''[28]

How would Ms. Held's construct be applied? In the instance of the regulation of television programming, for example, there would be at least two levels for consideration. First, the question of the *preferences* of a majority of the population would be determined empirically. Similarly, the *interests* of the majority could also be determined empirically, but

> [b]oth of these questions would be distinct from that of whether existing programming practices are in the *public interest*. It might or it might not be considered in the interest of the polity to satisfy *majority* interest in this field. The question of majority interest might well be the one with which we were concerned, in a particular discussion, but if so, we would do well to use this term, not the public interest. We might conceivably decide, for instance, that it is not in the public interest for government to interfere with television programming, no matter what is produced, and that this decision has priority over any evaluation of program content. Discussion of the latter, then, might be in terms of majority interests, of the responsibilities of the networks to minority interests, or of aesthetic considerations, and perhaps not in terms of the public interest at all.[29]

The Held system depends, of course, on laws and regulations with the courts as a mechanism for adjudicating public interest disputes.

Perhaps the most useful distinction in this conceptual definition is the clear dividing line between *preference* and *interest*. What interests the public, in terms of its wants, desires, and tastes may necessarily be in the public interest. For example, in a developing nation, the immediate desires of pre-literate people for a certain content in television programming might not comport with the government's desire to use television as a channel for education and cul-

ture. Thus, even in a democracy, majority rule might be in conflict with the public interest. In American society, for example, freedom of speech is a fundamental tenet of constitutional law and of societal values. However, in a single instance the majority of the community might favor censorship. Under Ms. Held's system, public interest doctrine would dictate adherence to societal rules, overturning the immediate will of the majority. In many instances such an approach is essential to the preservation of minority rights, aesthetic values, and other public interest concerns.

SEARCHING FOR A STANDARD

Virginia Held's assumption that ''[only] the polity may be *understood as a system which validates public interest* claims,''[30] moves the definition of the public interest in relation to the press toward the legal sphere. This is appropriate since the courts frequently have invoked the concept in adjudicating conflicts between individuals and the press. A fragmentary definition of the public interest, based on an aggregate view of these cases, has provided what one legal scholar called ''a public interest doctrine''[31] that gives the press relief from damages in such areas as libel and privacy.[32]

The public interest, long a cornerstone of the English common law, was expressed in such terms as *pro bono publico,* the general welfare and others. However, the concept was always related to specific, pragmatic conflicts between individuals and/or social institutions. In his *Commentaries,* William Blackstone wrote, ''the public good is in nothing more essentially interested, than in the protection of every individual's private rights.''[33] For the term ''public interest'' the linkage between the common law and American judicial decisions came in the landmark case of *Munn v. Illinois* wherein private grain elevators located along railroad lines were said to be "affected with a public interest."[34] *Munn* established a basis for direct governmental regulation over certain businesses thought to involve the public business, and therefore, the public interest.

MEDIA INTEREST AND PUBLIC INTEREST

Over the years, spokesmen for the communications industry in America have maintained that they operate *in* the public interest. This is a traditional view of the first amendment and is solidly grounded in case law. It is, most commentators agree, a negative interpretation of the first amendment, focusing on the phrase, "Congress shall make no law," a command that has been interpreted as a shield against interference with the free flow of information. Clearly this interpretation favors the *issuer* of communication. It is an ultimate triumph for the "trickle-down" theory of mass communication and press freedom. By allowing the purveyors of communication maximum freedom, the means for the free flow of information to the public is determined.

Arguing for a positive interpretation of the first amendment, law professor Jerome Barron, an authority on mass communication law, takes sharp issues with the "trickle-down" theory. He sees this traditional interpretation of the first amendment as abrogating individual rights of communications access to a small number of vital voices in the marketplace of ideas. Barron's model is not unlike a pinball machine. He would add more voices to the marketplace and while they would shoot their

messages on different vectors, the ultimate result would be pinballs moving in the same direction and within a fixed range that may be designated as "press freedom." According to this view, the diversity of many voices rather than the stable force of a few, best serves freedom and the public interest.

While the argument centering on the question of whether the press interest and public interest are the same rages on, the work of public philosophers and jurists has helped to clarify its components. But they do not offer any objective criterion for deciding what is *in* the public interest. Since one ultimate source in adjudicating the public interest and sorting it out among a range of individual and private interests is the courts, one would expect to find guidance in judicial decisions. But any expectation for definition from this sector is quickly cooled since the courts have consistently blended public interest into an ambiguous rhetorical concept. As most court decisions indicate, the courts have said that what is *of* public interest is *in* the public interest.

In American society the Constitution is the ultimate statement of the public interest. The society and the media operates under the provisions of the Constitution, which imply and specifically state general goals. Under our system a free press is a means by which the public interest is transmitted and eventually achieved. It is the visible barometer, the expression of performance. If one accepts this general idea, the public's interest is much more than giving the public what it wants. Preferential choice needs to be consistent with constitutional rules. Inherent in our constitutional government is the assumption that the process of democracy is delegated—as a public trust—to public servants and officials. In delegating this trust, society takes an important step in the view of audience re-searcher Robert Silvey, who wrote:

> It is as though society says in effect to the public servant: "It is up to you to look after our interests. You must immerse yourself in your subject, because we haven't time to do so. There may come times when we shall demand that you take a certain course which you, having weighed it in the light of your knowledge and experience, will tell us is not in fact in our interest. Though you are our servant you must, in such a case, refuse to obey us. You will be right to do so, for though at the time you will be refusing to give us what we want, you will, paradoxically, be doing what in the long run we want you to do.[35]

So it is that the courts find themselves adjudicating press freedom cases. In this process they must be concerned not only with the aggregate preferences of society, but also with larger constructs of freedom for the social order—as well as for the individual. It has been in such a spirit that the courts have decided that:

a. The free flow of information is in the public interest.

b. Information about public affairs is of public interest and in the public interest.

c. The publication of newsworthy information is in the public interest.

d. Communications diversity is in the public interest.

e. Government regulation of certain communications activities "affected with a public interest" is in the public interest.

f. Matters *of* public interest or matters *in* the public interest are usually immune from libel and privacy recovery.

By the very act of being free, the press operates in the public interest. However, as Barron points out, because freedom of the press belongs to all of the people, the press, as an issuer of communication, has no right to prevent the communication of others. Activities by the press that drive out competition, encourage censorship, or prevent free discussion and debate on matters of public concern are at odds with the notion of positive freedom of the press. They are, therefore, not in the public interest. Thus the public interest and the media interest are congruent only when there is a viable relationship between issuer and consumer of communication that is operating to the satisfaction of both. This does not mean simply giving the public what it wants; rather, it means acquainting the public with the broad range of possibilities and then allowing it to make a free choice. When immediate whims and curiosity-seeking by the issuer or the consumer conflict with other social rights, the government, through the court system, should act as the regulator. For example, the interest in a celebrated trial may be quite high and the media may want to cover it in all aspects. However, such coverage might conflict with an individual's right to a fair trial. In such an instance it is up to the courts to sort out the conflicting interests and values.

If communication law cases were decided in a public interest framework, a quite precise, measurable definition of the public interest might emerge. That definition would be dynamic, flexible and accommodating, while at the same time it would provide a standard and a rationale for media behavior.

Government, however, is not the only check and balance between purely private interests and the public interest. In considering other activities that also advance and protect the public interest, the public health model of disease prevention is useful. The public health model suggests three levels of prevention—primary, secondary, and tertiary. When applied to the problem of the press and the public interest it can be expressed schematically as it is in Figure 10.1.

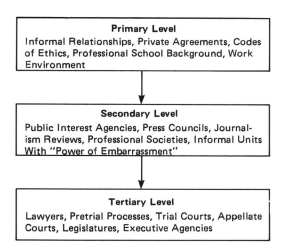

Figure 10.1 Adjudicatory Means for Public Interest Conflicts

At the primary level, prevention of public interest violations could be accomplished through informal educational processes in which the various parties in society would interact and settle their differences privately. In this arena, the universities, especially schools of journalism, have a broad mandate to teach ethics and responsible performance. Ideally, all disputes could be settled in this free and informal forum.

At the secondary level of prevention, watchdog agencies would monitor press behavior and attempt to curb abuses and point out public interest violations. These agencies would include such public interest bodies as Ralph Nader's Center for the Study of Responsive Law and Common Cause. Further, the press could be more directly influenced through press councils, communications task forces and foundations, journalism reviews, and professional groups.

Finally, and only after the other two levels had failed, would the prevention measures of the tertiary level be employed. This would include the courts as well as the legislature and the executive branches of government.

The public interest and the press interest would be the same when maximum freedom and minimal interference exists for both. The press interest/public interest would be measured by the degree to which the press fostered the free flow of information and satisfied the justifiable information needs of its consumers. Only when such a balanced ratio is achieved will the interest of the press and the interest of the public be one and the same.

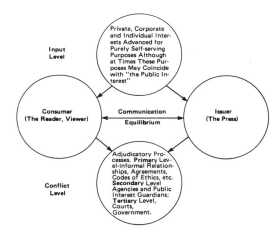

Figure 10.2 A System of Public Interest/Press Interest

Figure 10.2 illustrates such a scheme in which the public interest would begin to define itself. It would be the reaction of the press to higher-order interests expressed in the Constitution, blended with the interests of individuals and groups in society. The sources of this information pool would be the expressions of public and private interests related directly to the issuer of communication or indirectly to the issuer through the consumer. This interplay between issuer and consumer would determine the appropriate messages to be communicated to society and hopefully would solidify the public interest content of those messages. All conflicts would be sorted out and resolved through the primary, secondary and tertiary processes indicated above. Monitoring such an operational system would yield a system of public interest/ press interest.

SUMMARY AND CONCLUSION

Drawing together strains from most of the preceding chapters, this chapter discusses the concept of the public interest as it applies to the mass media. It is, of course, the resolution and definition of this concept that is at the root of much communication research and media criticism. Thus, its study is of great importance in unravelling research and criticism. Questions regarding scholarly inquiry about the interests of the consumer of media versus the interests of the issuers are considered. The literature of political science, economics and philosophy as it applies to public interest definition is also explored. The search for a public interest standard, particularly in the law is also treated. Finally, a system and model for sorting-out public interest-media interest questions is proposed.

It may seem at first glance an over-simplification to suggest that our understanding of mass media and society from a research perspective might be best served by an analysis of the public interest. However, as this chapter indicates the resolution of the puzzle of the public interest is highly complex and may always be central to a dynamic society and its media system. Research provides new information that may be a basis for decisions about the press and the public interest. In this book we have traced the internal and external probings of communications researchers as well as the critical commentaries of the scholar-critics. Concerned with different aspects of mass communication, employing different methods for their soundings and conclusions, the communications researchers are offering explanations where few have existed in the past. With their help we will know more about the interface of mass communication and communication systems with the larger society in the years ahead.

Notes

[1] The National News Council, *In The Public Interest, A Report by The National News Council;* New York: 1975, p. 108.

[2] Ibid., p. 110.

[3] William Ernest Hocking, *Freedom of the Press, A Framework of Principle, A Report from the Commission on Freedom of the Press* (Chicago: University of Chicago Press, 1947), p. 164.

[4] Francis E. Rourke, *Secrecy and Publicity, Dilemmas of Democracy* (Baltimore: John Hopkins Press, 1966), p. 31.

[5] Hocking, *Freedom of the Press,* p. 31.

[6] *New York Times v. Sullivan,* 376 U.S. 254, 270 (1964).

[7] Jerome A. Barron, *Freedom of the Press for Whom?, The Right of Access to the Mass Media* (Bloomington: University of Indiana Press, 1973), p. 12.

[8] The National News Council, *In the Public Interest,* p. 44.

[9] Daniel Bell and Irving Kristol, "What is the Public Interest?," *The Public Interest,* Fall 1965, p. 4.

[10] Frank Sorauf, "The Conceptual Muddle," in *The Public Interest,* ed. Carl J. Friedrich (New York: Atherton Press, 1962).

[11] Walter Lippmann, *The Public Philosophy* (New York: Mentor, 1955), p. 40.

[12] Robert Skidelsky, "Politics is Not Enough: On the Dying Metaphor of the National Interest," *Encounter,* Jan. 1969, p. 47.

[13] Stephen K. Bailey, "The Public Interest: Some Operational Dilemmas," Friedrich, *The Public Interest,* p. 106.

[14] Anthony Downs, "An Economic Theory of Political Action in a Democracy," *Journal of Political Economy,* April 1957, pp. 135-50.

[15] Anthony Downs, "The Public Interest: Its Meaning in a Democracy," *Social Research,* Spring 1962, pp. 1, 2.

[16] Ibid., p. 4.

[17] Gerhard Colm, "In Defense of the Public Interest," *Social Research,* Autumn 1960, pp. 294, 296.

[18] Ibid., pp. 294-97.

[19] Ibid., pp. 297-99.

[20] Ibid., p. 307.

[21] Alan Altshuler, "The Potential of 'Trickle-Down,'" *The Public Interest,* Spring 1969, pp. 46, 47.

[22] Glendon Schubert, *The Public Interest* (Glencoe, Ill.: The Free Press, 1960), pp. 223-24.

[23] Virginia Held, *The Public Interest and Individual Interests* (New York: Basic Books, 1970).

[24] Ibid., p. 43.

[25] Ibid., p. 44.

[26] Ibid., p. 136.

[27] Ibid., pp. 176-77.

[28] Ibid., p. 183.

[29] Ibid., p. 192.

[30] Ibid., p. 176.

[31] W. H. Flamm Jr., "Further Limits on Libel Actions—Extension of the *New York Times* Rule to Libels Arising From Discussion of Public Issues," *Villanova L. Rev.* 995, 961 (1971).

[32] For a discussion of case law regarding libel, privacy and the public interest, *see* generally, Everette E. Dennis, "The Press and the Public Interest: A Definitional Dilemma," 23 *DePaul Law Review* 937 (Spring 1974).

[33] William Blackstone, *Commentaries,* 139 (1769).

[34] *Munn v. Illinois,* 94 U.S. 113 (1877).

[35] Robert Silvey, "Giving the Public What it Wants," *Contemporary Review,* May 1961, p. 261.

"There was a wise man in the East whose constant prayer was that he might see today with the eyes of tomorrow."

—Alfred Mercier

Chapter 11

Toward a Media Society

From an office that looks out over a Korean pagoda set against the blue mountains of Honolulu's misty Manoa Valley, Wilbur Schramm quietly answers his visitor's questions. The tall, easy-mannered Schramm talks about mass communication technology and its effect on our lives. He talks about the revolutionary developments he has seen in his lifetime and of his efforts to sort them out, to study them. "This century," he says, "will be remembered as the communications century—or at least it should be."[1]

For more than an hour Schramm elaborates on his favorite topic—communication and its central role in civilization, especially modern civilization. He ticks off the major innovations of communication technology from wireless transmitters to communication satellites and beyond. And he recalls how researchers eyed these developments, trying to calibrate their influence and impact. Some of the researchers, he says, were in search of ideas; others were more interested in developing tools for measurement. But both were about the business of learning, and the advancement of knowledge, and to both we owe a debt for enhancing understanding of mass communication as it integrates with the lives of individuals and the society.

It is hard to imagine anyone better qualified than Schramm to explain these things. He is in a real sense the consummate personification of the communication century. An intellectual leader in the field of communications for more than three decades, he has been a practitioner, (reporter, magazine journalist, author), a scholar, and (author of major works in mass communication), an educator developing programs at three major universities, and a policymaking adviser on children and television, mass communication and national development, and education.

His work has embraced all of the major themes articulated in this book. His research and writing on mass communication processes and effects has made major contributions to knowledge about the external relationships of the media and the society. His concern with communication process, gatekeeping and the nature of news and journalistic work broke new ground in illuminating the internal aspects of communication organizations and enterprises. Similarly, books and articles about ethics in mass communication have added an important critical dimension to his overall contribution.

In addition to his own original research and that which he directed, Schramm was the great synthesizer of mass communication. He took abstruse theories and research reports written by others in tortured language and integrated them into crisp, readable prose. This was not merely a job of translation, but an inspired integration that offered context and continuity.[2]

Communication researcher Wayne Danielson, a student of Schramm's, says that one needs to remember five things in order to understand and appreciate his mentor's work.

Schramm, he maintains, was motivated, pushed, and directed by (1) a sense of urgency about the need to unravel communication problems, (2) the need to be practical—to conduct research not to satisfy idle curiosity but to solve pressing human problems, (3) the urge to pioneer "in opening up new ground, in running toward life rather than away from it,"[3] (4) the hope for technology—the faith that innovations would be "great weapons against a recalcitrant natural and social environment,"[4] and (5) the unreachable stars—a Quixotic desire to seek out difficult problems and solve them. As Danielson put it:

> To pick up any book or article by Wilbur Schramm is almost immediately to feel a sense of tension, of unease, of time scurrying on, of important tasks undone, of urgency. In India, people are starving because they cannot get simple and useful agricultural information; in South America and Samoa, governmental inefficiency and obstinancy is preventing the implementation of vitally needed programs. Whole nations are developing slowly or not at all because of our inability to discover what needs to be done and to mobilize the resources to do the job.[5]

What were the results of Schramm's inquiries? Danielson says that in making tracks on four continents and in dozens of countries, Schramm "has left behind many true and enduring accomplishments."[6] Among them: "Children are reading who would have been illiterate. Old men and women are alive who would have been dead. Scholars, countless scholars, here and abroad, are asking Schramm-type questions about communication, practical questions they would not have asked had he not instilled in them his own sense of the urgency of events."[7]

Although Schramm's work was far more broad-based and extensive than any other single communication scholar, it is clearly reflective of the shape, direction, and utility of communication research. And Schramm's straightforward explanations about research are convincing:

> There is nothing especially esoteric about research. It is simply the best way we have yet found to gather information systematically, accurately, and with safeguards that permit one to estimate how reliable the information is. This is accomplished through scientific sampling, adequate research design, uniform asking of questions or making observations, skillful reduction of data, and the application of suitable statistics. It is not something that one undertakes without study or training; but neither is there anything magical or mysterious about it.[8]

We have in this book inventoried several areas of communication research and scholarship. An overview of the inquiries that have probed questions of the impact, influence, and effect of media generates new perspectives for understanding what the mass media do to people and their society. Studies of internal decision making by media personnel explain how and why messages are generated by media organizations. Add to this the critical factor of scholars and other commentators offering evaluations of media performance and a fuller picture of media and society is at once evident.

THE REACTION TO RESEARCH

Not everyone agrees with Wilbur Schramm's persuasive "case for communication research." There is, as we pointed out in Chapter 1, a considerable distance between communication practitioners and communication researchers with regard to the value of research. Part of it stems from the fact that most communication research is conducted in schools of journalism and mass communication and practitioners feel that this preoccupation with research detracts from the business of training reporters, editors, broadcast journalists and advertising personnel. Educators say that it does not, that research in fact enhances teaching with obvious benefits to students.

There is a know-nothing flavor to many of the attacks by media professionals on communication research. "Lord, help us all," wrote columnist Lynn Ashby of the *Houston Post* in February 1977, the last thing any decent school of journalism needs "is for professors to spend less time in the classroom and more time writing opaque reports on obscure subjects for a tightly knit group of fellow professors who won't read them."[9] Ashby continues:

> Such learned treatises might cut a path through the academic jungles, which already have more than their share of poseurs, charlatans, deadbeats and dropouts, but what possible good do such interoffice memos have to do with better journalism? I have never seen a scholarly research paper on journalism in a city room. I have never heard a reporter quote a line from such publications. They do no good, have only an artificially incubated market and constitute nothing but make-work for frightened faculties which must publish or perish.[10]

While acknowledging the need for scholarly research and professional writing in other fields, Ashby decries their presence in journalism and communication. No mention is made of the urgent problem of television and children, of the political impact of advertising, of persuasion and propaganda. These things, not to mention the considerable research on newsroom problems and the critical literature that charts directions for a better press, are ignored.

Fortunately, most of the communication industry is more enlightened, especially personnel at the higher levels. Declines in newspaper circulation, for example, led the American Newspaper Publishers Association and the Newspaper Advertising Bureau, Inc. to push for more research on readership patterns, the youth audience, and other topics with immediate and practical implications. A number of major publishers have invited management scientists and communication researchers to examine their organizations' inner workings. Journalists themselves have led the small but growing movement for a "precision journalism" whereby reporters use the methods of the social sciences in gathering news and utilizing survey and other data. Broadcasting networks and local stations make regular use of research data in determining program choices. And, of course, advertising agencies have been making heavy use of research for almost as long as they have been in existence.

Still, old canards don't die so easily. More imagined than real, for example, is the chi-square versus green-eye shade battle between research-oriented professors in schools of communication and those who are more concerned with professional practice. This battle, which is seen as very real by a few quite isolated researchers and a few isolated teachers of communication skills courses, is quite passé. Some observers doubt that it ever really existed. The need for research in advancing knowledge about journalism and mass communication is clear—it is the only pathway that takes the practitioner beyond parochial local patterns. Yet there is a misunderstanding and the researchers are by no means free from guilt in this matter. Some researchers, especially those working on interpersonal communication problems, have been reluctant to translate the purpose and worth of their research to those who do not immediately understand its implications—whether theoretical or practical.

Communication researchers over the years have had to seek a place for themselves in journalism schools which were sometimes hostile environments. The reaction was sometimes an angry striking-back, an arrogance that dismissed the value of the work of their more practical-minded colleagues. Among researchers there is some of this snobbery and arrogance. Some researchers concerned about theoretical and methodological matters ignore or playdown the systematic work of their colleagues who prefer to use historical, literary or legal methods in their work.

Fortunately, many of these old animosities are dying. Books about journalistic practice these days rarely fail to include relevant research. And similarly, books and articles produced by researchers often focus on real-life professional situations. The value of interaction between and among researchers and media professionals is evident, of course. Trade journals and professional magazines are making more of an effort to popularize research findings and books based on communication research data are getting reviewed in large circulation publications.

Because researchers and practitioners have somewhat different goals, they will probably never agree on all things, but there is evidence that they are viewing each other with more understanding, and that is cause for hope.

This is not to suggest that research should not be vigorously analyzed and criticized. Obviously, it should. Researcher Maxwell E. McCombs, for example, has criticized his fellow researchers for "whacking away" at trivial, fragmented problems while ignoring those of greater and more sustained importance. McCombs calls for greater commitment to intellectual inquiry and explains:

Since research costs money, a "practical" research question must be broad in scope. It must be abstract. That is, it must cover a general situation so that the answer obtained can be applied in a large number of specific situations. This means that every question in which it is practical to invest research time and money is abstract. It is theoretical.[11]

McCombs is right, of course. In the long run everyone will be better served by research of high quality that probes highly generalizable questions. And as research turns in this direction it should inspire more confidence among media professionals.

In this book we have urged a recognition that research is systematic inquiry, but that the researcher may use many tools. Research using social science tools is research. So is historical research, legal research, literary research, and visual research. We are cognizant that there is good research well-conducted and bad research poorly conducted. The discerning student of mass communication must make a thoughtful evaluation of research, sorting out in order to determine what a particular piece of research means. This is as important to the student who is a consumer of research as it is to one who looks for a career in research activity. And it is equally important to the student who seeks a career in professional journalism where the ability to evaluate research is becoming necessary at all levels.

TOWARD THE MEDIA SOCIETY

What we have been discussing in earlier chapters is highly complex. Not only are the patterns of research and the tools used by the researchers and commentators complex, but so are the massive changes in society against which they must be measured. We have made frequent reference to communication technology and the revolutionary changes which it has undergone. This technology and its almost immediate integration into our daily lives makes the need for thoughtful commentary and systematic scholarship essential. What we understood about television yesterday, we may not understand today because its nature and its potential impact may be changing. One medium replaces another or alters the role of another. What we knew about magazines in 1900 has little bearing today without consideration of the changing role and function of the modern magazine. Of course, historical research helps us gain that perspective.

There is a tendency in the midst of changing communication technology to want to predict the future. What will the "media room" in the home of tomorrow be like? How soon will massive changes come? How soon will they really affect our lives? The difficulty with prediction is our inability to sort out what is technologically feasible from what is necessarily desirable or likely from a social and political standpoint. Many of the predictions about the runaway pace of cable television ten years ago were hopelessly wrong, not because technology wasn't capable of moving that fast, but because public policy suggested another course. Happily research helps guide our portrait of the future.

We know that we are in a communication revolution. We know that it is changing our lives and in this book we have attempted to perceive those changes as researchers have in a systematic fashion. That intelligence—the findings of the researchers—is in itself a cautious, highly qualified view of the present and the future. The patterns of activity we have observed suggest relevant questions for the future.

The future, pregnant with possibility, will be determined by many forces, chief among them the role of economic and governmental institutions—the private and public sectors. They will be the key variables that will guide us all—our media, our society, and ourselves toward an uncertain destiny.

Notes

[1] Personal interview with the author, August 1976, Honolulu, Hawaii.

[2] *See* generally, Steven H. Chaffee, ed., Godwin C. Chu, Jack Lyle, and Wayne Danielson, "Contributions of Wilbur Schramm to Mass Communication Research," *Journalism Monographs,* No. 36, Oct. 1974. Essays by former Schramm students shortly after Schramm's retirement from Stanford University and move to the East-West Communication Center, Honolulu. Schramm left the East-West Center in 1977 to become a distinguished research professor at the Chinese University in Hong Kong.

[3] Ibid., Wayne Danielson, "Wilbur Schramm and the Unreachable Stars: The Technological Papers," in Chaffee, et. al., p. 27.

[4] Ibid., p. 28.

[5] Ibid., p. 24.

[6] Ibid., p. 30.

[7] Ibid., p. 30.

[8] Wilbur Schramm, *The Role of Information in National Development* (Paris: UNESCO, 1965), p. 33.

[9] Lynn Ashby, "J-School Not An Ivory Tower," *The Houston Post,* Feb. 17, 1977. For a somewhat broader, but still highly critical view, *see* generally, Ben H. Bagdikian, "Woodstein U., Notes on the Mass Production and Questionable Education of Journalists," *The Atlantic,* March 1977.

[10] Ibid.

[11] Maxwell E. McCombs, "J-Researchers Appraises, Too Many 'Whack' at Problems, Fail to Think Creatively," *Journalism Educator,* April 1974, pp. 44.

Bibliography

General Works

Reed H. Blake and Edwin O. Haroldsen, *A Taxonomy of Concepts in Communication,* New York: Hastings House, 1975.

W. Phillips Davison, and Frederick T. C. Yu, *Mass Communication Research: Major Issues and Future Directions,* New York: Praeger, 1974.

Melvin L. DeFleur and Sandra Ball-Rokeach, *Theories of Mass Communication,* Third Ed., New York: David McKay Co., 1975.

Ithiel de Sola Pool, Wilbur Schramm, Frederick W. Frey, Nathan Maccoby and Edwin B. Parker, eds., *The Handbook of Communication,* Chicago: Rand McNally Co., 1973.

Wilbur Schramm, *Men, Messages and Media, A Look at Human Communication,* New York: Harper & Row, 1973.

Wilbur Schramm and Donald Roberts, *The Process and Effects of Mass Communication,* Second Ed., Urbana: University of Illinois Press, 1972.

Influence and Effect of Mass Communication

W. Phillips Davison, James Boylan and F.T.C. Yu, *Mass Media, Systems and Effects,* New York: Praeger, 1976.

Denis McQuail, *Towards a Sociology of Mass Communication,* London: Collier-Macmillan, 1969.

F. Gerald Kline and Phillip J. Tichenor, eds., *Current Perspectives in Mass Communication Research,* Beverly Hills, Ca: Sage Publications, 1972.

Steven H. Chaffee, *Political Communication: Issues and Strategies for Research,* Beverly Hills, CA: Sage Publications, 1975.

Charles R. Wright, *Mass Communication: A Sociological Perspective,* Second Ed., New York: Random House, 1975.

L. John Martin, ed., ''Role of the Mass Media in American Politics,'' a special issue of *The Annals of the American Academy of Political and Social Science,* Sept. 1976.

The Press as a Social Institution

Chris Argyris, *Behind the Front Page, Organizational Self-Renewal in a Metropolitan Newspaper,* San Francisco: Jossey-Bass, 1974.

Lou Cannon, *Reporting, An Inside View,* Sacramento: California Journal Press, 1977.

J. Edward Gerald, *The Social Responsibility of the Press,* Minneapolis; University of Minnesota Press, 1963.

John W. C. Johnstone, Edward J. Slawski and William W. Bowman, *The News People, A Sociological Portrait of American Journalists and Their Work,* Urbana: University of Illinois Press, 1976.

Bernard Roshco, *Newsmaking,* Chicago: University of Chicago Press, 1975.

Leon V. Sigal, *Reporters and Officials, The Organization and Politics of Newsmaking,* Lexington, Mass.: D.C. Heath, 1973.

Media Criticism and Analysis

Lee Brown, *The Reluctant Reformation, On Criticizing the Press in America,* New York: David McKay, 1974.

William Ernest Hocking, *Freedom of the Press: A Framework of Principle,* Chicago: University of Chicago Press, 1947.

John C. Merrill, *The Imperative of Freedom: A Philosophy of Journalistic Autonomy,* New York: Hastings House, 1974.

William L. Rivers and Wilbur Schramm, *Responsibility in Mass Communication,* New York: Harper & Row, 1969.

Index

Abelson, Robert, 57
Access to the media, 145
Acquaintance—with, 81
Adversarial journalism, 87-90
Adversary relationship, 80
Advertiser pressure, 71
Advocacy journalism, 83
Agenda-setting hypothesis, 12, 13, 104
Agenda-setting study, 12-13, 43
    criticism of, 13
Agnew, Spiro, 41, 88, 132
All powerful influence of press, 3
All the President's Men, 71, 88
"All the President's Men," film, 35, 93
Alternative journalism, 85, 112
Alternative, The, 132
American Newspaper Guild, 112, 119
American Newspaper Publishers Assn., 32, 122,
    138, 153
America's House of Lords, 131
Anderson, David, 124
Anderson, Jack, 88
Antioch Review, 129
Applied research, 102
Argyris, Chris, 70, 75, 101
Aristotle, 141
Armies of the Night, 85
Aronson, James, 66, 119, 129, 130
Art of Writing Nonfiction, The, 86
Ashbury Park (N.J.) *Press,* 123
Ashby, Lynn, 153
Ashmore, Harry, 134
Aspen Institute Program on Communication
    and Society, 134
Associated Press, 130
Associated Press daily budget, 97
Associated Press Managing Editors Assn., 123,
    134
Association for Popular Culture, 49
Association of Tribune Journalists, 112
Atlantic, The, 35, 120
Audience effects, 6
Audience predispositions, 7
Autobiography of Lincoln Steffens, The, 71

Backtalk, Press Councils in America, 117
Bagdikian, Ben, 72, 117, 123, 124, 133, 134
Bailey, Samuel, 141
Ball-Rokeach, Sandra, 4, 8, 11
Barron, Jerome A., 116, 141, 145
Bauer, Raymond and Alice, 80
Becker, Lee B., 37
Beer, Stafford, 68
Behind the Front Page, 101
Bell, Daniel, 141
Benchley, Robert, 131
Bentley, Eric, 55
Berelson, Bernard, 6, 36
Berger, Arthur Asa, 58
Bernstein, Carl, 35, 88, 90
Bertrand, Claude-Jean, 118, 119
*Between Fact and Fiction: The Problem of
    Journalism,* 133
Bias in news coverage, 38
Bias of Communication, The, 60
Blackstone, William, 144
Blackstone's *Commentaries,* 144
Blake, Tiffany, 78
Blanchard, Robert O., 104
Blankenberg, William, 117
Bobrow, David, 43
Bonaparte, Napoleon, 2
Boorstin, Daniel, 56, 58, 94
Bowers, David, 73
Boys on the Bus, The, 135
Bradlee, Ben, 93
Brass Check, The, 73, 129
Breed, Warren, 69, 96-97
Brennan, William, 141
Breslin, Jimmy, 85
British Press Council, 116
Brown, Donald, 116
Brown, Lee, 123
Browne, Ray, 49, 60
Brucker, Herbert, 134
Buckley, James L., 139
Buckley, William F., 132
*Bulletin of the American Society of Newspaper
    Editors,* 134

Bureaucratic aspects of press, 71, 103
Bureaus of accuracy and fair play, 122
Business-journalistic relationships, 74

Cannon, Lou, 134
Capote, Truman, 85
Carbine, Patricia, 68
Carey, James, 132, 133, 136
Carlysle, Thomas, 55
Carpenter, Edmund, 60
Cater, Douglass, 27, 28, 68
CBS News, 71
Celebrities and the press, 54, 55
Celebrities, journalistic, 88, 94
Center for the Study of Democratic Institutions, 134
Center Magazine, The, 134
Chain ownership of newspapers, 130
Charnley, Mitchell V., 80, 89
Chicago Journalism Review, 111, 112
Chicago Tribune, 78
Children and advertising, 29-31
Children and politics, 15
Children and television, 27
Chisman, Forest P., 43
Churchill, Sir Winston, 75
Circulation of newspapers, 32
Cirino, Robert, 133
Civil disorders and the press, 22-23
Clarke, Peter, 9, 10
Cockburn, Alexander, 90, 135
Cognitive dissonance, theory of, 5
Cohen, Bernard, 12
Cold war and press, 129
Coles, Robert, 15
Collier's, 78
Colm, Gerhard, 142
Columbia Journalism Review, 119, 121, 132, 133
Columbia University Graduate School of Journalism, 129, 131
Commentary, 132
Commission on Freedom of the Press, 114-15, 141
Commission on Obscenity and Pornography, 25
Commonweal, 132
Communication century, 151
Communication history, 59
Communication in history, role of, 58
Communication research
    criticism of, 153-54
    funding, 27, 31
    methods, 6
        content analysis, 6, 9, 22, 23, 24, 28, 30, 50, 87

experimental method, 6, 9, 24, 26, 28, 30
survey research, 6, 9, 10, 22, 26, 30, 36, 39, 73, 87, 94, 118, 122, 132, 133
    value of, 152
Communication satellites, 151
Communication technology, 151
Communicator studies, 105
Community Press in an Urban Setting, The, 72
Conflict reporting, 72
Congress and the News Media, 104
Congressional sex scandals, 35
Content analysis, see Communication research methods
Content of mass communication, 79-90
Content of news, 79
Control-analysis studies, 71
Cool medium, 58
Coorientation research, 43
Court reporting, 104
Cowles publishing interests, 112
Craft attitudes in journalism, 79
Crescendo journalism, 88
Crouse, Timothy, 135
Cultural media criticism, 132, 133

Daedalus, 79
Dailey, Peter H., 42
Daily Planet, The, 70
Danielson, Wayne, 151-52
Darnton, Robert, 79
Davison, W. Phillips, 14
Deadline for the Media, 119
Decision-making in the newsroom, 69
Decline and Fall, 71
"Deep Throat," 93
DeFleur, Melvin L., 4, 8, 11
Delayed-reward news, 81
Denver Post, 121
Determinations by the Council, 117
Dilliard, Irving, 139
Dimmick, John, 69, 96, 97
Dodson, Don, 54
Donohew, Lewis, 72
Donohue, George A., 11, 72
Downs, Anthony, 142
"Dragnet," 84
Due to Circumstances Beyond Our Control, 71
Dunn, Delmer, 103
Durkheim, Emile, 83

Eastman, Max, 130
Economic influences on press, 71
Edelstein, Alex S., 72
Editor & Publisher, 39

Editorial cartoon, impact, 4, 37
Editorial endorsements, 37-39, 40
Editors, roles of, 102
Efete Conspiracy and Other Crimes by the Press, The, 133
Effects of mass communication, 3-63
    political impact, 35-45
    popular culture effects, 49-63
    public policy and effects, 21-33
    research perspectives
        agenda-setting, 12-13
        attitude change, 5-8
        re-interpretation, 8-11
        political socialization, 15-16
        uses and gratifications, 13-15
Elections, communication research on, 35
Electoral endorsements, 37-39, 40
Elmira study, 36
Epstein, Edward Jay, 35, 88, 133
Erie County study, 5, 6, 36
Ethics of journalism, 74
Event-centered news, 81
Exposes, 88

Fact and Fiction, the New Journalism and the Nonfiction Novel, 87
Fact versus opinion, 83-84
Fairbanks, Douglas Sr., 55
Federal Communications Commission, 29, 143
Federal Trade Commission, 29
Feminism, images of, 57
Feminist values, in press, 67
Festinger, Leon, 5
Final Days, The, 90
First Amendment, 68, 117, 132, 133, 141, 145
Fishwick, Marshall, 55, 86-87
Fontaine, Andre, 86
Form of media, 58
Fortune, 134
Four Theories of the Press, 116
Fourth branch of government, 68
Free and Responsible Press, A, 117
Freedom of the Press, 114
Freedom of the Press for Whom?, 116
Freedom of the Press v. Public Access, 116
Freud, Sigmund, 57, 81
Friedrich, Otto, 71
Friendly, Fred, 71
Front Page, The, 93
Fuld, Stanley, 117, 118, 135
Functional approach to media study, 53
Functions of mass communication, 11-12, 53
Funding, of communication research, 22, 44
"Fuzz," 3

Gans, Herbert, 48, 51, 53
Garvey, Daniel, 96-97

Gatekeeper, 71
Gatekeeper, gatekeeping studies, distinguished, 95
Gatekeeper studies, 69, 94-97
Gatekeeping studies, 69
Gavin, William F., 139
Gerald, J. Edward, 74, 97, 116, 133
Gerbner, George, 31
Ghiglione, Loren, 124
Goebbels, Joseph, 5
Goldschlager, Seth, 104
Gossip, 80, 90
"Great man" theory of history, 55
Green, Theodore, 55
Greenstein, Fred, 15
Gregg, James E., 38
Grey, David L., 97, 104

Hahn, Taeyoul, 71, 73
Harding scandals, 56
Harper's, 120
Harper's Weekly, 4
Hawley, Searle, 97, 98
Hays, Wayne, 35
Hearst, Patricia, 136
Heider, Fritz, 57
Held, Virginia, 143-44
Hennessy, Bernard, 38
Hero study, 54-56
    heroes, in popular culture, 50
    heroes in popular magazines, 55
    heroes, types, 55
Heuristic method, 30, 51, 133
Hidden Persuaders, The, 6
High culture, 54
Historical method, 44, 50, 80, 113
History of business, 74
History of journalism, 74
Hocking, William Ernest, 114, 132, 140
Hoffman, Dustin, 35
Hohenberg, John, 92
Hollowell, John, 87
Hook, Sidney, 55
Hot medium, 58
Houston Post, 153
Howe, Allen, 35
Hughes, Howard, 56
Hulteng, John L., 88, 132
Human communication, 50
Humanistic scholarship, 57
Hunt, Todd, 81
Hutchins Commission, 114-16
    Recommendations, 115-16
    Report, 126
Hvistendahl, J.K., 72
Hyman, Herbert, 16

Ickes, Harold L., 131
Image Candidates, The, 41
Image or Whatever Happened to the American Dream, The, 56
Image study
    image-making capacity of media, 50, 55
    images, 44
    images in popular culture, 50
    images, women, racial groups, 50
Images of Asia, American View of China and India, 56
Immediate-reward news, 81
Imperative of Freedom, The, 116
Imperial Hearst, 131
Impressionistic study, 44
Improvised News, 20
In the Public Interest, 117
Information Machines, The, 133
Information theory, 68
Information types, 10
Informational impact of media, 79
Innes, Harold, 60
Interpretation of Dreams, 57
Investigative journalism, 35, 80, 87-90, 94
Irwin, Will, 131
Isaacs, Harold, 56, 57
Ismach, Arnold, 82
Ito, Shin-Chi, 102
Ivins, Molly, 111, 112, 139

Janis, Irving L., 27
Janowitz, Morris, 72
Jaros, Dean, 15
"Jefferson Airplane," 54
Jensen, Jay, 132-33
Jobson, Thomas W., 123
Johnson, Fred J., 118
Johnson, Gerald W., 55
Johnson, Lyndon B., 22, 34
Johnson, Michael, 85
Johnstone, John, 68, 98-100
Journal of Popular Culture, 60
Journalism education, 124
Journalism reviews, 111-13, 119-20
Journalistic image, 93
Journalists in America, 98-101
Judge, 130

Kansas City Star, 120
Kansas City Star and Times, 121
Kato, Hidetoshi, 49
Katz, Elihu, 14
Kerner Commission, 22-23
Kirk, Russell, 132
Kissinger, Henry, 88
Klapp, Orrin, 55, 58

Klapper, Joseph T., 6, 25, 27, 59
Kline, F. Gerald, 9, 10
Knowledge-about, 81
Knowledge-gap hypothesis, 11
Kraus, Sidney, 16
Kristol, Irving, 89, 141

Lacey, Carol, 112
Langston, Kenneth B., 15
Larsen, Otto, 25, 72
Lasswell, Harold D., 5, 12, 71
Lazarsfeld, Paul, 5, 36
Legal research methods, 113
Legislator-reporter relations, 103
LeMonde, 121
Lenin, Nikolai, 5
Levels of analysis, 4, 8, 95
Libertarian theory of the press, 116
Liebling, A.J., 131, 135
Liebling, A.J. Counter-convention, 111
Lindbergh, Charles A., 56
Lippmann, Walter, 57, 83, 128, 132, 141
Literary criticism, 50
    as a scholarly method, 59, 60, 87
    literary devices, 85
Living system, press as, 70
Lockhart, William P., 26
Lords of the Press, 131
Louisville Courier-Journal, 122
Low culture, 54
Lowenthal, Leo, 55
Lundberg, Ferdinand, 131
Lyle, Jack, 28

McCall's, 68
McCarthy, Joseph, 83
McCarthyism, 129
McClure, Robert D., 42, 43
McCombs, Maxwell, 11, 12, 13, 38, 58, 154
MacDougall, Curtis D., 38, 80
McGuire, W.J., 4
McLeod, Jack, 97, 98
McLuhan, Marshall, 50, 58-60, 61, 79
    criticism of, 59
    study of, 58-60
McQuail, Denis, 6, 14, 52, 70
Madden, David, 49
Magazine Publishers Assn., 32
Magic Writing Machine, The, 85
Mailer, Norman, 85
Management practices of media, 68
Management science study, 73, 101-3
Marbut, Frederick, 96
Marxism, 52
Mass behavior, 49
Mass communication, functions, 11

Mass culture, 49
Mass news, 68
Mass society, 49
Mass society/mass culture critics, 50-54
Mass society theory, 52
Masses, The, 130
Masthead, The, 41, 134
Matthews, T.S., 8
Media as business, 68
Media as social system, 68-69
Media criticism, 132
Media sociology, 86
Mellett Fund, 117, 118
Mendelsohn, Harold, 8, 15
Mercier, Alfred, 150
Merrill, John, 116, 132, 133
Merz, Charles, 128
Midura, Edmund, 131
Midwest Working Journalists' Forum, 111
Miller, Jack, 112
Miller, Jonathan, 59
Mills, C. Wright, 50
Mills, Wilbur, 35
Milwaukee Journal and Sentinel, 121
Minneapolis Star, 100
Minneapolis Star & Tribune, 121, 122
Minneapolis Tribune, 111, 112
Minneapolis worker participation committee, 121
Minnesota Press Council, 112, 117, 118
Mollenhoff, Clark, 88
"Monkees, The," 54
Monopoly press, 129
(More) 102, 120, 132
Mott, Frank Luther, 37
Ms., 67-68, 74
Muckraking, 4, 67, 88
Munn v. Illinois, 145
Murphy, James E., 86
Murphy, Reg, 136
Myth of media power, 8

Nast, Thomas, 4
Nation, The, 130
National Advisory Commission on Causes and Prevention of Violence, 23-25
National Advisory Commission on Civil Disorders, 22-23
National Association of Broadcasters, 29, 32
National Conference of Editorial Writers, 41, 134
National Guardian, 129
National News Council, 117, 139
National Observer, 42
National Review, 132
New England Daily Newspaper Survey, 124

New journalism, 80, 83, 84-87
New Journalism, The, 85
New nonfiction, 85
New Republic, The, 128
New York, 67, 120
New York Times, 3, 43, 70, 88, 97, 101, 102, 103, 104, 117, 118, 129, 139, 141
New York Times v. Sullivan, 140
New York World, 122
New Yorker, 131
Newland, Chester A., 104
News, 79-82
    defined, 80
    discussed, 82
News from the Capital, 96
News from Nowhere, 133
News-gathering process, 79
    news-making process, 81
    properties of, 80
    selection, 71
    sources, 103
    strategies and tactics, 80
    types, 81
Newspaper Advertising Bureau, 153
Newspaper chains, 40-41
Newspaper circulation, 153
Newspaper news, 82
Newspaper-television news, distinguished, 82
Newsroom policy, 69
Newsroom technology, 68
Newsweek, 84, 90
Noelle-Neumann, Elisabeth, 8, 9
Normative analysis, 85

Objectivity, 79, 80, 82-84
Obscenity and pornography, 25
O'Keefe, Garrett J., 44
Olien, Clarice, 11, 72
Ombudsman, 121-23
"One Party Press," 38
Opinion formation, 5
Opinion Makers, The, 104
Organizational study, of press, 67-71
Other Voices: The New Journalism in America, 85, 119
Ownership, chain, 40-41, 72

Packaging the News, 66, 129
Packard, Vance, 6
Park, Robert E., 69
Parker, Edwin, 28
Parker, Harley, 60
Partisanship, of press, 41
Pastore, John, 27
Patterson, Thomas E., 42, 43

Pearson, Drew, 88
Pentagon Papers, 88
Perry, James, 42, 135
Peterson, Theodore, 87, 116
Piaget, Jean, 30
Plato, 141
Pleasure principle, 81
Policy in newsrooms, 69, 96
Political communication, 44
Political socialization study, 11, 15-16
Pool, Ithiel de Sola, 5, 27, 29, 57
Popular Culture and High Culture, 51
Popular Culture Assn., 60, 61
Popular culture study, 49-63
    critics of, 14, 52
    cross-cultural studies, 52
    differentiated from mass culture, 54
    defined, 49
    effects of, 51
Porter, William, 103
Powerful mass media, return to concept of, 9
Power-goal studies, 72
Power of the press, 5, 8
Powers, Thomas, 132
Power structure, community, 72
Praegar Publishers, 134
Precision journalism, 85, 153
Press, The, 131
Press and the Cold War, The, 129
Press as kingbreaker, 40
Press as kingmaker, 40
Press as living system, 70
Press as social institution, 67-75
Press councils, 116-19
Press, dual structure of, 71
Press-government conflict, 74
Press-government relationships, 89
Print, impact of, 43
Pro bono publico, 144
Process-centered news, 82
Process of media, 58
Professionalism, in mass communication, 71, 74,
    83, 97
Propaganda and the News, 131
Propaganda study, 4, 5, 7, 8
Providence Journal and Bulletin, 121
Pseudo-events, 56
Public health model, 146
Public interest, 139-49
    formulations, 142
    of public interest distinguished
        from in public interest, 146
    preference v. interest, 144
    theories, 143
Public Interest, The, 89, 134, 141
Public Officials and the Press, 103

Public Opinion, 57, 83
Public policy and research, 31
Public relations practice, 56
Publishers, power of, 72
Puck, 130
Pulitzer Prize, 88

Quasi-folk culture, 54
Quill, The, 134

Race relations and the press, 22
Radio and Television News Directors Assn., 134
Rand Corporation, inquiry on future of media,
    133
Realism, 85
Reality principle, 81
Redford, Robert, 35, 93
Reedy, George, 134
Reform journalism, 83
*Region's Press: Newspapers in the San Francisco
    Bay Area,* 124
Reigle, Donald, 35
Reilly, Thomas, 96
Reluctant Reformation, The, 123
Reporter as Artist, The, 86
Reporter-official relationships, 103-5
Reporter power movement, 120
Reporter-source relationships, 80-83
Reporters, 100-101
Reporters and Officials, 103
Representative picture theory, 116
Rights, 129
Rivera, Geraldo, 93, 94, 102
Rivers, William L., 68, 85, 94, 104, 117, 119,
    124, 133
Roach, John, 121
Robinson, John P., 10, 39, 45
Robinson, Michael, 135
Rogers, Will, 79
Roosevelt, Franklin D., 37
Rose, Arnold, 72
Rosenberg, Bernard, 53
Roshco, Bernard, 80, 83
Rosten, Leo, 83, 94
Rourke, Francis E., 140-41
Rubin, David, 102, 118, 124
Rubinstein, Eli A., 27
Rusher, William, 139

Sage Annual Reviews of Communication Re-
    search, 15
St. Louis Post Dispatch, 139
St. Paul Pioneer Press and Dispatch, 112
St. Petersburg Times, 122
Samuelson, Merrill, 97
Sanders, Keith, 122

Saturday Evening Post, 71
Schickel, Richard, 55
Schmidt, Benno, 116
Schoebel, Jean, 121
Schools of journalism, 123-24
Schramm, Wilbur, 5, 11, 28, 31, 81, 96, 116, 151-52
Schramm-type questions, 152
Schultz, J. Blaine, 72
Schwartz, Alan U., 35
"Schwindel," 5
Scientific media criticism, 132-33
Seldes, George, 130
Selective exception, 58
Selective identification, 58
Selective interpretation, 58
Selective perception, 5, 9, 36, 58
Sensationalism, 83
Seymour-Ure, Colin, 44
Shannon, C.E., 68
Shaw, Donald L., 11, 12, 13, 58
Shibutani, Tamotsu, 20
Shilen, Ronald, 83
Shils, E.A., 52
Shobowale, Ola, 121
Sieb, Charles, 123
Siebert, Fred, 116
Sigal, Leon V., 103
Sigma Delta Chi, 124
Silvey, Robert, 146
Sinclair, Upton, 73, 129
Skidelsky, Robert, 141
Social control, of newsroom, 71
Social Responsibility of the Press, The, 74
Social responsibility theory, 113, 132
Social Science Research Council, 44
Social typing, 56
Socialization, 15
Socialization, political, 11, 15-16
Socialization to Politics, 16
Society of Professional Journalists, 124, 134
Sociology of journalism, 94
Sociology of knowledge, 81
Sociology of media, 82
Sociology of news, 81
Sociology of organizations, 70
Some Newspapers and Newspaper Men, 130
Sorauf, Frank, 141
Specialist reporters, 95
Steffens, Lincoln, 130
Steinem, Gloria, 67
Stereotypes, functions of, 57, 58
Stevenson, Adlai, 38
Stop the Presses, I Want to Get Off, 134
Strentz, Herbert, 124
Strickland, Stephen, 27

Structural control of press, 73
Sugar Pill, The, 8
Supreme Court and the News Media, The, 104
Supreme Court coverage, 104-5
Supreme Court press corps, 95, 104-5
Surgeon General's Report, 25, 27
Survey research, 6, 9, 10, 22, 26, 30, 36, 39, 73, 87, 94, 118, 122, 132, 133
Survey Research Center, 10, 36, 37, 39
Susann, Jacqueline, 49
Swedish press council, 121
Swedish press ombudsman, 121
Symbolic leaders, 55

Talese, Gay, 21, 85
Taste publics, 54
Television advertising, 42
Television and social behavior, 27-29
Television and Social Behavior, 27
Television news, 42, 43, 82
Texas Observer, 139
Theories of mass communication, 60
Theory of cognitive development, 30
Theory of cognitive dissonance, 5
Theta Sigma Phi, 124
Tichenor, Phillip J., 11, 72
Time, 85
Towards a Sociology of Mass Communications, 70
Traditional media, 14
Trickle-down theory of public interest, 143, 145
Tuchman, Gaye, 83
Tweed, William Marcy, 4
Twentieth Century Fund, 117
Twin Cities Journalism Review, 111-13, 120
Twin Cities Newspaper Guild, 112, 121

Underground press, 67, 85
Us and Them: How the Press Covered the 1972 Election, 135
Uses and gratifications study, 11, 13-15, 43, 52, 53, 60, 61

Van den Haag, Ernest, 50
Vanocur, Sander, 134
Village Voice, 90, 120, 135
Villard, Oswald G., 130
Violence and the Mass Media, 23
Violence and the news media, 23-25
Violence Commission, 23-25
Violence Commission Report, 23-24
Violent content, of media, 3, 21
Voltaire, 110

Voter decision-making, 44
Voters, independent, 41

WABC-TV, 93
Wackman, Daniel, 30
Ward, Scott, 30
"War of the Worlds," 5
Wartella, Ellen, 30
Washington, George, 22
Washington Post, 35, 88, 93, 103, 122, 123, 133, 134
Washington Press corps, 94
Watchdog, role of press, 89
Watergate crisis and the press, 4, 35, 68, 87
Wayward Pressman, The, 131
Waxman, Jerry J., 95
Weaver, Paul, 89, 133
Weaver, Warren, 43
Webb, Jack, 84
Weber, Max, 83
Weber, Ronald, 86

Weiss, Walter, 39
Welles, Orson, 5
Wells, H.G., 5
White, David Manning, 95
Wiggins, Charles, 103
Wilhout, G. Cleveland, 38
Wireless transmitters, 151
Wolfe, Tom, 85
Women in Communications, 124
Woodrow Wilson Center for Scholars, 134
Woodward, Bob, 35, 88, 90, 93
Worker participation committees, 114, 120-21
Worker Participation: New Voices in Management, 121
Wright, Charles, 53
Wycoff, Gene, 41

Yarbrough, J. Paul, 103
Yellow journalism, 88
Young, Art, 130